GOTHIC QUEER CULTURE

EXPANDING FRONTIERS:
INTERDISCIPLINARY APPROACHES TO
STUDIES OF WOMEN, GENDER, AND SEXUALITY

Series Editors:
Karen J. Leong
Andrea Smith

GOTHIC QUEER CULTURE

Marginalized Communities *and the* Ghosts *of* Insidious Trauma

LAURA WESTENGARD

University of Nebraska Press | Lincoln

A portion of the preface was previously published
in "Gothic Gaga: Monstrosity, Trauma, and the
Strategic Artifice of Lady Gaga's Pop Stardom," in
Star Power: The Impact of Branded Celebrity, vol. 2,
ed. Aaron Barlow (Santa Barbara: ABC-CLIO/Prae-
ger imprint, 2014), 175–99. Used with permission of
ABC-CLIO, through the Copyright Clearance Center.

A portion of chapter 3 was previously published in
"'Conquering Immortality': Gothic AIDS Literature
as Queer Futurity in Gil Cuadros' City of God," *JNT:
Journal of Narrative Theory* 45, no. 2 (2015): 274–300.

Library of Congress Cataloging-in-Publication Data
Names: Westengard, Laura, author.
Title: Gothic queer culture: marginalized
communities and the ghosts of
insidious trauma / Laura Westengard.
Description: Lincoln: University of Nebraska Press,
[2019] | Series: Expanding frontiers: Interdisciplinary
approaches to studies of women, gender, and sex-
uality | Includes bibliographical references and index.
Identifiers: LCCN 2018057900
ISBN 9781496202048 (cloth: alk. paper)
ISBN 9781496217028 (pbk: alk. paper)
ISBN 9781496217424 (epub)
ISBN 9781496217431 (mobi)
ISBN 9781496217448 (pdf)
Subjects: LCSH: Gay culture. |
Goth culture (Subculture)
Classification: LCC HQ76.96 .W47 2019 |
DDC 306.76/6—dc23
LC record available at
https://lccn.loc.gov/2018057900

Set in Minion Pro by Mikala R. Kolander.
Designed by L. Auten.

For J, my light that never goes out

CONTENTS

ILLUSTRATIONS

PREFACE

I have to admit that I am generally immune to commercial pop music and its artists. As someone who is a self-professed "goth at heart," if not in outward appearance, I tend to favor art and music with a little more darkness and complexity. But in 2010, when Lady Gaga, known as "Mother Monster" to her fans, walked the red carpet at the MTV Video Music Awards wearing a dress made entirely of stitched-together hunks of raw meat, paired with meat-covered platform boots and clutch and topped with a demure steak hat, she captured my attention.[1] What monstrous excess! What morbid camp! What does it all mean?

As a pop culture figure, Gaga is overdetermined by her multiplicity of meanings to fans and critics alike. Her adoption of a morbidly excessive aesthetic and her use of the rhetoric of monstrosity has established her as a gay icon, a spokesperson for the marginalized, and a target for virulent criticism. I believe Lady Gaga epitomizes the historically conflicted uses of gothicism in relation to queerness, and my personal fascination with her rise to fame reflects some of the larger questions I ask in this book. What is it about gothic aesthetics that so captures the public imagination? How has gothic rhetoric been used to capitalize on the violent marginalization of difference, and how has that same rhetoric been used to speak back to violence and create queer communities? How do these contradictory purposes work together to create queer culture that is dazzlingly and powerfully incoherent? Gaga's multiplicity speaks to the many purposes of gothicism that I explore in this book as well as gothicism's refusal to settle, its rebellious resistance, and its inherent queerness. A brief overview of Gaga as a cultural figure sets the stage for the conversations occurring throughout this book and brings into focus the way gothicism rooted in eighteenth-century popular culture continues to infiltrate contemporary conversations around difference, traumatic marginalization, and queerness.

Lady Gaga shot to pop music stardom with the release of her debut album, *The Fame*, in 2008. Since then she has released several more albums, appeared on the television series *American Horror Story*, founded a nonprofit foundation, and served as a fascinating and notoriously contentious cultural icon. She is perhaps best known for her outrageous and unpredictable fashion choices and public appearances that border on performance art. The meat dress instantly polarized the public, generating a flurry of media conversations about its meaning, and has become so representative of Gaga's position in popular culture that curator Meredith Rutledge-Borger selected it to be displayed in the Rock and Roll Hall of Fame's 2012 national touring exhibit, *Women Who Rock: Vision, Passion, Power*. Regarding its meaning, Brett Zongker of the *Huffington Post* explains, "When Gaga wore the dress, she was accompanied by U.S. soldiers impacted by the 'don't ask, don't tell' policy to protest the ban on gays serving openly in the military. She explained that if people don't stand up for their rights, 'pretty soon we're going to have as much rights as the meat on our own bones. And, I am not a piece of meat.'"[2] In an interview with Anderson Cooper, Lady Gaga declared, "And, you know what? What I was really trying to say was dead meat is dead meat. And anyone that's willing to take their life and die for their country is the same. You're not gay and dead, straight and dead. You are dead."[3] Although the reading of the dress as a commentary on "don't ask, don't tell" has now been cemented as the official interpretation, the internet still offers speculation about its meaning—from claims that it was a feminist statement to the argument that it was simply a publicity stunt for spectacle rather than politics.[4]

In addition to the debate over the political implications, many discussions of the meat dress stray into the territory of the morbid, pondering details about its creation, smell, decomposition, and preservation. The meat dress immediately attracted scrutiny from People for the Ethical Treatment of Animals, who postulated that "meat is the decomposing flesh of a tormented animal who didn't want to die, and after a few hours under the TV lights, it would smell like the rotting flesh it is and likely be crawling in maggots—not too attractive, really."[5] Dress designer Franc Fernandez responded to the "big debate of whether it smelled or rotted under the lights" by explaining that "Gaga herself said it smelled good, because it smelled like meat." In terms of its preservation, Fernandez noted that he hoped the dress would be put in the Gaga Archive with all of her other dresses and allowed to decompose naturally there, so when "it is brought out again . . . it will be a different dress."[6] The logistics of that fantasy storage situation, however, were never fully worked out. For its inclusion in the Rock and Roll Hall of Fame, the dress was in fact preserved, its rapidly decaying raw meat taxidermied by placing it in a vat of chemicals and then molding it around a body form to dry. Once the meat was dried, it darkened significantly and had to be painted to assume its fresh, raw meat color. The dress now stands, an empty shell of hardened flesh and chemicals, in the shape of Lady Gaga's form with "the lifespan of beef jerky."[7]

The dress has journeyed from pungent hunks of conjoined animal flesh to its current state as empty husk flamboyantly defying decomposition. This story may sound vaguely familiar. It is also the tale of Frankenstein's creature—pieced together from the meat of dead humans and animals, oozing, stinking, and splitting but also featuring technology that persists despite its abject fleshiness that should by all accounts rot before our eyes. Like her meat dress, Lady Gaga's persona is a patchwork creation made of cultural bits culled and pieced together in a new, excessive form. Many critics claim that Gaga's music and aesthetics are derivative, even plagiarized from other cultural figures. Rossen Ventzislavov points out that Lady Gaga's persona relies heavily on the appropriation (or perhaps, more kindly, the citation) of musicians, artists, and other public figures who have come before her and adds that she is both "an explosion of idiosyncrasy and a veritable Frankenstein patched up from parts of easily identifiable pop culture parentage."[8] As a result, Lady Gaga signifies drastically different things to different people as a kind of Frankensteinian creature, her patchwork meat dress not only viscerally evoking Frankenstein's monstrous progeny but also representing the multiple meanings playing out on her body.

In an extension of her Frankensteinian monstrosity, Lady Gaga has also famously taken on the role of "Mother Monster" to her legions of fans, or "Little Monsters." This persona, too, functions both as public relations stunt and as an extension of her social politics. The social media site littlemonsters.com frames Mother Monster's relationship with her fans as an attempt to support and embrace those who identify as freaks and misfits and to provide a sense of community for those on the social margins. Lady Gaga's Little Monster community has coalesced around the notion of difference, suffering from alienation based on the perceived inability to fit into normative society for one reason or many. Gaga's fans are queer outsiders in the broad sense of the term—queering norms and often being socially ostracized as a result. They are also often queer in the narrower sense of the term as well—embodying nonnormative ways of being in relationship to gender and sexuality. And while the monstrosity of Gaga polarizes her critics, it is precisely what appeals to her Little Monsters dealing with the struggles of social marginalization. Indeed, many fans (and Gaga herself) sport tattoos that mark them as Little Monsters, a permanent aesthetic choice that proudly displays their "monstrous" difference.

Lady Gaga herself is openly bisexual, and she developed a large gay male following in the early years of her career. In his ethnographic study of gay male veneration of female music icons, Craig Jennex explains that many of the fans he interviewed identified Lady Gaga's fashion choices, "particularly her famous meat dress, as 'challenging what is considered proper' for presentation of self in public." This flamboyant aesthetic outrageousness marks Gaga as a model for being out and proud and links her fashion choices to a kind of visible "anti-normal" politics.[9] OUT magazine lists her among "The 12 Greatest Female Gay Icons of All Time" for gay men among such notables as Judy Garland, Madonna, and Barbara Streisand.[10] Jennex's respondents cite Lady Gaga as "*the* influential figure in their lives," often referring to her music (especially the 2011 anthem "Born This Way") as inspiration for coming out, as much-needed representation of identities not otherwise visible in mainstream media, and as motivation to continue living when contemplating suicide. "Born This Way," Gaga's self-proclaimed "this-is-who-the-fuck-I-am anthem," has served as the theme song for many a Gay Pride event, encouraging revelers to "just love yourself" because "God makes no mistakes."[11]

Like the multiplicitous semiotics of the meat dress, Gaga's politics have more than one reading. Gaga's message of radical self-acceptance through "heightened biological metaphors"—that each individual was "born this way" and should be proud of their inherent difference—reduces highly complex social constructions and interactions to inherent individual idiosyncrasies.[12] Without a more revolutionary deconstructive framework, people are left to interpret Gaga's message through the lens of a fully internalized social narrative about what it means to be brave or to love oneself rather than as a means of reimagining those marginalizing narratives and structures. In spite of her liberal individualist "born this way" rhetoric, Gaga might still be read as transgressive by those fans who are perhaps more well informed about Gaga's citationality and recognize that her artifice draws attention to the constructedness of identity and the performative nature of gender and sexuality. One fan in Jennex's study explains, "I see connections to Andy Warhol and other gays of days gone by. Some people get pissed and say she's stealing other people's looks, but I think she's paying respect AND keeping them relevant."[13]

Just as designers pieced her meat dress together from several dead creatures to create a new hybrid creation, Lady Gaga's entire pop persona has been quite obviously pieced together from musical, artistic, and cultural referents. Yet she still claims to be both real and authentic, drawing attention to the forces and influences that work together to create the selves we perceive as inherent and unchanging but that are truly contingent and constructed. In this reading Gaga embodies the kind of monstrously threatening queerness of Lee Edelman's *No Future*, a figure that "exposes the obliquity of our relation to what we experience in and as social reality, alerting us to the fantasies structurally necessary in order to sustain it and engaging those fantasies through the figural logics, the linguistic structures, that shape them." Perhaps Gaga uses the logics of liberal individualism and the glorification of essentialized difference to subtly alert us to their construction as fantasies. Edelman likens this role to exposing the knotted underbelly of the sequined dress of cultural ideology, offering us "fantasy turned inside out, the seams of its costume exposing reality's seamlessness as mere seeming, the fraying knots that hold each sequin in place now usurping that place."[14] The reading of Lady Gaga as intentionally performative, strategically artificial, is a revolutionary one, and one that is, perhaps, the most threatening to those invested in perpetuating the "seamlessness" of a hierarchical social structure that marginalizes difference in the service of maintaining systems of power that benefit some and oppress others.[15]

More recently, however, Gaga has adopted a more conservative persona, ditching her outlandish fashion choices first for a classic Hollywood, jazz-standard aesthetic and then for a Barbie-pink country-and-western one, but her champion-of-the-alienated function still remains, as she attempts to give voice to the silenced survivors of campus rape by penning the Oscar-nominated song "Til It Happens to You" for the film *The Hunting Ground* (2015). Admittedly, pop star images and causes are mutable, but Gaga's shift from her original political cause as supporter of gay rights implies that she might imagine that project to be complete. After all, her meat dress purportedly addressed the now-repealed "don't ask, don't tell" policy, and her assimilationist "born this way" message asked society to usher queer folks into the folds of culture ("same DNA but born this way"), a call the 2015 Supreme Court decision to uphold gay marriage arguably answered.[16] Gaga's past political rhetoric undertheorized the systems that create inequality, marginalization, and violence by first focusing on a passive, essentializing narrative of biological difference and then asking people to respond to their problems through bravery rather than systematic social change. With the narrative of bravery, Gaga places the burden for change on the individual rather than society, and it also promotes the comforting illusion that once certain individuals are able to successfully assimilate there is no need for larger, structural change. Perhaps there is no longer a need for the avant-garde, queer, quirky Mother Monster to fight for gay rights now that the LGBT community has been properly assimilated. She can now address the next group of alienated and traumatized people and call on them to be brave in the face of systemic violence. It is certainly a comforting narrative of progress, albeit one that feels a bit hollow in the face of undeniable ongoing discrimination (such as the recent tide of laws aimed at policing binary gender norms in public spaces such as bathrooms) and overt violence (such as the mass shooting on Latin Night at the Orlando gay club Pulse in June 2016).

Gaga's rhetoric may be ultimately conservative in its message of feel-good individuality that pacifies any revolutionary sentiments, or it may be transgressive and denaturalizing in its overt performativity. She adds sparkle and flair to the ideological systems already in place, but she may also construct that sparkle using the language of dominant discourse to draw attention to its very artificiality, thereby exposing the construction. The sparkle may also simply reflect the razzle-dazzle of pure capitalism, her persona a series of strategic decisions to generate and maintain what Jackie Huba calls "monster loyalty" as business strategy.[17] When filtered through the lens of commercial aspiration, Gaga's choices certainly read as crass commercialism.

David Halperin claims that Gaga's resonance represents the gay male cultural practice of reading queerness into cultural objects that "contain no explicit gay themes, that do not represent gay men, that do not invoke same-sex desire, but that afford gay men opportunities for colonizing them and making them over into vehicles of queer affirmation." This description maps directly onto the historically queer appeal of eighteenth- and nineteenth-century Gothic novels—popular fiction that was created for heteronormative audiences but that has been repeatedly adopted and converted for "queer uses."[18]

Like a proper Gothic monster, the surface of Gaga's Frankensteinian meat dress reflects the fears and desires of a society concerned with questions of authenticity raised by the new realities of a virtual world. She offers a titillating image of transgression, temporarily eschewing cultural beauty and behavioral norms but always, ultimately, returning to the fold in one way or another. In her appropriative mode she embodies the individualist Gothic villain who uses anyone or anything he comes in contact with to achieve his aims—a capitalist supreme. She is a queer cultural producer as well, identifying as bisexual and writing songs (often infused with gothicism) that reflect pride in an identity founded on difference, both sexual and otherwise. She also depicts queerness in her music and her philanthropy; as Mother Monster, she takes on the responsibility of convincing her fans that nonnormative genders and sexualities are "brave" and encourages them to persist in the face of bullying. In this sense trauma is central to her music and her causes, from this initial focus on bullied and ostracized teens to her more recent focus on the trauma of sexual assault, something she speaks to as a survivor herself. Throughout her career she has offered both a resistant queer gothicism and an adoption of neoliberal individualism.

After reflecting on her existence as a queer icon who trades at times in the monstrous and the morbid, I have come to see that Gaga's significance as icon, champion (and profiteer) of the queer and alienated, and voice of the traumatized is in large part due to her adoption of gothicism as a way of queering traumatic experience. In this way she represents the complex phenomenon in twentieth- and twenty-first-century U.S. culture that I explore in detail in this book: queer performers, artists, writers, and thinkers have turned again and again to gothicism to navigate and express the trauma of queer experience in the United States. In the following pages I investigate a broad range of queer cultural production that, like Gaga and like myself, may not always seem gothic on the surface but is certainly "goth at heart."

ACKNOWLEDGMENTS

This book was formed, dismembered, and stitched back together over the course of many years. I sat down one day to reflect on the trajectory of my interests, and it slowly dawned on me that there was a clear theme to my work: from sadomasochism in Anthony Trollope to Frankensteinian monstrosity in AIDS literature—a veritable cabinet of curiosities. I looked up from my computer screen and gazed around my apartment and at my collection of oddities: a Victorian hair broach, human teeth, tintypes of anonymous people with dead eyes. It clicked. Gothicism was part of my worldview, an aesthetic and rhetoric that allowed me to navigate my place in academia and beyond as a queer cis femme. At that moment this book received the spark of life.

Unlike Victor Frankenstein, who toiled over his creation in isolation and solitude, I could not have accomplished this book without the people in my personal and professional life who have provided me with support, ideas, and feedback over the years. My mentors in the English Department and the Gender and Sexuality Studies Department at UCR— George Haggerty, Tiffany Ana López, Steven Axelrod, Alicia Arrizón, and Jennifer Doyle—generously oversaw my writing and professionalization. Michael Podolny and Emily Mattingly read each chapter of my work in our ad hoc writing group, and my friends Janise Roselle, Deborah Sims, and Shelley Garcia listened without (visible) judgment to my incessantly dark and morbid musings.

My friends and colleagues at the City University of New York also stepped up with invaluable feedback. Carole Harris, Robert Lestón, and Benjamin Shepard generously read drafts, and Jill Belli provided accountability and a writing companion for summer library sessions. My project took on its present visage during my time in the CUNY Faculty Fellowship Publication Program under the mentorship of Shelly Eversley and with the thorough and challenging feedback of my peers Jacqueline Jones, Brian Thill, Natalie Havlin, Laura Barberan Reinares, Swan Kim, and Heidi Bollinger. Through happenstance I met Christopher Ian Foster—equal parts brilliant and metal—who thoughtfully read every word of this manuscript and pushed me to simultaneously be a better scholar and to live deliciously.

Most important, my family has offered love, conversation, and inspiration that allowed me to turn my macabre proclivities into a profession. My mom gave me the gift of writing and an appreciation for the "treasure hunt." She may not always relate to my interests but continually responds with loving, respectful wonder. My dad read every paper I ever wrote and chatted endlessly with me about philosophy and spirituality over coffee and beer. His death left an intellectual void that has been filled only by my cocktail-infused conversations with Kirsten Richter. My sister, brother-in-law, and nephew offer me perfectly wry love and dry humor that has lightened my life without being cloying and provided me with breaks from my exhausting earnestness. From my aunts I learned a willingness to embrace my weird and to pursue the beauty in that which others might find creepy or perverse. Thank you to Angela, James W., Kirsten, Kate, James C., Michael, Chrissie, and Dodo.

Jamerson, my partner of over a decade, has stuck with me throughout this extended process, from joining me on sadistic performance art "dates" to discovering me typing away in a dark apartment after writing in solitude all day, sallow face, vacant eyes, glued tongue. With patience and engagement, Jamerson has truly been my muse—the formative ideas and suggestions they have contributed to this project are too many and too engrained to enumerate. Their intellectual blood runs through the veins of this manuscript. The biggest gift they have given me, however, is a lesson about gentleness, both to others and to myself. This lesson has created a much kinder life, in which I have been able to thrive personally and professionally.

The University of Nebraska Press has been a pleasure to work with, especially the enthusiasm, consistency, and responsiveness of my editor, Alicia Christensen. I would also like to thank the anonymous reviewers of this manuscript, who provided useful commentary and suggestions that have taken my book to the next level. I am honored to have been invited to be part of the Expanding Frontiers series, and I extend special thanks to the series editors, Karen J. Leong and Andrea Smith, for their generous invitation and for their feedback on this project.

Finally, my home institution, New York City College of Technology, has supported the development of this book through reassigned time for new hires. I would like to thank my chair Nina Bannett, Dean Justin Vazquez-Poritz, Julia Jordan, Provost Bonne August, and President Russell Hotzler for creating an environment that allowed me to complete this scholarship while continuing to serve our students. New York Public Library's Manhattan Research Library Initiative in collaboration with New York University and Columbia University has given me invaluable access to research resources, without which I could not have completed this book, and the ONE National Gay and Lesbian Archives at the University of Southern California Libraries granted me access to their archival holding of lesbian pulp fiction. Thanks to Ron Athey, Cassils, Zackary Drucker, M. Lamar, and the ONE Archives for permission to reproduce the images in this book.

GOTHIC QUEER CULTURE

INTRODUCTION

Queer Cultures and Insidious Trauma

The ghost is not simply a dead or a missing person, but
a social figure, and investigating it can lead to that dense
site where history and subjectivity make social life.

AVERY GORDON, *Ghostly Matters*

On the eve of his marriage to Isabella, poor young Conrad is crushed by
a monstrously large helmet that falls from the sky, sparking his father,
Manfred, to begin a paranoid scramble to escape the prophecy of a family
curse. Manfred's first order of business: to divorce his wife, Hippolita, who
has not given him a male heir and to take Isabella, the young woman who
was to become his daughter-in-law, as his new wife. Through drafty subterranean passages connecting the castle to a nearby monastery, Manfred
chases Isabella, who is frightened into desperate flight by his incestuous
intentions and aggressive sexual advances. The supernatural abounds, from
the appearance of giant appendages to ancestral ghosts wandering the castle
halls to the slow reveal of the "fleshless jaws and empty sockets of a skeleton,
wrapt in a hermit's cowl."[1] In addition to the setting—a gloomy medieval
castle in Catholic Italy with darkened, twisting underground passageways—
The Castle of Otranto (1764) by Horace Walpole mints the currency of the
Gothic with its sexualized power dynamics, supernatural elements, and

terrorized and vulnerable women. Many of these themes reflect both social and psychological nostalgia for and fear of a lost or repressed past that erupts into the narrative in frightening and unexpected ways.

Otranto is a story driven by trauma—the narrative trauma of Conrad's sudden death and the sexual terror of incestuous pursuit, yes, but also the trauma visited on all the characters as an outcome of the patriarchal system in which they function. The women in the narrative are completely vulnerable to the system, in which they are valued as objects tied to property accumulation. Their failure to properly marry and bear male children means they are in constant threat of destitution, rape, and violence. To a certain extent even Manfred is a victim of his circumstance, as he is miserably and desperately driven to maintain his wealth and paternal power at any cost, demonstrating, as George Haggerty notes, that the "normativity of paternal power itself is the perversion."[2] The novel is also certainly informed by Walpole's experiences as a queer author during a period of intense surveillance of sexual and gender deviance through sodomy persecutions.[3] Was Otranto a way for Walpole to critique the normative structures that threatened him? I argue that there is something about gothicism that resonates with the experience of queer precarity in a system built to maintain normativity, a connection between existing in a world built to deny and devalue queer expression and the creation of gothic content. In other words, if something is both queer and gothic, look under the surface to disinter the insidious trauma buried there.

On its surface Gothic fiction offers traumatic moments that erupt into the narrative and jolt readers with terrifying and titillating surprises, but between these eruptions exist an ongoing atmosphere vulnerability and its attendant low-level, internalized terror. Conrad's death is shocking, and Manfred's rampage is a crisis for the women he threatens with violence and ruin, but I am more interested in the spaces in which characters negotiate their own precarity to survive a system in which they are always at risk. For me the fascinating part of gothic narrative appears in the interstices that convey normalized, daily trauma rather than in its punctuated moments of shocking spectacle. To focus on the crannies and crevices of the gothic is to take a new approach to trauma, for so much discussion of trauma focuses on its horrific events without examining the accumulated daily assaults arising from systemic refusals and invalidations.

The metaphors, settings, and conventions that appear in eighteenth- and nineteenth-century Gothic fiction appear again and again in twentieth- and twenty-first-century cultural production, something I identify broadly as "gothicism." Gothicism, I argue, provides a particularly resonant means of expressing those mundane experiences that often fly under the radar of trauma in the traditional sense. In this book I consider what it would mean to read gothicism in a new way, focusing not on its inciting shocks and its satisfying resolutions but on the moments between as expressions of insidious trauma, specifically the trauma of being queer in a system built to invalidate and destroy anyone who strays from the norm. In this sense Walpole's *Otranto* serves not only as the epitome of the Gothic novel but also as a prototypical representation of what I call "gothic queer culture," or queer creative production in which gothicism is used as a strategy for expressing ongoing, accumulated traumatic experiences.

This book explores the queer use of the gothic in more contemporary times, proposing that twentieth- and twenty-first-century U.S. queer culture is gothic at the core. Using an interdisciplinary cultural studies approach to examine the gothicism in queer art, literature, and thought— ghosts embedded in queer theory, shadowy crypts in lesbian pulp fiction, monstrosity and cannibalism in AIDS poetry and art, sadomasochism in queer performance—the book argues that the twentieth and twenty-first centuries have seen the development of queer culture that responds to and challenges traumatic marginalization by creating a distinctly gothic rhetoric and aesthetic.

It is undeniable that queer people have been the targets of violence and oppression because of their place outside of the mainstream. Gothicism not only reflects antinormative queerness but also serves as a response to the systematized exclusion and violence that has plagued U.S. queer communities in the twentieth and twenty-first centuries. Those with non-normative genders and sexualities have faced persistent and insidious trauma, and, as a result, queer culture has developed that responds to this trauma with an aesthetic that uses gothicism to acknowledge violent marginalization while challenging the structures that create it. This book examines the complex intersections between the systemic marginalization of U.S. queer communities, the trauma tied to this oppression, and the development of rich queer culture infused with a gothicism that is both informed by and resistant to that traumatic marginalization.

Both Gothic fiction and late twentieth-century trauma theories rest on certain assumptions about a subject or system that has been disrupted by an event and must be repaired. The Gothic narrative obsession for a nostalgic past in reaction to the rise of the middle class, for example, imagines that the medieval period offered an idealized social model that was unified and orderly, a world of "organic wholeness" in comparison to an emergent individualized bourgeois society. In the Gothic imagination the "medieval individual was defined by his relation to other groups and the world outside of himself," whereas the "modern identity is defined in terms of autonomy and independence," a frightening prospect in relation to a comforting, if fantasmatic, past founded on order and unity.[4] The villain of the Gothic narrative acts out this fear, exhibiting a monstrous predatory desire for power and fulfillment and representing the extreme adoption of corrupt individualism. Villainous behavior disrupts the social order, threatens the conventions and mores of the time and place, and sets the narrative into action. There is, of course, the eventual restoration of the predespotic wholeness and social order, and in the process the narrative *produces* an idealized fantasy of the past. The use of gothicism to produce fantasy norms to which society must revert recalls Jack Halberstam's definition of the gothic as a "technology of subjectivity, one which produces the deviant subjectivities opposite which the normal, the healthy, and the pure can be known."[5] In its conservative mode, gothicism exhibits a nostalgic drive to recreate idealized subjects and histories that offer a return to some idea of past wholeness.

Similarly, the dominant narrative of trauma and recovery imagines a pretrauma individual as whole and not yet fragmented by traumatic experience. Judith Herman, following Sigmund Freud's logic, explains that traumatic experiences have historically been associated with fragmentation as the "human system of self-defense becomes overwhelmed and disorganized" in the face of powerlessness in the traumatic situation. Fragmentation appears again and again in descriptions of hysteria, shell shock, and post-traumatic stress disorder. In Maurice E. Stevens's examination of trauma as a cultural object, or an "ingathering of practices," he observes that these practices explain and respond to the overwhelming realization of the "everyday precariousness and brutality of the social," which collapses the "*myth of the independent and isolated ego, the coherent and seamless self, the proper citizen-subject.*" In response to the frightening traumatic fragmentation of the coherent self, "the idea of trauma provides explanatory narratives that, by offering one telling of how the subject achieved its ruination, support fantasies of an originary time before the fall; a time of whole, coherent, innocent selfhood, and uncorrupted, clean, and proper subjectivity."[6] In other words, the narrative of trauma and recovery imagines that there is a pretrauma coherent self to which the recovered subject can return. Like the Gothic narrative's eventual restoration of normative social order after a momentary rupture, this idea of trauma is conservative in that it looks back to an imagined moral past, hoping to erase the anxieties of the present social reality through a return to a place that never actually existed.

This traumatic nostalgia, and the Gothic one, refuses to pause in the space of fragmentation and disruption, favoring instead a fantasy of the moral past, the normative subject, the coherent self. This book refocuses the optics of trauma from a focus on the overwhelming *event* from which one must recover to a focus on the overwhelmingness of existence in a heteronormative, homophobic society in which marginalization and oppression are compounded by other intersecting aspects of social location (such as race, class, ability, etc.). Event-based trauma and the horrific surprises in Gothic fiction are only part of the story. Gothic narrative might start with a trauma and end with a resolution, but buried in the pages is an ongoing state of disruption that reflects insidious trauma, or "the traumatogenic effects of oppression that are not necessarily overtly violent or threatening to bodily well-being at the given moment but that do violence to the soul and spirit."[7] I pause in the midst of the gothic narrative, the traumatic moment of overwhelming anxiety, of contingency, of incoherency, of swirling uncertain affect, to locate the space where gothicism emerges out of insidious, persistent queer traumatic experience. To settle here allows us to visualize how queer gothicism is a refusal of traditional conservative narratives. Gothicism queers both trauma and normative fantasies of what it means to be fully and coherently human.

What Is Gothic and How Is It Queer?

Gothic literature originated in eighteenth-century Britain as titillating popular fiction, causing social conservatives to clutch their pearls and those whose proclivities included the morbid, lurid, or perverse to consume the stories with greedy abandon. Its tales of incest, family curses, obsessive desires, convoluted supernaturalism, female vulnerability, horror, and terror led Gothic literature to be associated with perversity and human depravity. It also offered a space for women to enter the public sphere as authors and consumers, leading to the broad feminization (and subsequent devaluing) of the genre.[8] Nevertheless, Gothic fiction found broad appeal, resonating with the public's fears and desires, both known and latent, and initiating centuries of recurring metaphors, tropes, and aesthetics that we have come to recognize as "gothic." While the Gothic can be read strictly as a literary and historical period, gothicism can also be understood as a literary device or aesthetic sensibility that may have originated from but is not strictly tied to any historical or geographic location.[9] For this book I use the capitalized *Gothic* to refer to the historical literary period and the uncapitalized *gothic* to refer to gothic aesthetics and rhetorics (shifting symbols, themes, and metaphors) that find their root in eighteenth- and nineteenth-century British and U.S. Gothic literature but that are dislocated from any specific historical period. One need only to look at the overwhelming number of contemporary television shows and movies that evoke the undead, dark sexualized power struggles, paranoid doublings, supernatural occurrences, live burials, and gloomy and foreboding atmospheres to be convinced of the refusal of the gothic to be contained within a specific historical moment.

In his day famed Gothic writer Matthew Lewis, author of *The Monk: A Romance* (1796), faced charges of plagiarism, sparking eighteenth-century conversations about the (im)possibility of creating anything truly new. The structure and themes of many Gothic texts intentionally reflect their status as works that newly combine elements of form and content rather than as works that display original innovations, resulting in a piecemeal genre that "feeds upon and mixes the wide range of literary sources out of which it emerges and from which it never fully disentangles itself."[10] Haggerty claims that Gothic literature is primarily an "affective form" concerned with the objective manifestation of psychic realities that are often inexpressible by other means, something that Eve Kosofsky Sedgwick also identifies as the Gothic "unspeakable."[11] Because of the unspeakability of its affective register, Gothic fiction is notoriously indeterminate and "structured so as to heighten this multiplicity of interpretive possibilities."[12] The Gothic's main concern, Maggie Kilgour echoes, "is not to depict character but to create a feeling or effect in its readers by placing them in a state of thrilling suspense and uncertainty."[13] Its characteristic depiction and readerly experience of heightened and disorganized emotion made Gothic fiction controversial, and many eighteenth-century thinkers believed reading these tales corrupted young readers and undermined structures of authority within society. Many also thought the form disrupted the eighteenth-century notions of aesthetics, "rendering aesthetic borders unclear and stimulating unlimited imaginative expansion" in contrast to the classical aesthetics of symmetry and order. Its resistance to aesthetic norms, its sensational emotionality, and its willy-nilly incorporation of other forms and genres not only caused critics to deride Gothic fiction as failed writing but also led to the designation of both the form and its effects as monstrous.[14]

The monstrosity of Gothic form and aesthetics functioned on many levels—from its cannibalistic incorporation of other literary forms and topics to its overdetermined, unspeakable emotions to its depiction of the perversity of human desires. The Gothic responded to British anxieties and fears about race, class, gender, and sexuality in the face of an emerging modern cultural identity and dealt with such anxieties through the use of supernatural, psychological, and highly sexualized themes and recurring symbols. As a complex reaction to nascent Protestant bourgeois culture and its attendant shifts in social norms, Gothic narratives usually involve a fascination with the past and a plethora of mysterious and supernatural metaphors that work through the newly (and differently) resonant anxieties accompanying social upheaval.[15] Many of these supernatural metaphors work with historically and spatially specific meanings regarding race, class, and sexuality. While they might signify differently with present-day readers, the characteristic indeterminacy of gothicism means that its metaphors and aesthetics can offer each generation of readers means for negotiating the complexities of anxiety and desire. Or, as Nina Auerbach argues in her study of vampires, every age embraces the vampire (read gothic metaphor) it needs.[16]

Beginning with the first arguably Gothic novel, Horace Walpole's *The Castle of Otranto* (1764), and continuing into such nineteenth-century novels as Mary Shelley's *Frankenstein* (1818) and Bram Stoker's *Dracula* (1897), eighteenth- and nineteenth-century Gothic literature emerged as a genre obsessed with themes such as paranoia and doubling, terror, incarceration and live entombment, sexualized power dynamics and torture (often within the context of the Spanish Inquisition), monstrosity, ghostliness and haunting (especially in dark, mysterious castles), the grotesque, and the uncanny.

Even as nineteenth-century Gothic texts began to depict settings other than castles and monasteries, the atmospheric gloom remains a staple, as does the structure of embeddedness through stories within stories and frames of found manuscripts and letters. And though the power-hungry sexually predatory older male does not appear in precisely the same form as Walpole's Manfred or Ann Radcliffe's Montoni in *The Mysteries of Udolpho* (1794), in nineteenth-century texts such as *Frankenstein* or Robert Louis Stevenson's *The Strange Case of Dr. Jekyll and Mr. Hyde* (1886), driving paranoia and an obsession with power continue to appear, as does a newly inflected version of monstrosity. Victor Frankenstein, for example, is compelled at first by the desire to control the spark of life, and his obsessive need to acquire scientific fame and a godlike power costs him his mental and physical health as well as relationships with friends and family. Once he has successfully created his creature, Victor's obsession shifts to a kind of hysterical paranoia, as he imagines his own monstrous creation lurking behind every door and outside every window. Paranoia, the grotesque, and the uncanny take center stage in *The Strange Case of Dr. Jekyll and Mr. Hyde* as well, when upstanding Dr. Jekyll's chemistry experiments cause him to slip uncontrollably into his baser self, manifesting in a monstrous body that elicits an unspeakable sense of horror in all those who interact with him. Doubling and paranoia resonate in both of these tales of splitting, replicating, merging, fear, and desire making indistinguishable the line between "murderous or amorous."[17]

A spectacle of perversity usually occupies the majority of Gothic narratives, exposing readers to transgressive modes of being and often reveling in a highly stylized gothic queerness. Though Gothic fiction certainly caused an uproar among those who feared its wild supernaturalism would have deleterious effects on impressionable readers, many critics recognize Gothic fiction as predominantly conservative in its aims and functions. Eighteenth- and nineteenth-century Gothic narratives indulge in the figurative or literal representation of difference and transgression, be it sexual, racial, class or otherwise, and then ultimately destroy that difference only to return to the safety of the status quo. The subversive elements of the plots titillate readers with a temporary deferral of norms and laws—both social and natural—but that "momentary subversion of order" is followed by "the restoration of a norm, which after the experience of terror, now seems immensely desirable."[18] While the Gothic villain may be killed in the end and while the vulnerable woman trapped in the dark recesses of the castle may eventually enter into her proper domestic role as wife, the twisted path that leads to this reestablishment of norms is, nonetheless, queer. Max Fincher explains that the "formal characteristics of Gothic writing, such as its Chinese-box narrative structures, its multiple narrators and interrupted stories, invite a circuitous reading attitude," adding that because of their form, "Gothic stories never follow a 'straight' course, a fact that in itself makes them queer."[19] When taken as a whole, Gothic fiction's queerness—its deformation of form and aesthetics, indeterminate meanings, and affective uncertainty—make the Gothic, from its start, formally, aesthetically, and topically queer.

For this project I use *queer* to reflect this nebulous gothic meaning, generally to refer to nonnormative genders or sexualities while keeping in mind that gender and sexuality are always shaped by other intersecting aspects of experience. Sedgwick's definition reflects queer's gothic indeterminacy perfectly, as "the open mesh of possibilities, gaps, overlaps, dissonances and resonances, lapses and excesses of meaning when the constituent elements of anyone's gender, of anyone's sexuality aren't made (or can't be made) to signify monolithically."[20] This definition allows us to think of folks in various historical, social, and spatial locations as queer in relation to their specific circumstances, leaving its meaning productively contingent and resisting any attempt to make the term *queer* itself monolithic.

The symbols and themes associated with the most famous Gothic texts have retained their associations with nonnormative gender and sexual expression, even in their reiterations in newer literary and popular cultural forms (think of the many queerly sexualized twentieth-century vampire figures, for example). Gothic themes and metaphors function—both in the eighteenth century and today—to "evoke a queer world that attempts to transgress the binaries of sexual decorum" in part by offering "transgressive social-sexual relations" as "the most basic common denominator."[21] Many have argued that the nearly universal presence of transgressive sexuality in Gothic fiction stems from its psychoanalytic resonance, a means of processing certain human drives.[22] Whether or not one wishes to universalize the appeal of the Gothic using a specifically psychoanalytic framework, there is certainly a compelling psychological element to the cross-cultural, cross-historical span of gothicism that speaks to human fears and desires—fears and desires that may be rooted in repression but that may equally be rooted in the highly contingent fears and desires arising out of intersectional social experience. What is remarkable is gothicism's ability to reflect human anxieties and fantasies in ways that resonate with people across times and locations (both social and geographic).

Of course, Gothic fiction is not an exclusively British phenomenon. The emergence of Gothic fiction in the United States in the late eighteenth century echoed themes and metaphors deployed in the British Gothic, but with new variations reflecting the social anxieties unique to the colonial context of the United States. Allan Lloyd-Smith notes that many view U.S. Gothic writers as essentially British subjects who transplanted the genre to a new setting by "substituting the wilderness and the city for the subterranean rooms and corridors of the monastery, or the remote house for the castle, dark and dangerous woods for the bandit infested mountains of Italy." He asserts, however, that U.S. Gothic fiction emerged, not as an adaptation of British Gothicism, but in response to the unique conditions of U.S. experience, namely the violence and solitude of the frontier, Puritanism, tense relations with Europe, and racial issues involving slavery and indigenous relations.[23] Gothic writers from the United States such as Charles Brockden Brown and Edgar Allan Poe enjoyed relationships of reciprocal influence with their British counterparts, indicating a more complicated relationship between British and U.S. Gothic forms than simply an American replication of the British genre.

Nonetheless, many iconic Gothic themes and metaphors appear in both British and U.S. Gothic fiction in one way or another, speaking to the remarkable shape-shifting abilities of a form built on indeterminacy. In Poe, for example, the paranoid double takes shape in the narrator's splitting and dissociation in "The Tell-Tale Heart" (1843), and the subterranean passage appears as a site of vengeance, guilt, and live burial in "The Cask of Amontillado" (1846) and "The Black Cat" (1843).[24] The gloomy castle that confines the vulnerable woman in a maze of intricate passageways and locked doors is replaced with the locked doors of the top-floor nursery in which the narrator of Charlotte Perkins Gilman's

"The Yellow Wallpaper" (1892) slowly becomes the raving hysteric her doctor husband expects her to be. The dark and cavernous compartments of the literal castle come to light as the twisted recesses of the psyche when the homestead in the woods, cozy and austere, becomes uncannily threatening in Brown's *Weiland* (1798), as Theodore Weiland gives in to his obsessive religiosity at the expense of reason and compassion. The monstrous supernatural creature takes shape as the devil and his followers in texts such as Nathaniel Hawthorne's "Young Goodman Brown" (1835), the story of a man struggling, like Manfred, with the corruption of his paternal ancestors. The themes and aesthetics of British Gothic fiction may shift and slip in their U.S. appearances, but they do indeed appear. Gothic fiction coming out of the United States not only trades in the conventions of the British form but also offers an expansion of the genre by adapting gothicism to respond to the unique fears and desires of the colonial context.

As a field of academic inquiry, gothicism has served as a kind of rite of passage for scholars who have eventually found broad recognition as theorists of gender and sexuality, including Nina Auerbach, Richard Dyer, Eve Kosofsky Sedgwick, and Jack Halberstam.[25] There is also a significant body of critical work among scholars whose primary field is literary but whose work on Gothic fiction uses a queer cultural studies methodology to locate queerness, perversity, and sexual and gender transgression in eighteenth- and nineteenth-century Gothic fiction.[26] There is no doubt that the texts these Gothic-cum-queer scholars analyze speak to the presence of transgressive genders and sexualities in Gothic fiction, whether for the purposes of representation or for the purposes of censure and marginalization, and they also represent a gothic thread in queer theory, an academic field that arose in the 1990s to examine ideas, philosophies, and materialities around nonnormative genders and sexualities.[27] In other words, not only is queerness categorically embedded in eighteenth- and nineteenth-century Gothic fiction and its more contemporary reverberations, but the Gothic in turn serves as a theoretical bridge, spanning thinking on cultural production and queerness.

If gothicism (both Gothic fiction and its more contemporary thematic and aesthetic iterations) is categorically queer, then is queerness itself somehow gothic? Gothicism as an aesthetic device has certainly been a trend in the U.S. cinematic relationship with queer characters. As Vito Russo explores so convincingly in *The Celluloid Closet*, queer characters have appeared in films throughout the twentieth century, but the predominant narrative pattern depicts queer characters as monstrous—an object of derision for comic relief, a predator, a miserable depressive—and destined for an early death.[28] Russo explains that although the concept of monstrous queerness plays on the public understanding of gays and lesbians as creepy, sick, and villainous, these characters were sites of clandestine representation for queer writers, directors, and viewers. Gothicism in twentieth-century U.S. cinema, like its eighteenth-century predecessors, generally titillates audiences with transgression and then returns to the comfort of normative values in the end. But in this contemporary context, we begin to see the redeployment of these conservative gothic tropes within the queer communities marginalized by them. Like the reclamation of the term *queer*, originally used as an abusive epithet and then reappropriated by some members of the LGBT community to signify a proud and often politicized nonnormative identity, gothic reclamation serves to remove some of the linguistic and aesthetic violence committed by queer dehumanization in popular culture.

Gothicism is not simply a vehicle for transgressive sexual content but also an example of queer cultural production. Recall the controversial creativity of the Gothic form that challenged conventions, disrupted linguistic and conceptual structures of meaning, reflected the psychological desires and anxieties of its time, and opened up both the novelistic form and the history of sexuality to new interpretations and unexpected futures. In *The Culture of Queers*, Richard Dyer notes that it is not just sexually transgressive themes that make their appearance in Gothic literature but that "homosexual *writers* have often been drawn more generally to the Gothic" as a mode of expression.[29] The excesses of the Gothic—its ability to place readers in an unsettled affective space, its indulgence in those thoughts and behaviors considered lurid and perverse, its tendency to dismember cultural norms and reform them in visibly parodic ways—offer queer ways of being that resonate with those who find themselves outside of the mainstream and those driven to resist normativity and to embrace the fluidity of movement that this resistance allows.

Gothic Trauma and Queer Failure

Why would queer cultural producers be drawn to the gothic, especially when gothicism has so often been used to censure nonnormative genders and sexualities? It is precisely in the gothic's conflicted purposes that we find an answer. The normalized, unquestioned, and repeated destruction of queer characters in U.S. cinema is simply one example of the constant messages queer folks receive about their right to exist and live happy lives. Within the social and behavioral sciences, the term *microaggression* describes this type of persistent and often unacknowledged assault experienced by people who fall outside of the hegemonic norm. Derald Wing Sue and David Rivera's eight-year research study at Columbia University investigates the relation between racial microaggressions—a term originally developed to describe the everyday slights and insults directed at people of color by well-intentioned white people—and the forms of microaggression experienced by those whose gender and sexuality make them targets of bias. Sue argues that while overt forms of discrimination continue to exist, "the greatest harm to persons of color, women and LGBTs does not come from these conscious perpetrators . . . but instead [from] well-intentioned people, who are strongly motivated by egalitarian values, believe in their own morality, and experience themselves as fair-minded and decent people who would never consciously discriminate." Kevin Nadal examines how microaggressions impact the mental health of those within the LGBT community, specifically. Daily forms of discrimination, he argues, function as stressors that can lead to depression and anxiety, cognitive disruptions, hypervigilance, and rage. Further, the awareness of LGBT hate crimes can cause members of the LGBT community to experience "vicarious traumatization," shaking their belief in the "benevolence and meaningfulness of the world (and of other people)." The accumulation of microaggressive experiences and vicarious traumatization has significant negative impact on worldviews and mental health, meaning that overt violence impacts both the survivor and those community members who experience the trauma vicariously. Micro-aggressions and vicarious trauma often operate alongside more overt forms of violence used to police and oppress those who exist outside of the culture's mythic norm—what Audre Lorde describes as "white, thin, male, young, heterosexual, christian, and financially secure"—but the survivor of accumulated microaggression and vicarious trauma is rarely acknowledged in the way survivors of overt trauma are.[30]

Feminist psychologist Maria Root coined the term "insidious trauma" in the late twentieth century to focus attention on the disavowed traumas experienced by marginalized people, and it offers a way to think about the repetitive, daily injustices and vulnerabilities queer communities have faced but that have not been widely acknowledged. Laura Brown later took up the concept to challenge more traditional notions of trauma as an event "outside the range of human experience."[31] She argues that the concept of "human experience" implies an invisible, privileged norm: "the range of human experience becomes the range of what is normal and usual in the lives of men in the dominant class; white, young, able-bodied, educated, middle-class, Christian men."[32] Insidious trauma, she claims, is a common experience among marginalized subjects who feel constantly threatened by the prospect of violence. This type of trauma is constant and internalized, but it creates a traumatogenic reaction that is similar to reactions to the more "traditional" event-based traumas such as war, rape, or life-threatening accidents. Brown argues that not only are LGBT folks constantly aware of the possibility of physical violence but that their vulnerability is not taken seriously by a justice system that often implies that they bring violence on themselves through risky choices or flamboyant behavior.[33] This book resurrects the concept of "insidious trauma" as a productive term for examining the accumulated effects of small, persistent acts of microaggression combined with unacknowledged institutional and systemic violence to claim that gothic queer cultural production is a traumatic response to accumulated microaggression and insidious trauma.

As there are links between queerness and gothicism, there are also resonances between gothicism and trauma. A traumatic event is "not assimilated or experienced fully at the time, but only belatedly, in its repeated *possession* of the one who experiences it," explains Cathy Caruth; "to be traumatized is precisely to be possessed." She later explains that trauma is often "*not known* in the first instance" and "returns to haunt the survivor later on."[34] Roger Luckhurst notes that the memory of a traumatic event is "rather like a ghost, a haunting absent presence of another time in our time," and he coins the term "trauma Gothic" to explain how "trauma psychology frequently resorts to the Gothic or supernatural to articulate post-traumatic effects." Post-traumatic experience is "intrinsically uncanny" and emerges in cultural production through images of "ghostly visitations, prophetic dread, spooky coincidence or telepathic transfer."[35] In *Postcolonial Witnessing*, Stef Craps attempts to correct for trauma theory's heretofore exclusive focus on Western subjects and experiences, but despite Craps's break from problematically universalizing approaches to trauma, gothicism remains. Craps returns to spectrality, claiming it as a productive mode for investigating the lingering traumatic effects of colonial structures. Gabriele Schwab's work on transgenerational trauma similarly takes haunting as its critical framework, but the book's gothicism extends beyond the singular ghostly metaphor. The epigraph alone contains the words "grave," "tomb," "ghosts," "haunt," and "monsters."[36] I point to these instances of contemporary trauma theory to illustrate that even though thinking in trauma studies continues to evolve, the persistence of gothic language, imagery, and metaphor in writing on trauma illuminates an important link between trauma and the gothic.

Whether theorists conceptualize trauma as a singular event or as an accumulated response to histories of oppression, trauma haunts and possesses, driving its recreation in both traditional and unexpected forms.[37] The most contemporary work in "critical trauma studies," pushes beyond the privileging of the bounded traumatic event to explore the complex meaning of trauma in a culture that is infused with trauma and its vocabulary.[38] Stevens, for example, investigates trauma as a cultural object that produces subjects and in turn drives subjects to produce: "At its base is the notion that *trauma* is not simply a concept that describes particularly overwhelming events, nor is it simply a category that 'holds' people who have been undone by such events; but it is a cultural object whose function produces particular types of subjects, and predisposes specific affect flows that it then manages and ultimately shunts into political projects of various types. *Trauma does not describe, trauma makes*."[39] By recognizing the many functions and effects of trauma, we can begin to question the responsibilities of a field of inquiry that does not simply describe but acts on its subjects and can better acknowledge the connection between traumatic experience, social marginalization, and the cultural production coming out of that experience. In other words, traumatic experience and trauma discourse "make" subjects, knowledge, and political action, and those groups that experience systemic trauma and marginalization also "make" in the form of reclaimed histories and other creative expressions that represent traumatic experience.

While the discussion of microaggression is a fairly recent phenomenon, queer cultural producers have been pointing to this type of trauma for some time now, though the underpinning of insidious trauma has not always been recognized. Institutionally produced trauma, the insidious and persistent marginalization created by institutional structures that value certain subjectivities over others, is largely unexamined in traditional trauma studies, making the field subject to criticism that it privileges a universalized "racially unmarked citizen-subject." Stevens offers two important findings in relation to these limitations in trauma discourse: "First, the denigrated and the degraded, if only to beat back the loathing, must create histories that feature themselves and their loved ones as vindicated whole beings who possess the stuff of historical merit—will, self-awareness, culture, humanity, and so on. And second, the absence of this kind of confrontation in traditionally authorized settings (e.g., universities, capitol halls, state archives) has forced the work of representing, and potentially working through, difficult historical events, to fall to cultural production as a focus for memory management."[40] By locating and analyzing the thread of gothicism in queer cultural production, this book disinters the traumatic undercurrent of queer culture while drawing attention to the undertheorized aspect of critical trauma studies that Stevens points out. Through an intersectional analysis of the effects of accumulated and persistent institutionalized and structural traumas on queer folks in the United States, I present the histories, memory making, and cultural production that have come out of queer communities in response to persistent and insidious denigration and degradation.[41]

The concepts of microaggression and insidious trauma work together to provide a vocabulary for analyzing those notoriously tough-to-pin-down experiences that reinforce social hierarchies, create environments in which certain people feel alienated and indirectly threatened, and maintain the status quo while effectively gaslighting the disempowered and marginalized. Traumatic experience, by definition, resists language and narrativization because it cannot be fully assimilated. Caruth identifies trauma as an "aporia," or paradox, because the "force of this [traumatic] experience would appear to arise precisely, in other words, in the collapse of its understanding," and Luckhurst summarizes it as a "crisis of representation" because the traumatic event is characterized by its very inability to be represented.[42] In spite of the "crisis of representation" associated with trauma, a person who has experienced trauma is often driven to communicate the event and its subsequent effects, resulting in an almost obsessive need for testimony and an inability to do so effectively.[43] The expressive difficulty presented by explicit traumatic experiences is compounded when trauma is insidious and accumulated—an experience developed over time and through invisible structures and microaggressive interactions.

Despite the differences between traditional and insidious trauma, both create subjects who are driven to express the inexpressible. While Irene Visser argues that trauma theory must move beyond the limiting notion of traumatic narrative failure, this project takes the position that the difficulties of traumatic narrative push individuals and groups toward increasingly creative responses to traumatic experience. Ann Kaplan explores the drive to narrativize individual and collective trauma as "translation" that produces communities and cultural artifacts (such as art and literature), and Donna McCormack points to the corporeal, or the "role of the body," as a mode of "shar[ing] the unspeakable."[44] I would add that the role of critical theory and material cultural production must also be taken seriously as creative and unexpected forms of traumatic communication. The motley archive I have collected in this book traces traumatic cultural production across all these registers to show how queer folks have attempted to communicate the slippery experience of insidious trauma in a wide range of media in an almost obsessive endeavor to express the inexpressible. In these pages I show that gothicism, as a means of expressing microaggression and insidious trauma in queer lives, is the thread linking the disparate forms gathered here. The notion of unspeakable trauma does not necessarily shut down creativity; the insidiousness of accumulated trauma appears in unexpected ways that, in turn, accumulate into visible and recognizable cultural forms.

Indeed, the failures of traumatic expression have become a queer mode. As Jack Halberstam argues in *The Queer Art of Failure*, failing is "something queers do and have always done exceptionally well; for queers failure can be a style, to cite Quentin Crisp, or a way of life, to cite Foucault." Though Halberstam does not address queer failure as the failure of traumatic expression per se, he does position failure in relation to memory by cautioning against memorialization and positioning failure to appropriately remember as "a way of resisting the heroic and grand logics of recall" that "unleashes new forms of memory," a kind of resistant negativity. Lauren Berlant and Lee Edelman reflect on negativity itself—"the psychic and social incoherences and divisions, conscious and unconscious alike, that trouble any totality or fixity of identity"—as a failure of sovereignty often experienced as unbearable. Trauma, too, disrupts sovereignty, as people experience unbearable fragmentation and ruptures in myths around coherent selfhood and agency. Berlant and Edelman link these ruptures, not to isolation and apathy, but to the social and the queer, and they reflect on the way negativity functions as "resistance to forms of sovereignty and so in its status as an impediment to normativity's will to social closure and coherence."[45] Gothic queer culture accepts and uses the failures of traumatic remembering to linger in the "negative" sociality of traumatic rupture and to refuse "normativity's will" by remaining open to the traumatic wound as a queer space of indeterminacy and revision. Queer failure, when read through persistent and accumulated traumatic experiences, reveals a queer approach to trauma that recognizes its negativity and unspeakablity while remaining receptive to the antinormative possibilities of communicating trauma queerly. In this way trauma and failure emerge as a queer style in relation to the complex, intersectional insidious trauma experienced by queer folks in twentieth- and twenty-first-century U.S. society, leading to traumatically informed queer aesthetics and rhetorics, as community members work to create their own histories and manage their own memories in the face of a pervasively indifferent society.

I do not claim that queer folks have adopted gothic rhetorics and aesthetics to recover from trauma or to return to an idealized pretraumatic moment. Instead, gothic queer culture resists liberal narratives of wholeness and progress, envisions ways of being that push against assimilationism and limiting conceptual binaries, and gives voice to innumerable experiences of queer insidious trauma. Gothic queer culture has developed to construct and reconstruct memories whose absence is a result of both traumatic aporia and structural erasure. In these pages I examine how gothicism allows queer folks to live in an unsettled space that honors their traumas and that offers a vision of queer past, present, and future that resists neoliberal and neoconservative narratives of temporality and subjectivity. If, as Kilgour points out, the gothic is "better at dismemberment than re-memberment," then I would like to propose the existence of always already disparate, incoherent, and fragmented gothic queer culture that occupies a dismembered space, that fails to properly re-member, and that speaks to trauma while calling out and challenging those indifferent and violent structures that shape subjective queer experience.[46]

The chapters in this book are organized by gothic tropes—haunting, burial, monstrosity, and sadomasochism. Each chapter offers careful historical and cultural contextualization for the pieces at hand while supporting the book's overall claim that queer culture queers trauma through an applied gothicism that directs our gaze past the eruption of event-based traumatic experience to focus instead on the underlying insidious traumatic experience always vibrating in the margins.

Chapter 1, "Haunted Epistemologies: Gothic Queer Theory," examines the overlooked presence of gothicism in contemporary queer theory and argues that, as an outgrowth of underlying insidious trauma within academia, queer theory itself is expressly gothic. While critics have identified the presence of transgressive sexuality in eighteenth- and nineteenth-century Gothic fiction, this chapter proposes that there is an inverse relationship, a decidedly gothic presence in queer theory. Haunting is a queer temporality and a traumatic one. It implies a penetration of the present moment by ghosts from the past who refuse to settle, and it reflects the disruption of linear temporality that occurs with traumatic experience. Because of this, haunting is an apt metaphor for trauma. During a traumatic event, time is contorted, and following a traumatic event its memory intrudes "rather like a ghost, a haunting absent presence of another time in our time."[47] I argue, however, that queer writers and artists often deploy haunting to queer the experience of trauma, not by pointing to any specific bounded events but by describing the ongoing insidious trauma that infuses queer experience. Haunting in queer epistemology allows writers and thinkers to acknowledge the ongoing reverberations of historical traumas (what Carla Freccero calls "queer spectrality") while pointing toward the ways that insidious trauma queers time itself, creating a traumatically informed space for theorizing queer temporality.[48] In other words, insidiously traumatized time is haunted time is queer time.

Chapter 1 performs a unique reading of gothicism in contemporary queer theory texts, treating queer theory itself as a form of cultural production responding to the insidious trauma of queer marginalization. It argues that gothicism "haunts" and "possesses" queer thought in texts such as Lee Edelman's *No Future*, Jasbir Puar's *Terrorist Assemblages*, Elizabeth Freeman's *Time Binds*, and Karen Tongson's *Relocations*. The chapter analyzes various gothic tropes at work in queer theoretical projects that acknowledge and integrate traumatic histories while critiquing structures of normativity but settles on haunting as the primary manifestation of gothic queer theory, because haunting gets at the unique temporal registers of insidious trauma.

Chapter 2, "Live Burial: Lesbian Pulp and the 'Containment Crypt,'" examines the contradictory purposes of gothic burial during the "golden age" of U.S. lesbian pulp fiction—the mid-1940s to the mid-1960s. This period also notably coincided with the height of the Cold War United States and its foreign and domestic strategy of "containment," a policy that worked to control the spread of communism.[49] In Gothic fiction, subterranean passages, crypts, and catacombs hold double meaning. They offer vulnerable characters a place to hide or to escape, though their damp and dark passages are often nearly as terrifying as the men who roam them in rapacious pursuit. Though they offer the promise of escape, these concealed spaces also serve as prisons, places in which characters are buried alive, locked away just out of reach from those who might offer help. The nightmare of being buried alive in a catacomb alongside generations of rotting corpses at the ultimate mercy of your captor speaks to the queer experience of the closet. Though overt violence and traumatic assault has certainly been part of queer life in the United States, the sense of entrapment, of no possibility of escape, reflects the quiet and persistent experience of queer folks in mid-twentieth-century United States, who discovered quickly that they lived in a world structured to eliminate them, to exclude them from living a full life, even to destroy them. Internalization of the message that heteronormativity is the only way to thrive created an atmosphere of insidious trauma for those who could not (or would not) conform to "TV's idealistic 'Leave It to Beaver' image of the average American family."[50] Queers, however, have always been resilient and, in spite of their silent burial under the weight of heteronormativity, often found a way to form underground community within the metaphorical spaces created to isolate and contain them.

Chapter 2 examines how lesbian pulp novels deploy containment-inflected gothic tropes such as subterranean spaces, demonic manipulation, and live burial to fly under the radar of repressive censors while reappropriating the notion of containment to transform it into a space of community rather than one of marginalization. I read the cover art of first-edition pulp novels along with Ann Bannon's Beebo Brinker Chronicles, a series of five novels from the 1950s and 1960s that chronicle the life and love of Beebo, a Greenwich Village lesbian.[51] Analyzing the conflicting purposes of pulp cover art and the stories inside, I argue that lesbian pulp authors negotiate the structures of paranoia and domestic normativity by representing contained spaces, such as Greenwich Village's dark, subterranean bars, as opportunities for community formation, networking, and romance. Often appearing on cover art as lurid and pathologized places designed to pacify censors, within the text itself the "containment crypts" of lesbian pulp reframe the marginalizing narratives of the Cold War period to create gothic queer spaces and cultural practices.

Chapter 3, "Monstrosity: Melancholia, Cannibalism, and HIV/AIDS," examines the adoption of gothic monstrosity in cultural productions responding to the impact of HIV/AIDS on queer subjects, both during the AIDS crisis and today. The monster has become an iconic gothic trope precisely because it embodies the horrors of excess—unstable meanings, nebulous anxieties, unexpected desires. Like Gothic fiction itself, the monster serves both conservative and revolutionary purposes, straddling fear and desire, exclusion and belonging. Since it exceeds the singular, the monster threatens the understanding of a coherent self, and its refusal to be classified also makes it fundamentally queer. Monsters provide a manifestation of otherness against which the normal and the human can be defined, and the attribution of monstrosity creates scapegoats or sacrificial figures that can be excised from society in good conscience—after all, they are less than human.

It only makes sense that, as constantly shifting representations of cultural anxieties and desires, some of the most iconic Gothic monsters—Frankenstein's creature and Dracula—are composed of multiple bodies. The creature is literally pieced together from parts harvested from "the unhallowed damps of the grave" and the "living animal."[52] Dracula's multiplicity is less literal, however. Dracula lives by ingesting human blood in a cannibalistic form of monstrosity. Cannibalistic incorporation creates an uncomfortable disruption of boundaries because it "depends upon and enforces an absolute division between inside and outside; but in the act itself that opposition disappears, dissolving the structure it appears to produce."[53] In other words, both vampires and cannibals are what they eat. As representatives of otherness by which the norm is defined, monsters such as the patchwork creature and the cannibalistic vampire represent the dehumanizing othering that queer folks have faced as social outsiders and scapegoats. Especially in the context of HIV/AIDS, the use of monstrosity as an othering device has undermined the humanity of those tied to the disease in the public imagination, primarily gay men. In addition to the overt trauma of the AIDS crisis, the attribution of monstrosity creates insidious trauma among those who internalize ideas about their inhumanity. The queer extravagances of the monster, however, also offer a way of exceeding death and the limitations of normativity.

Chapter 3 begins with a text written at the height of the AIDS crisis, Gil Cuadros's mixed-genre *City of God* (1994), arguing that it is a piece of gothic AIDS literature that offers a Frankensteinian model for the queer subject in the face of overwhelming loss. The chapter then turns to the so-called post-AIDS era today, focusing on the work of queer punk–performance artist, Ron Athey, who tested positive for HIV in 1986 and continues a successful performance art career today. By analyzing Athey's performances featuring his own flowing blood, I argue that Athey deploys a vampiric, leaky queer body to address the ongoing material realities of HIV/AIDS. Both Athey and Cuadros work with cannibalistic consumption of infected bodily fluids, using the perceived threat of ingestion and infection as a gothic melancholic strategy that offers new modes of queer kinship and community in the face of widespread cultural indifference.

Chapter 4, "Sadomasochism: Strategic Discomfort in Trans* and Queer of Color Performance Art," argues that some queer artists respond to insidious trauma by creating aggressively uncomfortable live performances, using the materiality of the physical body in the performance space to elicit an affective response from the audience. Sexualized power dynamics are nearly ubiquitous in Gothic fiction. Sadomasochism is a controversial concept, and its practice is widely misunderstood, but that hasn't stopped theorists of sexuality, psychology, and sociology from obsessing over its meanings. Bondage/discipline, dominance/submission, sadism/masochism might seem to reflect and uphold oppressive social power structures, but its proponents point to the power of BDSM to denaturalize these dynamics while undermining binaries, often pointing to the power that the submissive player has in imagining, consenting to, and ending a scene in which they submit to the dominant player. Sadomasochism's complexity, its erotic charge, and its ability to appropriate and remix power make it a (gothic) queer go-to. BDSM can queer the oppressive binaries of normative social structures and practices, thereby giving it the potential to in turn queer the traumatic experience of existing within a dominant episteme that devalues nonnormative subjectivity.

Chapter 4 examines a body of queer art that deploys gothic sadomasochism through the complex negotiation of power and aggressive discomfort to force a change in the social myths that structure racialized and antitrans* violence. I first analyze artist M. Lamar's solo exhibition, *Negrogothic, a Manifesto, the Aesthetics of M. Lamar*, as gothic sadomasochism that forces viewers to encounter the then and now of histories that they might rather forget in favor of a liberal "postrace" contemporary consciousness. I then examine the work of two contemporary transgender artists—Cassils and Zackary Drucker—whose performances *Becoming an Image* and *The Inability to Be Looked At and the Horror of Nothing to See* address trauma through a productively incoherent blend of sadistic aggression and masochism. Ultimately, it is the deployment and disruption of sadomasochistic power that offer a paradoxical model of queer survival by recreating traumatic affect within the performance space.

The conclusion, "The Challenges of Neoliberalism," begins with a reading of Charlaine Harris's Sookie Stackhouse series, inspiration for HBO's *True Blood*. The series opens with a reference to vampires coming "out of the coffin" and integrating into human society. While this may appear to be a popular culture manifestation of gothic queer culture, I begin with this example to address the neoliberal appropriation of gothic queer culture. The conflict between the "mainstreaming" vampires in the series and those who refuse to conform to social norms serves as a representation of the current tension between those invested in homonormative values, most vocal in the marriage equality movement, and those who consider themselves more subversively queer in their resistance to normative cultural values, such as property ownership, private intimacy, monogamy, marriage, and family. The conclusion returns the conversation to the original motives of Gothic fiction in the eighteenth and nineteenth centuries as a means of censuring and containing queerness while at the same time offering titillation in the depiction and eventual destruction of nonnormative bodies. In queer culture's contemporary moment, the gothic once again serves as a battleground where society can work through its anxieties, where the marginalized can reappropriate dehumanizing narratives used against them, and where the battle between assimilation and queer resistance rages on. The conclusion points to the past and future of queer epistemology and culture, reinforcing that even when battles are raging, those battles involve the gothic language of monstrosity, haunting, containment, and power.

Gothic Queer Culture traces intersecting threads that point to the intricate and inextricable connections between queerness, trauma, and gothicism. Trauma is integral to the connection between the queer and the gothic, and gothicism itself is a way of queering trauma. By tracing gothicism as a through line in twentieth- and twenty-first-century queer cultural production, we can better understand the ways queer culture speaks to the invisible, insidious systems and practices that create myriad traumatic queer experiences—traumas that simultaneously demand and exceed expression. Gothic queer culture acknowledges the material realities and effects of violent marginalization and insidious trauma while developing a rich cultural aesthetic that makes visible structures of oppression and resists narratives of linearity and return in favor of radical contingency, dismemberment, failure, and incoherence.

1   HAUNTED EPISTEMOLOGIES

Gothic Queer Theory

Pockets of pain, burning rockets of pain—their pain,
her pain, all welded together into one great consuming
agony. Rockets of pain that shot up and burst, dropping
scorching tears of fire on the spirit—her pain, their
pain . . . all the misery at Alec's. And the press and the
clamour of those countless others—they fought, they
trampled, they were getting her under. In their madness
to become articulate through her, they were tearing her
to pieces, getting her under. They were everywhere now,
cutting off her retreat; neither bolts nor bars would avail
to save her. The walls fell down and crumbled before
them; at the cry of their suffering the walls fell and crumbled: "We are coming, Stephen—we are still coming on,
and our name is legion—you dare not disown us!" She
raised her arms, trying to ward them off, but they closed
in and in: "You dare not disown us!"

RADCLYFFE HALL, *The Well of Loneliness*

The final passage in Radclyffe Hall's *The Well of Loneliness* (1928), with its
melodramatic exclamations of pain and suffering and its clamoring ghosts

demanding vengeance for wrongs forgotten, would seem quite at home in an eighteenth-century Gothic novel. I include it here not merely to illustrate the gothicism in a text about gender and sexual nonconformity. I include it primarily because this final passage appears in a number of queer theory texts, serving as an illustration of this theory or that but persistently resurfacing, like the legion of suffering queers demanding Stephen's acknowledgement.[1] There is something about the demand of these ghosts of queer pasts that makes them particularly suited to theorizing about contemporary queerness and its futures.

Literary critics have frequently identified the presence of transgressive sexuality in eighteenth- and nineteenth-century Gothic fiction, usually highlighting its trajectory of temporary titillation followed by a comforting restoration of norms and pointing out that, even in its conservative mode, queerness is embedded in Gothic fiction. Trauma theory often uses gothic metaphors to describe the uncanniness of traumatic experience and its haunting aftereffects, something expressed both implicitly and overtly in theories such as Roger Luckhurst's "trauma Gothic," and queer cultural production (such as *The Well of Loneliness*) is also often infused with gothicism as an aesthetic and rhetorical mode.[2] In other words, the Gothic is queer, trauma is gothic, and queer cultural production is both queer and gothic because it responds to trauma, specifically insidious trauma or "the traumatogenic effects of oppression that are not necessarily overtly violent or threatening to bodily well-being at the given moment but that do violence to the soul and spirit."[3] As I argue throughout this book, gothic queer cultural production pulls together queerness, trauma, and gothicism as a way of acknowledging and communicating the insidious, structural traumas related to living queerly in the United States.

Traumatically driven cultural production takes myriad forms, but one type of creation usually overlooked as a kind of cultural production is queer theory itself. Eve Kosofsky Sedgwick begins *Tendencies* by linking the queer teen suicide rate, "the profligate way this culture has of denying and despoiling queer energies and lives," and the precariousness of those who "do" gay and lesbian studies, noting that "the survival of each one is a miracle." Notably, this discussion of unacknowledged insidious trauma, suicide, and academic queer studies begins with a gothicism that reflects the demands of Stephen's legion of suffering queer ghosts: "I think everyone who does gay and lesbian studies is haunted by the suicides of adolescents."[4] The academic production of queer theoretical texts is inextricable from the insidious trauma of professional and social marginalization of queer thought and being—more specifically the institutional silencing of queers in higher education, especially queers of color, who are most likely to receive unfair treatment in academic departments that are structurally and sometimes overtly racist and homophobic. Queer theory is an academic field developed in the 1990s, a time in which the AIDS crisis and culture wars raged and the possibility of federally recognized gay marriage seemed like a pipe dream after President Bill Clinton signed the Defense of Marriage Act. Traumatic circumstances such as these make the expression of theories around oppression difficult, if not impossible, since trauma tends to disrupt linguistic structures and meanings, but gothic queer theory is not confined to the 1990s. Queer theorists to this day often turn to gothic metaphors, resulting in a product containing gothicisms in form, content, or both.

In this chapter I read queer epistemological texts to locate gothic themes and forms, focusing specifically on paranoia, accretion, monsters, sadomasochism, and haunting. The gothic thread I trace through these texts points to the effectiveness of gothic metaphor as a means of elucidating insidious trauma, specifically around the institutional and structural microaggressions that impact queer folks. Paranoia and accretion are particularly suited to reflecting microaggression, since microaggressions often leave recipients feeling as if their responses are paranoid or overreactive (if you have ever been offended by someone's comment and then told, "It was just a joke!" then you may know this feeling). Accretion, the growth of a substance by an accumulation of layers, mirrors the way repeated microaggressions accumulate to create insidious trauma, an experience that can have significant negative impacts on mental health despite the "micro" nature of the offences. Monstrosity can itself be a form of accretion, as monsters are often cobbled together from various cultural anxieties and desires, allowing "for a whole range of specific monstrosities to coalesce in the same form."[5] The excesses of monstrosity and the hybridity of the living dead help visualize naturalized oppressive structures, making those structures uncanny and therefore intervening in the architecture of oppression. Both haunting and sadomasochism appear in queer thought as expressions of queer temporality that expose a particular type of traumatic temporality. Haunting manifests the swirling, fractured, intersecting temporality of ongoing low-level trauma, not just a singular traumatic event popping through into the present but a disorienting and overwhelming storm of traumatic intrusion.

The traumatic gothic shadow cast on queer theory is not always made explicit, however. Gothicism often subtly permeates contemporary queer theory—Gothic fiction does not necessarily serve as a source of primary examples, and theories sometimes explicitly engage gothicism but often do not. Rather, gothicism usually lurks under the surface, popping through texts in moments when its metaphoric power is needed to describe or theorize a concept or offering a structure that allows theorists to better communicate their ideas or to propose productive modes of resistance. In other words, queer epistemology is haunted by trauma, and the specter of "trauma Gothic" appears in the following texts in ways that exhibit preoccupation with gothic concepts. In this chapter I tell a story about queer thought's almost obsessive return to gothicism and how the insidious trauma associated with queerness and its intersections lends itself to gothic representation on multiple levels, often in a turn toward the grotesque, the uncanny, the monstrous, and the spectral.

Paranoia and Accretion

There is a deeply rooted relationship between gothicism, psychoanalysis, and theories of nonnormative gender and sexuality. Sigmund Freud's "Psychoanalytic Notes upon an Autobiographical Account of a Case of Paranoia (Dementia Paranoides)" is a foundational text that depends on gothic tropes and structures to theorize sexuality and its effects, specifically paranoia.[6] In this text Freud analyzes Dr. Daniel Paul Schreber's written autobiographical account of his struggles with paranoia and hypochondria (*Denkwürdigkeiten eines Nervenkranken*) to illustrate his emerging theory that "a defence against a homosexual wish was clearly recognizable at the very centre of the conflict which underlay the disease [paranoia]."[7] In this analysis Freud fundamentally links paranoia with homosexuality, but because of its gothicism Schreber's autobiography is particularly suited to Freud's task of describing the psychological trauma of having a "homosexual wish" in a homophobic culture.

Schreber's account contains the gothic elements of demonic manipulation, necrophilia, and fetishized decay that can be found in eighteenth-century Gothic novels. In Charlotte Dacre's *Zofloya, or The Moor*, for example, Victoria experiences uncontrollable sexual desires that drive her to become increasingly attracted to a forbidden object, her black servant Zofloya. Overtly, Victoria's sexual desires are directed at her husband's brother, Henriquez, but throughout the novel it becomes increasingly clear that she is, in fact, drawn to the majestic Zofloya as an object of sexual desire until they become (unconsummated) lovers by the end of the novel. At this point Zofloya reveals that he is actually Satan, and Victoria devotes herself to him for eternity just before he hurls her off a precipice. Similarly, Matthew Lewis's *The Monk: A Romance* includes demonic manipulation, when Ambrosio is seduced by Matilda, a woman who entered the monastery disguised as a young man and who turns out to be a servant of Lucifer, sent to encourage and support Ambrosio's sinful desires. When he grows tired of Matilda, Ambrosio then shifts his desire to the innocent Antonia, eventually giving her a potion to mimic death so he can rape her interred body, in a kind of simulated necrophilia. Ambrosio's necrophilia is paired with fetishized decay in the story line of Agnes, a young woman who, after becoming pregnant out of wedlock, is locked away in the catacombs underneath a convent, only to be later discovered in her burial chamber barely clinging to life, emaciated, and clutching the rotting corpse of her infant to her breast. Each of these iconic Gothic characters pursue forbidden sexual desires, leaving them vulnerable to decay and devilish manipulation. Schreber's autobiography is similarly concerned with his increasing drive toward sexual taboo paired with the sense that he was in communication with God and the "plaything of devils." Further, it contains descriptions of Schreber's "dead and decomposing" body and an allusion to necrophilia, in which Schreber imagined his "soul was to be murdered" and his "body used like a strumpet" by God, who "was only accustomed to intercourse with corpses."[8]

Freud heightens the gothicism of the account by focusing on the supernatural and divine manifestations of Schreber's delusions (in the "Case History" section of the text) and then explaining them away through psychoanalytic interpretation (in the "Attempts at Interpretation" section), a move that reflects the explained supernatural that often occurs at the conclusion of some Gothic fiction in which "all the incidents appearing to partake of the mystic and the marvelous are resolved by very simple and natural causes."[9] For example, Dr. Schreber hallucinates supernatural phenomena and develops delusions about the divine intention behind his emotional and physical sensations, each instance of which Freud describes (using direct quotes from the autobiography) and then systematically demystifies through interpretation. Schreber believes that "miracled birds" talk to him in "meaningless phrases they have learnt by heart" and then discharge a "load of ptomaine poison on to him" (a footnote clarifies that the literal translation would be "corpse poison"). Freud explains that what this ominous supernatural hallucination "really refers to must be young girls," whom "people often compare" to geese or "ungallantly accuse them of having 'the brains of a bird.'" Further, Schreber's sense that he is gradually transforming into a woman to be used by his doctor for "sexual abuse" and later to be used as a corpse "strumpet" by God is explained as a "feminine (that is, a passive homosexual) wish-phantasy, which took as its object the figure of his physician." Schreber even identifies the "call to sh—" and its attendant "voluptuousness" as supernatural, explaining that it is "evoked miraculously." Freud, of course explains that the persecuting God who manipulates Schreber's "evacuation," among other things, is merely the transfiguration of his father and an expression of a "father-complex."[10] In all these instances Schreber presents himself as passive, a vessel on which supernatural forces act, and Freud first presents them through this lens, allowing the supernatural to enter into the text as an imaginative possibility, only to explain each instance as a logical phenomenon stemming from Schreber's childhood experiences and repressed desires. This is what Freud does best—interpret apparent incoherencies within the rational frame of unconscious desires—but its resonance with the tradition of the explained supernatural provides a gothic cast to the work of analysis in this text.

Additionally, Freud's choice to analyze a published text rather than actual patient interaction creates a case study embedded with multiple voices and narratives, making "Psychoanalytic Notes" uncannily similar in form to Gothic literature from the eighteenth and nineteenth centuries.[11] Freud inserts Schreber's narrative within his own by beginning the piece with an introduction justifying his use of the autobiography, moving into a "Case History" section, in which he narrates Schreber's story using extended quotes from the autobiography (creating a kind of dual narration), then providing a second narrative of the events in the "Attempts at Interpretation" section, and finally ending with a generalization developed from this case in the section titled "On the Mechanism of Paranoia." Within this convoluted narrative, the lines between Freud's voice and Schreber's become blurred, since Freud moves between voicing his own position as narrator and voicing the reasoning behind Schreber's neurosis as if the paranoid logic were his own: "The behavior of God in the matter of the 'call to sh—' (the need for evacuating the bowels) rouses him to a specially high pitch of indignation. The passage is so characteristic that I will quote it in full. But to make it clear, I must first explain that both the miracles and the voices proceeded from God, that is, from the divine rays."[12] At the beginning of this passage, it is clear through the use of third person that Freud is summarizing Schreber's beliefs and feelings, and his position as a kind of omniscient narrator is quite overt when he explains that he will "quote" a passage from the autobiography "in full." The following sentence, however, does not maintain this authorial distance when it lapses into clarifying Schreber's logic as if it were a matter of fact ("both the miracles and the voices proceeded from God") and without qualifying the statement with any language such as "Schreber believes." While the first two sentences in this passage are clearly from Freud's perspective as narrator and analyst, the final sentence could just as easily have been written by Schreber himself.

This slippage of narrative voice occurs throughout the text—Freud inserts bits of poetry, lyrics, and plot summary in footnotes throughout and, at one point, interrupts Schreber's narrative with a story of another patient to illustrate the "father-complex," calling to mind those eighteenth- and nineteenth-century Gothic novels—*Melmoth the Wanderer*, *The Monk*, and *Frankenstein*, for example—in which lengthy embedded stories are narrated within embedded stories, often stalling the main narrative.[13] *Frankenstein*, for example, is famously structured with a multilevel frame narrative: the creature's narrative at the center, Victor's narrative framing the creature's, and Walton's epistolary narrative framing Victor's. Eighteenth-century Gothic novels tend to have even more circuitous narrative structures, offering texts-within-texts whose "structural correlate . . . is to be found in the structure of Gothic houses involving a succession of ruins, in the labyrinthine spatial enclosures of underground tunnels and secret chambers, and in the crossed lines of withering family trees."[14] One function of embedded narratives, especially those that incorporate found objects such as letters, prefaces, and first-person accounts, position the text as an authentic object of interpretation. Freud's adoption of embeddedness attempts to privilege the authenticity of his interpreted object while creating fragmented narrative, reflecting the "proliferation of fragments in Gothic fiction—abandoned houses, rusty locks, ill-fitting bolts, crumbling graves, incompleted manuscripts, half-formed sensibilities."[15] The fragmentation of the interrupted narrative mirrors both Gothic form and traumatogenic fragmentation, as Schreber desperately works to reconcile his taboo desires with the insidiously traumatizing strictures of his social context.

This traumatogenic gothic embeddedness and fragmentation create a kind of paranoid structure, making the text not only *about* paranoia but one that *embodies* paranoia in its gothic form. Sedgwick famously proposed that the Gothic is paranoid, coining the phrase "paranoid Gothic" to describe those novels that include paranoid homosexual content stemming from "homosexual panic" and that ultimately reinscribe homophobia by centering heterosexuality and "hav[ing] as their *first* referent the psychology and sociology of prohibition and control."[16] James Hogg's *The Private Memoirs and Confessions of a Justified Sinner* is a key example of the paranoid Gothic. Published in 1824, Hogg's novel is divided into three sections, all of which depict the same set of events but from different narrative perspectives—first, an "Editor's Narrative" conveys the events from an outsider's point of view; then an "original document" is inserted, providing an autobiographical account of the same events; followed by the editor attempting to justify the account with various rumors and theories quoted from (an apparently inaccurate) letter supposedly written by a man named James Hogg and eventually including an account of a grave-site excavation at which he discovers the autobiographical document he had presented in the previous section of the text. The structure of this text exhibits a multiplicity of nearly undifferentiated narrative voices and an account of a single event from multiple perspectives, one of which is an autobiographical account and the others as told by the editor, but stemming from information gathered in a fictional sleuthing and interpretive process. Freud's text mirrors this structure, a compilation of autobiography and outside interpretation divided into multiple sections that tell and retell a single set of events in an obsessive drive that mirrors the compulsion to narrativize an unassimilable trauma.

Indeed, not only is Freud's text gothic in its formal embeddedness, but its pathologization of homosexuality serves as a medicalized means of that "prohibition and control" Sedgwick describes as the central focus of the "paranoid Gothic." As is well established, Freud's work on homosexuality is peppered with misogyny and homophobia, frequently embodied in the pathologization of subjects like Schreber, who remarks that "it really must be very nice to be a woman submitting to the act of copulation."[17] By reading homosexual thoughts as psychological neuroses, Freud participates in the perpetuation of insidious trauma, as subjects like Schreber struggle to reconcile their desires with a culture that labels them sick and monstrous. In an extended analysis of "Psychoanalytic Notes," David Eng points out that Freud's analysis has been deployed as an argument against homosexuality rather than as a text highlighting the violent homophobia of a society that drives Schreber to his paranoid delusions, another feasible and more productive reading. Eng uses the framework of Schreber's paranoia to illustrate the contemporary assimilationist impulse in the LGBT community, specifically the "mental gymnastics" of those who fight for the right to be folded into a respectable liberal bourgeois lifestyle. In this sense Schreber's paranoia is not merely the homosexual wish fantasy Freud proposes but "a particular form of homosexuality that delineates the psychic compromises one might make in order to reconcile homosexuality to the moral demands of the ego-ideal—to blend into its confusion of voices through a particular form of family and kinship. Today, we might say that such a reconciliation defines the psychic structure and limits of queer liberalism."[18] Eng's reading also speaks to the psychological and emotional labor that nonheteronormative subjects must perform in a society structured to marginalize them through medical, social, and legal means—a burden all too easily dismissed by folks whose privilege allows them to remain blind to the violence of this perpetual negotiation and the inevitable exhaustion it causes.

Read as a paranoid gothic text, "Psychoanalytic Notes" reinscribes homophobia and controls sexuality through paranoia-as-diagnosis. Read as a piece of gothic queer theory, Freud's work responds to the unacknowledged trauma of queerness through paranoia-as-gothic form. For example, Freud notes that splitting, or "decomposition," is a central characteristic of paranoia that follows a sense of catastrophe stemming from the withdrawal of homosexual libidinal cathexes considered inappropriate. "*The delusion-formation*," he goes on to note, "*is in reality an attempt at recovery, a process of reconstruction*."[19] The paranoid "decomposition" and "reconstruction" of narrative is certainly present in the fractured, multiple structures of both *Justified Sinner* and "Psychoanalytic

Notes," a form that serves to illustrate and explain the complexities of nonnormative identity formations. Echoing Eng's reading of the text as an indictment of homophobic society, the "internal catastrophe" Freud names may function as an early exploration of traumatic fragmentation for a subject whose sexual desires are deemed pathological and unacceptable. Threatened by social rejection, career loss, institutionalization, legal punishment, and physical violence, a nonnormative subject in Schreber's time and place might certainly exhibit the kind of fragmentation that characterizes those who experience traumatogenic reactions. The process of traumatic fragmentation, or dissociation, followed by the drive to somehow reconstruct what was shattered is a common narrative in studies of trauma, and this process could very well be mapped on to what Freud describes as "catastrophe," followed by "delusion-formation" in paranoid neurosis.[20] Notably, the drive that moves a narrative from disruption to the reconstruction of a coherent and comforting originary condition is also a characteristic of those conservative Gothic novels that begin with a disruption to the order of things and end with order's restoration. In other words, "Psychoanalytic Notes" participates in the marginalization of homosexuality while simultaneously allowing those who read queerly to see the text as an indictment of the structures that cause Schreber to psychologically scramble in response to his desires. The unintentional gothicism implies that the text may also expose the insidious trauma of Schreber's homosexual subjectivity, though the nature of trauma means that this reading merely announces itself in the periphery, like a shadowy presence that flickers just out of sight.

Like Freud, Sedgwick too spent a significant amount of time exploring paranoia. One particularly influential essay, "Paranoid Reading and Reparative Reading, or You're So Paranoid, You Probably Think This Essay Is about You," cogently parses and critiques paranoid reading practices, and subsequent theorists have returned to her formulation of paranoid and reparative reading again and again.[21] Sedgwick began her career with an exploration of Gothic conventions (*The Coherence of Gothic Conventions*), moved on to examine the presence of homosexuality and homosociality in Gothic novels (*Between Men*), and continued with highly influential interventions in queer theory (*Epistemology of the Closet*). In *The Coherence of Gothic Conventions*, Sedgwick identifies paranoia itself as a Gothic convention, and in her later essay on paranoid reading, she subtly quotes from *Coherence* to point out the paranoid qualities (anticipatory, mimetic) in the feminist and queer uses of psychoanalysis.[22] She implies that the quote arises out of a feminist, queer, and psychoanalytic context but does not indicate that the quote she provides is pulled from a conversation specifically about Gothic fiction. She does, however, point out that paranoia, as a "hermeneutics of suspicion," dominates critical theory and notes that "queer studies in particular has had a distinctive history of intimacy with the paranoid imperative."[23] Sedgwick explicitly links queer studies with paranoia while imbuing that claim with unspoken gothicism. Sedgwick, of course, is not advocating for paranoid (or gothic) reading practices. Instead, she critiques the anticipatory paranoia that dominates queer theory to advocate for the consideration of reparative reading practices, a move that turns away from the negativity of gothic paranoia to a more productive mode of inquiry.

This move seems to detach queer thought from its gothic roots; however, her description of the reparative practice that she proposes as another option for queer epistemology is itself unintentionally gothic. Indeed, she states clearly that she is moving away from the Freudian "transhistorical" association between paranoia and "gay/lesbian issues," "suggesting that the mutual inscription of queer thought with the topic of paranoia may be less necessary, less definitional, less completely constitutive than earlier writing on it, very much including my own, has assumed." One motivation of paranoid reading, Sedgwick explains, is to be sure that "no horror, however apparently unthinkable, shall ever come to the reader *as new.*" To defend against this horror, a paranoid reader constantly anticipates future contingencies, an orientation that Sedgwick describes as a "rigid relation to temporality." Reparative reading, much like reading a Gothic novel, remains open to horror, shock, surprise, and even humiliation and allows past temporalities to haunt the present rather than remaining rigidly and exclusively future-oriented. Further, Sedgwick posits a link between this practice and traumatic experience, fragmented and temporally dislocated. The reparative approach surrenders to the horror of surprise and organizes itself around hope, which is itself a "traumatic thing to experience." Like gothicism and the traumatic fragmentation that gothicism can represent, reparative practices as a feature of queer reading "can attune it exquisitely to a heartbeat of contingency" precisely because of its ability to respond to insidious traumas, for example, "the brutal foreshortening of so many queer life spans" that has "deroutinized the temporality of many of us."[24] Here Sedgwick refers to the structures that actively cause or passively allow the deaths of those who do not adhere to normative temporalities and whose lives are seen as disposable.[25] Reparative reading, as Sedgwick describes it, contains horror, fragmentation, and contingency in relation to trauma—a description that attempts to move away from (gothic) paranoia but is itself decidedly gothic.

The horror that paranoid reading guards against braces the reader against the shock of a traumatic event, but the reparative concept of accretion more accurately reflects the ongoing traumatic accumulation associated with microaggression. Sedgwick describes the "reparative impulse" as "additive and accretive," a recombination of those "fragments and part-objects" encountered in a contingent and materially located queer epistemology that accounts for the insidious trauma of existing in a "culture whose avowed desire has often been not to sustain them."[26] This accretive approach reflects a kind of Frankensteinian accumulation of fragments, like the bits and pieces of flesh Victor gathered from "the dissecting room and the slaughter-house" to create an unimaginable creature out of the morbid conglomeration of accumulated materials.[27] Reparative reading pieces together the shards of traumatically fractured cultural objects and experiences to create new monstrous practices that attend to the horrors of humiliation, invalidation, and the undercurrents of a society in which queers are always already cathected to death and considered disposable and, as Judith Butler argues, ungrieveable.[28] Both paranoid and reparative reading practices respond to traumatic experience or are an attempt to brace oneself against a future trauma. But the inadvertently gothic description of reparative reading shifts the focus from the shock and horror of a shattering traumatic event to the accumulated, slippery, and often unrecognized experience of microaggression. In her move to open up reading practices from gothic paranoia to the contingent, traumatic, and additive reparative practices, Sedgwick—originator of the "paranoid Gothic"—has unintentionally proposed another type of gothic queer theory.

Monstrosity and the Living Dead

Sedgwick's reparative reading practices are subtly Frankensteinian, asking readers to acknowledge horror not as a surprise but as an ongoing internalized state or, as Victor Frankenstein might put it, to "make fear and unnatural horror the inmates of his breast."[29] Michel Foucault overtly theorized monstrosity in his lectures at the Collège de France (1974–75), in which he outlined a theory of the abnormal by describing the "human monster" at length. He explains that from the Middle Ages to the eighteenth century, the monster was conceived as a "mixture":

> It is the mixture of two realms, the animal and the human: the man with the head of an ox, the man with a bird's feet—monsters. It is the blending, the mixture of two species: the pig with a sheep's head is a monster. It is the mixture of two individuals: the person who has two heads and one body or two bodies and one head is a monster. It is the mixture of two sexes: the person who is both male and female is a monster. It is a mixture of life and death: the fetus born with a morphology that means it will not be able to live but that nonetheless survives for some minutes or days is a monster. Finally, it is a mixture of forms: the person who has neither arms nor legs, like a snake, is a monster. Consequently, the monster is the transgression of natural limits, the transgression of classifications, of the table, and of the law as table: this is actually what is involved in monstrosity.

By the end of the eighteenth century, he explains, the figure of the "sexual monster" emerges, in which the "monstrous individual and the sexual deviant link up," as the criminalization of monstrosity shifts from a focus on monstrous morphology to monstrous behavior. To illustrate this shift Foucault turns to the treatment of "hermaphrodites," once burned at the stake simply for existing (Middle Ages to early seventeenth century) and later criminalized only if, once their "true sex" had been determined, they "made use of their additional sex." In the late eighteenth and early nineteenth centuries, he points to an increasing focus on "monstrous criminality," leading to the concept of the "moral monster," which, he points out, "looms up in the gothic novel."[30] In these lectures gothic monstrosity serves as an epistemological foundation that haunts his subsequent work.

Foucault later deploys an indeterminate and hybrid body to illustrate the concepts he began to develop in his earlier lectures. In 1978 he compiled and published the memoirs of Herculine Barbin, a "nineteenth-century French hermaphrodite," to highlight the development of medical and juridical notions of "true sex" as inherent and identifiable. In a reflection of the gothic structure exemplified by *Justified Sinner* and "Psychoanalytic Notes," Foucault includes an introduction, Herculine Barbin's memoir, an archival "dossier," and a fictional nineteenth-century tale based on the memoir and told in the eighteenth-century Gothic style. Notably, the dossier includes notes from medical examinations performed on Barbin's living body and corpse by doctors specializing in "teratology," or the "science of monstrosities."[31] Foucault positions himself against the negative coding of the monstrous by glorifying the ambiguity of Barbin's gender and sexuality preceding the teratological examination at twenty-two, in which the doctors determined Barbin's "true sex" to be male. He calls Barbin's preexamination existence a "happy limbo of non-identity" and praises the fact that the memoir's "narrative baffles every possible attempt to make an identification" and rests more firmly on affect than on sexual identity.[32]

Though Foucault adopts the metaphor of monstrosity to theorize a counter claim to the nineteenth-century medical assumptions about sex, gender, and sexuality, his deployment of the monstrously coded body as a symbol of a desirable nonidentity stems partially from the very aspects that caused it to be marginalized during Barbin's lifetime. Foucault's compilation of materials highlights the marginalization and objectification of those who could not be easily categorized in terms of normative gender or sexuality, and the dossier's medical documents describing Barbin's genital structures and secretions in graphic detail call to mind the medicalizing and dehumanizing treatment of Saartjie Baartman, a nineteenth-century South African woman who was famously exploited and displayed across England as a "medical curiosity" for her large buttocks and genitalia. After her death Baartman's body was dissected, and her genitals and brain were placed in jars at the Musée de l'Homme in Paris. Baartman's usefulness rested on the dehumanizing use of her body-as-metaphor for racial inferiority, hypersexuality, and primitivism. Similarly, Foucault problematically uses Barbin's excessive body as a metaphor in a universalizing reading of Barbin's utopian "non-identity" (notably without an analysis of other intersecting factors such as race or class). The ambiguity and excess of a subject who defies binaries and troubles notions of gender and sexuality prompted medical and juridical figures of Barbin's time to deploy the gothic notion of monstrosity as a justification for their intrusion and reassignment, and Foucault redeploys this very same ambiguity as a symbol of what subjectivity might look like outside of these discourses. Though he does not explicitly label Barbin as monstrous in this text, within the context of his earlier lectures on monsters, Foucault's idealization of Barbin's morphology and sexual nonidentity rests on the implicit characterization of Barbin as monster.[33]

For Foucault the hybridity and ambiguity that monstrosity implies serve as a queer reminder of the limits of binary linguistic structures. He mentions in a footnote that Barbin's systematized use of gendered pronouns in the memoir (switching from "she" to "he" once ordered by authorities to live as a man) "does not seem to describe a consciousness of being a woman becoming a consciousness of being a man" but instead serves as an "ironic reminder of grammatical, medical, and juridical categories that language must utilize but that the content of the narrative contradicts."[34] In other words, the use of language follows the law imposed on Barbin but inadvertently exposes the limits of language to sufficiently describe the complexities of Barbin's experiences. Similarly, Foucault's adoption of monstrosity as a metaphor for idealized nonidentity works within the limited logic of the original medical discourse, inadvertently highlighting its limits. But his strategy performs a problematic deployment of the gothic, for it uses the body of an intersex person as a metaphor for utopian queerness, ultimately replicating the teratologists' objectification of Barbin's body. In his reappropriation of the traumatizing medical discourses striated with monstrosity that marginalized and ultimately drove Barbin to suicide, Foucault calls attention to the multiple interpretive possibilities of Barbin's body while simultaneously reducing Barbin to mere metaphor. Regardless, Foucault and others seem drawn to the monstrous as a means of exploring queerness, and his gothic framing of Barbin, both in content and in form, serves as an example of gothic queer theory while it illustrates how that theory might inadvertently replicate the traumatic structures it sets out to critique.

Though the lectures on abnormality are not among Foucault's most cited works, Jasbir Puar and Amit Rai take up his musings on the "human monster" in "Monster, Terrorist, Fag: The War on Terrorism and the Production of Docile Patriots." In this piece Puar and Rai tease out one of the concepts that later appears in Puar's 2007 *Terrorist Assemblages*—the post-9/11 creation of the "monster-terrorist-fag," a figure that tied "the image of the modern terrorist to a much older figure, the racial and sexual monsters of the eighteenth and nineteenth centuries." Because gothic monstrosity has traditionally functioned to solidify the mainstream in opposition to the othered monster, Puar and Rai argue that the monster-terrorist-fag "enables the practices of normalization, which in today's context often means an aggressive heterosexual patriotism." They rely on an extended citation of Foucault's concept of the "human monster" from *Abnormal* to show how monsters have always represented sexual transgression and to argue that monstrosity has been a regulatory apparatus that gets at the intersection of sexuality, culture, and race.[35] The "uncanny monster-terrorist-fag," in classic eighteenth-century Gothic fashion, allows once-marginalized groups to move toward a normalized center by shifting the coding of monstrosity to the figure of the terrorist.

Interestingly, the "monster-terrorist-fag" appears in Puar's chapter "The Sexuality of Terrorism," in *Terrorist Assemblages*, but the chapter subsumes the extended discussion of the sexualized Gothic monster that serves as the foundation of the Puar and Rai article. Like the article, the chapter too includes a lengthy citation of Foucault, but, rather than a quote from *Abnormal*, it includes an epigraphical quote taken from Foucault's *The History of Sexuality*. Instead of beginning with a discussion of the manner in which monstrosity quarantines the other while bolstering the normative center, Puar expresses the same sentiment as the "twin mechanisms of normalization and banishment" with no specific reference to the monstrosity that propelled the similar argument in her earlier article.[36] In a similar move to Sedgwick's in "Paranoid Reading," Puar depends on the gothic foundation of her earlier work to develop later theories but buries any explicit reference to gothicism in those later pieces. Like Sedgwick's, Puar's later work may not seem overtly gothic, but it is certainly informed by these gothic beginnings.

The roots of Puar's work around the monstrous sexualities characteristic in the eighteenth and nineteenth centuries are not all that marks her theory as expressly gothic. Puar's "queer necropolitics" relies on the metaphor of the "living dead" to describe existence as a population always already marked for death. Achille Mbembe's influential reframing of biopolitics within the colonial and contemporary contexts proposes "necropolitics" and "necropower" to describe how "weapons are deployed in the interest of maximum destruction of persons and the creation of death-worlds, new and unique forms of social existence in which vast populations are subjected to conditions of life conferring upon them the status of *living dead*."[37] Puar takes on this concept and inserts an explicit attention to sexuality in relation to the necropolitical drive, partially as a way to bring queer scholarly attention to biopolitics and to posit queer necropolitics as a "bio-necro collaboration" that moves beyond the framework of queer identity and visibility. This involves a decidedly gothic turn—focusing on the "interstices of life and death," including "the living dead, the dead living, the decaying living, those living slow deaths."[38]

Queer necropolitics and the attention to the "living dead" and "death-worlds" that mark some subjects as excess or disposable has resonated with other queer theorists, leading to work that specifically uses Mbembe's and Puar's concepts of (queer) necropolitics and its gothic associations, especially the notion of the living dead and cannibalism, to theorize the structural oppressions that produce insidious trauma in postcolonial and trans* of color communities.[39] Not only does necropolitics offer a theory infused with a kind of gothic monstrosity, but this gothicism also specifically arises to address structural oppressions and the insidious and accumulated traumas that attend systems in which some lives are cathected to death or marked for death as excess, disposable, and inhuman.

The living dead or undead are metaphors of monstrosity that work to acknowledge and understand the function of queerness in the face of structural oppression. These metaphors appear often in queer theory, even if their gothicism remains below the surface. Like Sedgwick's "Paranoid Reading," Foucault's *Herculine Barbin*, and Puar's *Terrorist Assemblages*, Lee Edelman's *No Future* never explicitly alludes to gothic literature or tropes but frequently employs monstrosity to explain and illustrate concepts. Edelman claims that contemporary culture is dominated by the ideology of reproductive futurity—the idea that all decisions must be made with the future generation of children in mind and that is characterized by terms that limit political discourse and make queer resistance unthinkable. In his now (in)famous antirelational, antisocial turn, Edelman posits that the value of queerness lies in its threat to the social order and the "logic of futurism on which meaning always depends." By threatening systemic logic, the system's fantasmatic construction is exposed. For Edelman, queers are *sinthom*osexuals—the sinthome being that which "connects us to the unsymbolizable Thing over which we constantly stumble, and so, in turn, to the death drive" and the *sinthom*osexual being those queers who embrace their own fantasy structures while revealing that these structures are, in fact, fantasies.[40] In other words, *sinthom*osexuals expose as mere fantasy the ideologies on which people base their existences, subverting the closed debate of reproductive futurity through their identification with the death drive and indulgence in *jouissance*. Edelman's queer threatens meaning by exposing the system that insists on its difference like Jeffrey Jerome Cohen's monster (akin to René Girard's scapegoat), a figure that reveals "that difference is arbitrary and potentially free-floating, mutable rather than essential, the monster threatens to destroy not just individual members of a society, but the very cultural apparatus through which individuality is constituted and allowed."[41]

Through its excess, its alienation from the ideology of reproductive futurity, queerness challenges meaning itself because it is simultaneously empty and overdetermined—a status that certainly recalls the multiplicity of interpretive possibilities that characterizes the gothic monster. As representatives of the death drive, *sinthom*osexuals become a kind of uncanny, undead figure in Edelman's text. Edelman quotes Slavoj Žižek's decidedly gothic explanation that the death drive itself "functions in exactly the same way as '*heimlich*' in the Freudian *unheimlich*, as coinciding with its negation," making the death drive representative of "what horror fiction calls the 'undead,' a strange, immortal, indestructible life that persists beyond death." Queers represent death in life, challenging the neat separation of oppositional binaries and exposing that very structure itself as a fiction. Further, as a positionality that sheds light on the fantasy of reproductive futurity, *sinthom*osexuality is uncanny because it "offers us fantasy turned inside out, the seams of its costume exposing reality's seamlessness as mere seaming, the fraying knots that hold each sequin in place now usurping that place."[42] In other words, *sinthom*osexuals turn the sequined fabric of society's fantasy structure inside out to reveal the knotted underbelly—to make what was once familiar and homelike horrifically exposed as something constructed and denaturalized, uncanny because it replaces the comfort of the fantasy with a perverse version of itself. As Edelman describes, *sinthom*osexuals are the "unacknowledged ghosts that always haunt the social machinery."[43]

Ten years earlier Susan Stryker made a similar claim, arguing that trans* folks expose the systems that marginalize them because their embodiment, "like the embodiment of the monster, places its subject in an unassimilable, antagonistic, queer relationship to a Nature in which it must nevertheless exist."[44] Stryker reappropriates the charge of monstrosity so often levied against trans* subjects: "I find a deep affinity between myself as a transsexual woman and the monster in Mary Shelley's *Frankenstein*. Like the monster, I am too often perceived as less than fully human due to the means of my embodiment; like the monster's as well, my exclusion from human community fuels a deep and abiding rage in me that I, like the monster, direct against the conditions in which I must struggle to exist." Stryker adds to Foucault's definition of the "human monster" as a hybrid mixture of two realms to wrest back its power, explaining that the monster's fabulous hybridity, like the sphinx, gives it the supernatural ability to warn and predict.[45] In other words, monsters help point out the social structures that are otherwise invisible to those who are privileged by them. In her definition Stryker brings together two dominant themes around queer monstrosity—its hybridity and its ability to make visible that which has been rendered invisible through naturalization.

Theorists have often turned to the reappropriation of monstrosity to illustrate trans* embodiment and experience, revising its pathologizing medical connotations to explore monstrosity's power to adopt, twist, and challenge concepts that have violently contained and marginalized trans* folks. The term *monster* appeared in the inaugural issue of TSQ: *Transgender Studies Quarterly* as part of a list of keywords that attempt to "elucidate a conceptual vocabulary for transgender studies" today. In the entry for *monster*, Anson Koch-Rein notes that monstrosity is particularly difficult to reclaim because its use as a marker of trans* difference is embedded with multiple intersecting markers of difference, including race, class, and disability. But it is "precisely the monster's ambivalent ability to speak to oppression and negative affect that appeals to trans* people reclaiming the monster for their own voices."[46] *In a Queer Time and Place*, for example, turns, like Stryker, to the monstrous, though Jack Halberstam does not characterize his illustrations as an overt reappropriation of Frankenstein's creature as Stryker does. Halberstam does turn to ambivalence in his definition of the transgender body as "an in-between body" that "retains the marks of its own ambiguity and ambivalence" through gesture and hybridity.[47] Halberstam goes on to describe *The Art(ificial) Womb* by art research group SymbioticA, a project that consists of Guatemalan worry dolls that are "seeded with endothelial, muscle, and osteoblast cell (skin, muscle and bone tissue) that are grown over/into the polymers. The polymers degrade as the tissue grows. As a result the dolls become partially alive."[48] As the tissue grows in unexpected ways, the polymer decomposes, creating a work of art that is simultaneously and unpredictably human and other. The result is a living dead object, not-dead and not-alive, part human and part plastic. The worry dolls represent "ambiguous states of being that can be summarized as transgender" because they are in the process of becoming something different without engaging in the myth of a predictable end point that might reinforce binary thinking, but they are also certainly abject, monstrous, and gothic. In fact, the descriptive language Halberstam uses—"semi-living," "mutant," "grotesque little conglomerates," with "Frankensteinian form"—clearly evokes the gothic within his discussion of postmodern spaciotemporality, even though an explicit deployment of monstrosity doesn't seem to be his intention.[49] Further, Halberstam describes SymbioticA's other "monstrous entities" such as growing unnecessary organs for animals and merging organic material with hardware, a practice that Halberstam labels a "living workshop of bodily mutation" and most certainly a kind of Frankenstein's laboratory in which the engineering of grotesque hybridity breeds unpredictable results.

To further illustrate this, Halberstam highlights Del LaGrace Volcano's work on "sublime mutations" as "glorifying bodies and body parts that might otherwise be read as freakish or ugly." Volcano both eroticizes the "neo-organs" of "testosterone enhanced clits" and displays traumatically scarred bodies of "patchwork flesh" that highlight the subject as an "assemblage, a rough draft, or skin and tissue pulled together around a literally de-centered self."[50] In Halberstam's description and visualization of trans* aesthetics as postmodern negotiations of flesh and technology, he once again gravitates toward language that evokes hybridity and monstrosity to represent in-betweenness without a destination as well as the glories and traumas that attend these embodiments.

Haunting and Sadomasochism

Though paranoia and monsters are easy to find when wandering through the queer theory landscape, haunting appears as perhaps the most frequent gothicism, flitting in and out of queer theory both under its surface and through frameworks that center haunting as a primary concept or methodology. Though Jacques Derrida's concept of "hauntology" in *Specters of Marx* and Avery Gordon's attention to the ghosts of sociology in *Ghostly Matters* are not queer theory per se, their gothic concepts certainly resonate with queer theorists.[51] Both Derrida and Gordon frame their attention to ghosts as an ethical orientation, specifically naming traumatic structural oppression, both overt and insidious. Derrida points to the violence of capitalism and totalitarianism: "No Justice . . . seems possible or thinkable without the principle of some responsibility, beyond all living present, within that which disjoins the living present, before the ghosts of those who are not yet born or who are already dead, be they victims of wars, political or other kinds of violence, nationalist, racist, colonialist, sexist, or other kinds of exterminations, victims of the oppressions of capitalist imperialism or any of the forms of totalitarianism." Gordon too ties haunting and ghosts to insidious violence, specifically of obscured or disavowed traumas: "Haunting is one way in which abusive systems of power make themselves known and their impacts felt in everyday life, especially when they are supposedly over and done with (slavery, for instance) or when their oppressive nature is denied (as in free labor or national security). Haunting is not the same as being exploited, traumatized, or oppressed, although it usually involves these experiences or is produced by them." Debra Ferreday and Adi Kuntsman note that because haunting allows theorists to imagine an ethical relation to the intersection of trauma, structural oppression, and history, ghosts emerge in work on "more contemporary and *seemingly mundane experiences* of oppression, injustice and daily structural violence—of class, or race, poverty or imprisonment."[52] Ferreday and Kuntsman, along with Derrida and Gordon, emphasize the structural, obscured, and mundane aspects of oppression, implying the resonance of haunting in accounts of insidious trauma, specifically.

Haunting certainly serves as a useful metaphor for those describing nonqueer histories (especially traumatic ones), but queer theory takes up haunting and ghostliness so frequently, more often than not one cannot make it through a full text without encountering at least a sprinkle of language referring to haunting, ghosts, or specters. For example, Angela Willey's *Undoing Monogamy* begins with an epigraph from Avery Gordon's *Ghostly Matters*; Joseph A. Boone's *The Homoerotics of Orientalism* describes the "ghostly textual voices" of same-sex desire that have been "marginalized and tabooed, censored and distorted" in literature about the Middle East, a gothicized description of the insidious trauma of erasure and punishment; and David Eng describes the "ghosts of miscegenation," "haunted history," and other ghosts throughout *The Feeling of Kinship*.[53] In *The Apparitional Lesbian* Terry Castle explicitly performs a search for the "ghosted" lesbian characters in literature, arguing that the pattern of disavowed female same-sex love turns the lesbian into an "apparitional figure [that] seemed to obliterate, through a single vaporizing gesture, the disturbing carnality of lesbian love. It made of such love—literally—a phantasm: an ineffable anticoupling between 'women' who weren't there."[54] Though haunting and ghostliness find their way into these texts, with the exception of those explicitly theorizing haunting such as Castle, these concepts generally do not appear in the books' indexes. References to ghosts and haunting often end up penetrating these texts without leaving the usual material traces.

Particularly fascinating is the pattern of integrating discussions of sadomasochism with language of haunting as a way of getting at queer temporal disruption and ethical historical imperatives. Sexualized power dynamics can be found throughout eighteenth- and nineteenth-century Gothic fiction. Though messy and not always legible as sadomasochistic per se, Gothic erotics deal "crudely" with the interplay of desire and power.[55] In Horace Walpole's *The Castle of Otranto*, for example, patriarch Manfred sadistically pursues almost daughter-in-law Isabella (she was engaged to marry Manfred's son before his untimely death by giant helmet) through the subterranean passages of a castle haunted by the ghosts of its wronged rightful owners. The power that Manfred wields, along with Isabella's vulnerability, create an atmosphere of sexualized power that opens the door to the vengeful return of the dead, who infiltrate the manor's hidden passages and chambers. This ghostly penetration eventually implicates Manfred in his past wrongdoings while creating an atmosphere of erotic fear that has taken on "talismanic importance in the history of gothic fiction."[56]

Sadomasochism's potential for queering power relations and illustrating what Leo Bersani identifies as the "self-shattering" aspects of sexuality means that sadomasochism also appears often in queer theory.[57] Foucault, for example, espoused sadomasochism's "mythical relations" as means of rethinking rigid active and passive sexual roles and challenging the idea that for gay men "the passive role is in some way demeaning."[58] To Foucault sadomasochistic practices allow for creativity in sexual play that opens up sexual possibilities and identities that are not rooted in authenticity discourse or identity politics because sadomasochism can appropriate and redeploy the power relations that are inherent in all relationships. The "s&m game," he explains, "is very interesting because it is a strategic relation, but it is always fluid. Of course, there are roles, but everybody knows very well that those roles can be reversed. . . . Or, even when the roles are stabilized, you know very well that it is always a game."[59] Gilles Deleuze might not characterize sadomasochism as a game, but he does point to the way sadism and masochism challenge assumptions about power since the masochists-submissives-bottoms design and enter knowingly into the scene of their own humiliation and pain, thereby holding the power to imagine, begin, and end the interaction.[60] I explore sadomasochism's relationship to power in chapter 4, but here I examine the intersection between sadomasochism and haunting as interrelated gothic tropes that appear in queer theory as a means of exploring traumatic queer temporalities.

In the shadow of the AIDS crisis, Bersani and Tim Dean turn to sadomasochism as a way to theorize loss and grief. Sadomasochism, it seems, allows for ghostly visitations. In "Shame on You," Bersani reflects on his observation that at a 2003 Gay Shame conference there was a jarring lack of discussion around AIDS and an outright denial of the "not insignificant number of gays" who participated in barebacking (having unprotected anal sex). Bersani explicitly links barebacking to the potential for role reversals that Foucault associated with sadomasochism, noting that barebacking reverses the idea that the recipient of anal sex occupies a shameful, because feminized, position and refocusing on the power of the bottom (or "bug-chaser"), who, like the masochist, designs the terms of his own demise in a kind of creative and "unfathomable spirituality." Though many would condemn the barebacking bottom as pathologically self-destructive, Bersani points out that "power has played no tricks on the bug-chaser: from the beginning he was promised nothing more, and he has received nothing more, than the privilege of being a living tomb, the repository of what may kill him." As an analogy to sadomasochism's potential for the creative and playful disruption of power, Bersani points to the creativity of the subculture of "gift-givers" and "bug-chasers," and he concludes with this particularly gothic characterization of the rectum, not simply as a grave but as a living tomb with the potential to become a "more sinister and more creative" version of the reproductive fantasy.[61]

To better understand why Bersani locates creativity and spirituality in the bug chaser as living tomb, it is best to turn to the source of his musings: Tim Dean's *Unlimited Intimacy*. In this text Dean exposes and theorizes barebacking as a subculture, "on the model of the SM community or the leather community (with both of which they overlap and exist in tension)." He explains, as Bersani points out, that the barebacking subculture "embraces masochism as proof positive of masculinity," creating a kind of mythology around hypermasculine bottoms who "sacrifice themselves on behalf of gay culture." Dean argues that barebacking subculture attempts "to use viral exchange to create kinship networks" and to replace the narrative of sickness and death around HIV with a "story about kinship and life" in which seroconversion is a "gift" that allows community members to "breed" since seroconversion is sometimes coded as impregnation.[62] In this context the masochistic practices of bug chasers allow the bareback community to access new approaches to reproduction and temporality.

Specifically, Dean links the masochism of barebacking with the concept of haunting to theorize how the practice can grant access to alternate temporalities. Active HIV transmission makes evident the connections between one's current partner and the "fragmentary, material traces" of their past partners, meaning that "the virus may be considered a particular form of memory, one that offers an effective way of maintaining certain relations with the dead." In a close reading of the bareback porn films *Breeding Season* and *Plantin' Seed*, Dean argues that these films are populated by the ghosts of the dead, meaning the "residual traces of persons" who form a lineage of seroconversion. He frames these porn films as a "ritual summoning of ghosts" in which the men are able to participate in a history that preceded them.[63] In this reading the masochism inherent in barebacking porn works to disrupt conventional investments in normative reproduction, instead looking to a future of kinship and community through viral impregnations. At the same time that the practice queers reproductive futurity it also provides material access to the past, those ghosts that represent a network of past sexual contacts, linking barebacking community members across time and space.

Sadomasochism as access point to traumatic pasts acts as a gothic encounter with both overt and insidious trauma. If the crude sadomasochism in *The Castle of Otranto* opens a portal for ghosts of generations past to penetrate its drawing rooms and subterranean passages, the sadomasochism rooted in queer theory allows texts and subjects to open themselves up to the specter of traumatic histories. Elizabeth Freeman's *Time Binds* is not described or marketed as expressly gothic, but like Dean, her musings on queer temporality through sadomasochism serve as an exemplary model of how gothicism works its way into a text that addresses the insidious and intersecting traumas of queer histories. This text on queer temporality and history is infused with gothicism—from its extended reading of *Frankenstein* to illustrate "erotohistoriography" and "temporal drag" to its use of Derridean hauntology and its explicit treatment of the gothic genre itself to describe queer temporalities: "the gothic traffics in alternative temporalites or a-rhythms that present themselves in concretely historical terms, as dead bodies coming back to life in the form of vampires, ghosts, and monsters." Though Freeman integrates monstrosity in her proposal that the "monster embodies the wrinkled time that marks both the gothic and . . . the queer" and that Frankenstein's monster specifically is "queerly hybrid in a temporal sense," perhaps most telling is her treatment of sadomasochism and haunting as gothic access points to queered temporalities.[64]

Freeman explicitly theorizes the temporal aspects of sadomasochism that Bersani and Dean merely imply in their discussion of masochistic barebacking kinship structures. She treats sadomasochism as "a deployment of bodily sensations through which the individual subject's normative *timing* is disaggregated and denaturalized," leading to sadomasochism's unique ability to allow participants to exceed their own temporality and access pasts and futures. Specifically, when sadomasochistic play takes up scenes of historical trauma (such as a master-slave scenario), it "may bring the body to a kind of somatized historical knowledge," thereby "refusing these moments the closure of pastness." We can see this playing out in the sadomasochistic aspects of barebacking Dean describes as community building in the shadow of the HIV/AIDS crisis, and Freeman likewise turns to haunting as a metaphor for the queered temporalities sadomasochistic practice offers to those inheriting the effects of historical trauma. In a close reading of Isaac Julien's short film *The Attendant*, Freeman explains that Julien "reanimates the dead" to create an "eroticized hauntology" that offers a queer of color intervention to the Derridean concept.[65] Freeman cites Carla Freccero's description of the role of passivity in historiography to illustrate her claims, without explicitly noting that Freccero frames this concept specifically in relation to haunting or, using Freccero's phrase, "queer spectrality."[66] Though Freeman does not completely disavow haunting as a guiding trope, this subtle omission exemplifies the implicit indebtedness that many queer theory texts have to gothic spectrality as well as the specific conceptual overlap between sadomasochism as queer temporal practice and haunting as an ethical relation to traumatic pasts. In the theoretical work of Bersani, Dean, and Freeman, texts that are in no way overtly gothic in content, the gothic tropes of sadomasochism and haunting work together to productively illustrate theories of queer temporality—in relation to traumatic history, the ongoing traumas of the present, and the damaging imperatives of reproductive futurity.

Although I have teased out gothic spectrality in the queer theories here, not all queer theory texts are as implicitly gothic in nature. In fact, many texts explicitly take on haunting as a primary framework. One of the most overt queer adoptions of haunting as gothic queer theory appears in Freccero's *Queer/Early/Modern*—the "queer spectrality" Freeman alludes to but does not explicitly mark as spectral. Haunting in Freccero's text functions in conjunction with traumatic histories—as in Bersani's, Dean's, and Freeman's. She proposes spectral queer historiography as a means of engaging with traumatic memories and violent colonial narratives, so the work of memory and history does not become entombed and therefore stabilized and silenced. Instead of a colonizing, melancholic approach to history, Freccero argues for historiography that is open to ghostly returns, allowing the agential dead to act on the living. She explains, "this willingness to be haunted is an ethical relation to the world, motivated by a concern not only for the past but for the future." Like sadomasochism, a spectral historiography queers temporality and opens up the boundaries of the self, granting access to both pasts and futures simultaneously. Like Dean's barebacking bottom, this approach to history requires a willingness to be penetrated by its ghosts. As the earlier texts explicitly treat sadomasochism with a ghostly subtext, the reverse is true for Freccero—her text is explicitly about haunting but brings in the subtext of masochism, evoking the figure of the bareback bottom whose receptivity becomes his power to reimagine relations with the dead. Indeed, Freccero connects "penetrative reciprocity" to the masochistic experience Bersani calls "self-shattering."[67] With this elevation of receptivity, we return to Freeman's use of Freccero's language to describe sadomasochism as "a suspension, a waiting, an attending to the world's arrivals (through, in part, its returns), not as guarantee or security for action in the present, but as the very force from the past that moves us into the future."[68] Through a close reading of the conversations happening among these queer theorists and the metaphors that work though traumatic queer experiences and their temporalities, it becomes clear that these intertwined theories have gothic roots, and, as Freccero points out, these "ghostly returns are thus a sign of trauma and its mourning."[69] Once again the gothicism of haunting and sadomasochism become a means to queer trauma and reflect its alternative temporality.

Though ghosts often provide queer theorists a way to reimagine temporality, Karen Tongson's *Relocations* turns to a rhetoric of haunting to attend to the insidious trauma of *spatial* displacement. Tongson's text oozes with implicit gothicism in its exploration of Los Angeles, its suburbs, and those queers of color who are both manipulated by the forces of urban gentrification and erased from narratives of suburban homogeneity. For example, Tongson cites Freeman's concept of queer temporality in an extended reading of the performance ensemble the Butchlalis de Panochtitlan (BdP), framing them as butch queers of color, embodying "'racialized' temporal drag" in relation to gentrified urban spaces. Tongson's description of the BdP sketch, *Lolo and Perla Return to Avenge Klub Fantasy*, describes Lolo and Perla as if they were ghosts haunting the "ruins" of what was once Latina lesbian Klub Fantasy at Nayarit in Echo Park but has since reopened as white hipster venue The Echo. Lolo and Perla begin the sketch by dancing to a "*banda* party anthem" until "Black Sabbath's 'Paranoid' interrupts their reverie," and they look around to realize that what was once a "lesbian Latina club . . . [or] a Latina lesbian club" has become a "punk rock dyke club." It dawns on them that the meaning of their community space has shifted underneath them. Their reaction, rather than to leave the venue, is to "act out" against the "indifferent" punk rock dykes through tasteless jokes about potential sexual conquests and recollections of what once was. Tongson explains that Lolo and Perla respond to their spatial loss and individual invisibility by deploying a queered temporality: "Lolo and Perla transport themselves from the scenes of spatial conquest unfolding in the present tense by activating their own memories, their own retrospective fantasies about owning the scene back in the day."[70] Though Tongson provides this example as a means of illustrating the deployment of temporal drag by queers of color, this temporal drag also frames Lolo and Perla as subjects from the past who continue to reside in the past through their "retrospective fantasies" and who spatially haunt the current incarnation of their old haunt. Temporal drag not only offers access to a queered temporality but also functions as a kind of agential queer haunting in the face of the insidious colonial violence of gentrification. Lolo and Perla, as displaced queers of color, begin like ghosts who go about their routines, failing to realize that they are dead, but then function increasingly like ghosts who haunt with purpose, as they continue to occupy those spaces to which they were once relegated but from which they are now alienated. In its shift from homeliness to *unheimlich*, Klub Fantasy becomes uncanny to Lolo and Perla, and in their ghostly refusal to fully disappear from its dance floor, they promise to make The Echo uncanny for others as well.

The BdP serve as representatives of queer folks of color navigating the economic, racial, and class shifts in "lesser Los Angeles" as "creative classers" move in to those spaces once marked as nowhere. They function as ghosts in limbo with no home in one world or another, and they are constantly on the move, "hoping to outpace the movements of gentrification." The BdP "ghosts" do not rest or disappear but remain in motion, moving in and out of spaces from which they have been displaced as well as those spaces as of yet ungentrified. Despite the fact that their movements are forced by and in response to urban gentrification, Tongson's subjects choose to locate pleasure in movement and even in the possibility of never actually arriving anywhere, a sentiment represented by The Smiths' lyric, "And if a double-decker bus, crashes into us / To die by your side is such a heavenly way to die." Reveling in the divine pleasure of "mutual annihilation" on the way from "nowhere" to "somewhere," the suburban and "lesser" urban queer folks of color that Tongson writes about are ghosts that never settle; "Maybe the light that never goes out is about *never* getting there, never arriving at that *some*where" but instead "protecting the nowheres you call your own." In a queering of the narrative of ghosts who have something to settle before they can rest, the BdP simply refuse to rest by remaining in limbo, disrupting temporality, and rejecting a peaceful departure from spaces from which they are expected to disappear or, at the very least, to become just "another atmospheric amenity."[71] The ghostliness of Lolo and Perla pops through Tongson's theorizing not only as a gothic queered temporality but also as agential queered spatiality; the paired spatial and temporal orientation works to make traumatic racial and colonial pasts and presents inseparable and undeniable.

The haunting that occurs in this sketch responds to the insidious trauma of those classed and raced social structures that relegate queer people of color to "nowhere" spaces and then later reclaim those spaces, alienating those who would like to remain attached to certain places and histories. This trauma places Lolo and Perla in the gentrified urban environment in which the trauma of relegation and displacement causes those who once occupied the space to lose their location in time and to become spectral as a result. Tongson's deployment of haunting not only creates gothic queer theory but also serves to illustrate the traumatic indifference of white, queer urban gentrification to the queers of color who occupied, and continue to haunt, those spaces to which they were once relegated. This spectral presence is an agential refusal to be silenced and erased by the process of gentrification. The haunting also becomes a source of empowerment because it allows Lolo and Perla the agency to remain tied to those places and memories through their lingering presence, and it allows Tongson to propose an alternate understanding of queer time and space that is not dependent on whitewashed notions of metronormativity—one that instead circulates around community and the "inevitably aimless transport of accidental reverie" that dominates her revision of queer time and space as a (ghostly) journey without a destination.[72]

Gothic Negativity

If we broaden our perspective for a moment to focus on trends in the field, it becomes clear that gothicism weaves through even supposedly oppositional theoretical approaches from the antirelational to the utopian. But the negative turn in queer theory seems to be particularly gothic in its focus on a kind of queer aesthetic and rhetoric of sadness, melancholy, failure, and other negative affects. For example, Jack Halberstam's *The Queer Art of Failure* advocates for "failing, losing, forgetting, unmaking, undoing, unbecoming, not knowing" since "for queers failure can be a style . . . or a way of life." One mode of resistance Halberstam proposes is the spectral. Calling on Toni Morrison's haunted novel, *Beloved*, and Gordon's *Ghostly Matters*, Halberstam suggests that we resist memorialization, since "forgetting becomes a way of resisting the heroic and grand logics of recall and unleashes new forms of memory that relate more to spectrality than to hard evidence, to lost genealogies than to inheritance, to erasure than to inscription." Beyond this nod to the spectral, Halberstam's call to resist through failure involves a rejection of accepted forms of knowledge to develop new counterhegemonic modes of being. This approach risks adopting modes that "dwell in the murky waters of a counterintuitive, often impossibly dark and negative realm of critique and refusal."[73] This "dark" and "murky" realm is a gothic activist aesthetic and its language of failure a gothic rhetoric that challenges dehumanizing marginalization, often activated through the label of the monstrous, the sadomasochistic, or the ghostly, by adopting those gothic failures as counterhegemonic strategies.[74]

Also dark and murky in focus and perhaps more overtly gothic is Heather Love's *Feeling Backward*. In this study Love chooses "to dwell at length on the 'dark side' of modern queer representation," and the first page of the introduction alone resorts to a gothic rhetoric of haunting and corpses to describe a "history of suffering, stigma, and violence." The rest of the introduction is littered with ghosts, haunting, darkness, melancholy, the dead, and trauma. Indeed, Love conflates an impossible longing for contact with history's queer dead with the "historical impossibility of same-sex desire."[75] Queerness here maps onto a desire for the dead, a relationship with corpses, and a rhetoric of burial and exhumation, the likes of which have graced the pages of many a Gothic novel. In an evocation of the ostracized, the monstrous, and the buried, Love's introduction ends with a refusal to "write off the most vulnerable, the least presentable, and all the dead," a drive that leads eventually to an analysis of the roiling undead horde that ends *The Well of Loneliness* and with which I began this chapter.

Failure and negativity have traumatic resonance in that traumatic experience demands narrativization while simultaneously confounding its expression. Part of the behavior that has been pathologized as post-traumatic stress disorder involves the intrusion of the traumatic experience, or what Freud called the "repetition compulsion," as an obsessive revisitation of the traumatic scene, whether through flashbacks, nightmares, or unconscious representations that emerge in speech patterns or creative expression.[76] Part of this traumatic return has to do with the persistent drive and inability to effectively communicate an experience that often involves fractured temporality, dissociation, and memory loss. The failure of traumatic communication is at the heart of queer epistemology. The writing I have explored here represents an obsessive attempt to get at the heart of the insidious trauma of marginalized queer experience, but the nature of trauma means these theorists can only get near it, exposing its contours perhaps but never finding its center. Gothicism, as a representation of the state of swirling incoherency that characterizes the mise-en-scène of Gothic narrative, speaks both to the decentering effects of trauma and the failure of naming those insidious traumatic experiences that slip from our grasp, evade our gaze, and make the space of queer existence itself uncanny. Yes, failure may be a queer style, but it is a style inflected by trauma and represented through the thread of gothicism that pervades queer thought and creative expression.

In this overview of texts I chose to perform a close reading of just a few of the queer theory texts deploying gothic rhetorics to illustrate the prevalence of the gothic within queer theory as a means of theorizing queer trauma. As Mair Rigby notes, queer theory certainly owes a debt to Gothic fiction, as both personal starting point and enabling mechanism for queer thought, but beyond its roots in Gothic literary criticism, I argue that queer theory is *itself* expressly gothic.[77] Many of the theorists appearing in this chapter might be surprised to be labeled as gothic, but I would remind them that gothicism sometimes creeps in around the corners of consciousness, often uninvited. Just as so many queer theorists have read Gothic texts as queer, the texts I outline in this chapter reflect a larger trend of gothicism in queer theory. Beyond Freud, who has received his share of close readings, queer theory texts are rarely read as cultural productions and potential subjects of analysis as such. If one reads with an eye for the presence of gothic tropes and forms, gothicism emerges to some degree in a majority of texts addressing queerness, mostly as descriptive language and implication rather than as anything intentional and explicit. But the prevalence of the gothic in queer theory is enough that I certainly could not cover all instances in this chapter. The story I tell here, through a curated selection of queer theory texts, is one that speaks to an impulse, a sensibility in queer theory, and a reflection of the accumulation of various intersecting daily traumas that queer theory attempts to speak to, even though the nature of insidiousness and of trauma resists narrativization. Gothicism emerges as a slippery, shadowy rhetoric that gets at, or at least around and near, those traumatic experiences that tend to dissipate before our eyes and slip from our grasp.

2

LIVE BURIAL

Lesbian Pulp and the "Containment Crypt"

With "morality" seemingly pervasive in the land, lurid
covers of paperbacks screamed sex from every retail
bookshelf and Americans gobbled up the books by the
millions. For lesbian books, cover copy proclaimed our
evil in order to meet morality requirements while the
come-hither illustrations beckoned the reader into their
pages and promised lascivious details.

KATHERINE V. FORREST, *Lesbian Pulp Fiction*

Beneath the dark and rocky peaks of an imposing mountain landscape, a
break in the gathering storm clouds illuminates a man with an agonized
face, reaching out toward something he seems driven to possess. The man
casts a shadow that draws the eye toward the object of his desire; a young
woman with loose blond waves, lavender blouse, and dove gray skirt is
resting on a couch framed by the craggy precipice, ominous clouds, and
masculine pursuer—all threaten to engulf her. She faces away from him but
casts her eyes back toward the approaching threat. Shielding her from these
encroaching forces, however, is another woman, dressed in an elegant black
gown, cigarette in hand. She places her hand on the seated woman's shoulder, a gesture of comfort and ownership, and looks down at her knowingly.

The image I just described is the cover art of Patricia Highsmith's (aka Claire Morgan) 1953 novel *The Price of Salt*, a story "of a love society forbids."[1] The cover's sublime and threatening landscape, male aggressor, and passive, vulnerable young woman could easily grace the cover of an eighteenth-century Gothic novel such as *The Italian* or *The Monk*, though the copy, fashion, and unmistakably midcentury sofa suggest otherwise. This novel is an example of a twentieth-century genre of tawdry, popular fiction known as paperback originals, pocket books, or pulp fiction.

Originally associated with hardboiled mystery and crime novels, "pulp" names the genre of cheap, mass-produced paperback novels that began to gain popularity after World War II, as the United States became more interested in portability and disposability. The genre evolved to predominantly feature novels that "emphasized violence, sex, and paranoia" as well as blatantly queer sexual themes such as bisexual love triangles, gay male and lesbian romances, sadomasochism, and other supposedly sordid "perversities."[2] Queer pulp, as Susan Stryker calls the 1940s and 1950s paperback novels with LGBT themes, was a primary outlet for exploring taboo subjects, their queer gothicism emerging as "brooding content that lingered beneath the bright, false, chrome-plated surfaces covering much of postwar American life."[3] Because of their disposability and affordability, pulp novels allowed readers to pick up a copy at the drug store or bus station for twenty-five cents, slip it in their pocket, read it on the bus or a park bench in anonymity, and leave it there when finished.[4] This proved to be a life-saving practice in an era of deep prejudice against gays and lesbians. In this chapter I focus specifically on examples of lesbian pulp fiction.[5] Sometimes called "survival literature," lesbian pulp served as the "only public source about the codes of existence of urban lesbian communities" and offered a glimmer of representation for many lesbians who felt deeply isolated by the narratives of heterosexuality and domesticity circulating in the United States at the time.[6]

Paperback originals were developed when publishers accepted original manuscripts submitted to them by unknown or little-known authors or commissioned work from writers who would be willing to conform to their standards to avoid obscenity charges and to maximize sales. Often this meant that the novels were written by people eager to earn the publisher's advance fee above all else, so they were willing to create sensational story lines that objectified, fetishized, and mischaracterized the sexualities they portrayed. Story lines frequently exploited lesbianism for the straight male pornographic gaze and then concluded with pathologizing or violent resolutions. Even the most lurid of these exploitative texts provided a degree of lesbian visibility (however fraught), but there was also a small segment of lesbian paperback originals written by lesbian or bisexual women who attempted to portray lesbian sexuality with some accuracy and sensitivity even in the face of editorial and juridical pressures. The "unprecedented and unexpected success" of novels centering on lesbianism "later led paperback fans to label the period between the mid-1940s and the mid-1960s, when these lesbian PBOs flourished, as a 'golden age' for the representation of sexual diversity in mass-market paperbacks."[7]

Of course, the lack of lesbian visibility in mainstream culture was achieved by a concerted effort by government, its censors, and the norms of decency that they constructed and enforced. Though pulp often contained fetishistic LGBT content, it was not generally in the service of celebrating queer life. Indeed, the highly charged atmosphere of the Cold War period created a toxic and restrictive environment for gay and lesbian citizens, one replete with both explicit and insidious traumatic experience. Warnings against queerness were embedded in pulp form itself, from the cover art and copy to the narrative limitations imposed on the content within their pages. For example, the exteriors of first-edition paperback originals from lesbian pulp—elements of the writing and publication process almost entirely outside of the authors' control—depict gender and sexual nonconformity with a gothic-infused blend of horror and fetishization. When we venture under the book covers, however, we see that the highly vocal and vividly depicted denunciation of queerness provided lesbians with a vocabulary and a geography, both physical and virtual, with which to understand themselves and their community. This was not a matter of simply internalizing the pathologizing narratives of immorality and desperation that characterized mainstream depictions of queerness. Instead, some pioneering lesbians chose to adopt the, often gothic, language they found in popular, medical, and legal culture to recognize and name themselves and to locate others like them. Tracing the gothic thread in pulp novels makes visible a conflicted use of gothicism in midcentury popular culture that mirrors its conflicted function in eighteenth- and nineteenth-century Gothic fiction. As I explore in this chapter, the gothic elements in lesbian pulp worked to contain and control queerness, a drive that certainly caused insidious trauma for those who saw only despair and destruction ahead of them or, perhaps even worse, saw only a void when they looked for others like themselves. Some, however, reappropriated that gothicism to express the very trauma created by it, thereby finding ways to connect and survive despite all the forces working to isolate and destroy them. To illustrate this tension, I first analyze the conservative, traumatizing use of gothicism in pulp cover art and copy within the context of Cold War–era United States. Next, I delve under the covers to read Ann Bannon's iconic lesbian pulp novels as examples of gothic queer culture responding to insidious trauma.

During the Cold War era heightened notions of decency and censorship found the biggest threats not simply in those who were blatantly anti-establishment (for they were easy to spot and keep track of) but frequently in those who were in the "closet," passing as "normal," defying surveillance practices, and possibly secretly corrupting those exposed to them. In this sense the closet was a deeply contested and ambivalent space, as dominant cultural forces worked to keep queer folks metaphorically (and sometimes literally) locked away to contain the spread of homosexuality while simultaneously feeling threatened by the ability for queers to operate under cover. This ambivalence made existence for LGBT folks virtually impossible and certainly did "violence to the soul and spirit."[8] Representations of betweenness on pulp covers reflected the dual resonance of the closet and functioned as gothic-inflected containment strategies, what I will call "containment crypts," created to surveil and control those who might queer normative gender and sexuality.[9] Lesbian pulp containment crypts allowed for control over an element of society that slipped between knowable poles of behavior, identity, and embodiment by creating a new region between the cracks of the binary, a "third" region that served as both prison and viewing area and in which the complexities of lesbian sexuality could be named, fetishized, policed, and controlled.

Notably, the "golden age" of lesbian pulp coincides precisely with "peak cold war America" and the height of containment culture (1946–64), as delineated by Alan Nadel.[10] Eighteenth- and nineteenth-century Gothic novels often deployed containment as a trope through the depiction of live burials, inescapable subterranean passages, and imprisonment within crypts, castles, and convents, but during the Cold War period containment took on a new valence as an overt strategy of foreign and domestic policy. In the famously sensational cover art and copy of lesbian pulp texts, unscrupulous publishers crafted conceptual catacombs to capitalize on readers' appetites for lesbian sex while satisfying the censors by framing that sex as monstrous, abnormal, and pathological. But within the pages of some pulp novels, lesbian writers utilized the containment discourse of the day as a means of communication and survival in reaction to the insidious trauma of marginalization, deploying containment crypts as a gothic reworking of Cold War narratives and thereby fostering visibility and building community through the very language and imagery deployed to contain difference—a form of gothic queer culture.

Containment was a U.S. Cold War foreign policy strategy first postulated by George Kennan in his famous 1947 essay, "The Sources of Soviet Conduct," in which he outlines the motivations and values of the Soviets as well as how forces of democracy might best respond to maintain global dominance. He describes the Kremlin's political action as an oozing, "fluid stream which moves constantly, wherever it is permitted to move, toward a given goal. Its main concern is to make sure that it has filled every nook and cranny available to it in the basin of world power." In response to this threat, he suggests a "long-term, patient but firm and vigilant containment of Russian expansive tendencies," and this containment practice came to include widespread political and military intervention in countries that indicated sympathy or alliance with the Soviets as well as in those countries in which the United States imagined the *potential* for leftist politics to take hold.[11]

Nadel reads Kennan's language of fluidity as seminal and frames the U.S. response as one driven to demonstrate its own virility and potency in comparison to global Soviet insemination. Kennan's metaphor created a national narrative in which the United States must provide a strong counterexample to communism, thereby "making the Soviets look less potent and attractive" and necessitating the extension of this containment-based foreign policy into the realm of the domestic. Nadel explains that in addition to foreign policy, containment "also describes American life in numerous venues and under sundry rubrics during that period: to the extent that corporate production and biological reproduction, military deployment and industrial technology, televised hearings and filmed teleplays, the cult of domesticity and the fetishizing of domestic security, the arms race and atoms for peace all contributed to the containment of communism, the disparate acts performed in the name of these practices joined the legible agenda of American history as aspects of containment culture." The containment narrative infiltrated nearly every aspect of U.S. life during the height of the Cold War period, reflecting a paranoid national consciousness and an obsessive desire to shut down dialogue and dissent by emphasizing an us/them binary and instituting practices that attempted to ferret out the "other" hidden within the ranks of the "same." This notion of duality dominated what Nadel calls a "nuclear gaze," or a gaze able to define the "difference between dangerous and nondangerous activity," to contain any nonnormative behaviors that might put national security at risk.[12] It is easy to see how queer folks could become a symbol of dangerous difference and suspicious secrecy and a prime target of the nuclear gaze.

According to this logic, the key to national security was to identify the inherent dual nature of all things, prohibit any behavior or identity that threatens to migrate to the "dangerous" side of that duality, and question any hint of ambiguity or duplicity that might outwit or confuse the nuclear gaze. Paranoid surveillance in the form of McCarthyism became the method for containing humanity's dual nature and controlling any subversion that might be lurking within the ranks of those supposedly "normal" and "loyal" citizens, and it is well known that Senator Joseph McCarthy and the House Un-American Activities Committee spearheaded the campaign to root out subversives by, among other things, identifying citizens suspected of having "homosexual tendencies." McCarthy's policing of sexuality might simply be the most public and infamous example of homosexual containment, but policing of social norms regarding gender and sexuality occurred on all levels of society, primarily though the narrative of the cult of domesticity—leading to "strictly censored television programming, the drop in average marriage age, the suburban housing development, the public elaboration of dating etiquette, and the rigidly constrictive and restrictive structure of female undergarments."[13] The idyllic, white, suburban, Christian, middle-class, heteronormative nuclear family became the picture of health and happiness, and anything that deviated from this structure—or functioned within the structure but failed to achieve happiness as a result—became the face of the enemy subversive.[14]

This era of paranoia, containment, and domestic normativity gave birth to the popular genre of gay and lesbian pulp fiction, as publishers began to recognize a clandestine demand for literature that exploited the very limitations established by containment practices. Katherine V. Forrest explains the alienating aspects of the cult of domesticity for anyone falling outside of the norms of gender and sexuality: "I grew up in the post-war 1950s, an idyllic world if you were a straight white male or if you were naïve enough to believe TV's idealistic 'Leave It to Beaver' image of the average American family."[15] Queer folks, however, found that they had no place in this world, and in addition to the stringent cult of domesticity, the widespread popularity of Freudian psychoanalysis pathologized their difference as neurotic and indicative of arrested psychosexual development. These cultural forces combined to create an environment of insidious trauma, as notions of "normal" worked to alienate and isolate those who fell outside of its narrow definition. The release of Alfred Kinsey, Wardell B. Pomeroy, and Clyde E. Martin's *Sexual Behavior in the Human Male* in 1948 opened up a new public conversation about sexual behavior, and though the authors attempted to present their study of human sexuality as objectively as possible, the popular application of their research often sensationalized, pathologized, or criminalized the sexual behaviors they brought to light. For example, scandal magazines used headlines such as "Hidden Homos and How to Spot Them" to capitalize on the public conversation about sexuality that the authors, along with Freud, fostered.[16]

Simultaneously, however, the prevalence of psychoanalytic and medical discourse circulating throughout popular and medical culture also provided people with a new vocabulary for talking about sexuality and gender, and the contradictory effects of psychoanalytic language certainly appear in the text of pulp paperbacks. Jaye Zimet points out that medicalized language also gave otherwise sensational novels an air of legitimacy, allowing them to escape censorship, for a "book could not be censored if it was, or could pretend to be, a serious scientific study."[17] Front- and back-cover copy promised content such as the "psychoanalysis of a female homosexual," "detailed case histories of the third sex," or "a frank and penetrating study of habits and practices among lesbians—their causes, cures and clinical histories."[18] This language helped evade censorship, but it also provided lesbian readers with a framework for understanding their feelings and desires, albeit one that cast those desires as disease.

Though pulp provided some much-needed visibility and knowledge for lesbians, it is because of this visibility that strict antipornography censorship laws targeted pulp fiction in an attempt to contain the "perverse" side of humanity: "According to one U.S. Senator, 'alien-minded radicals and moral perverts' had infiltrated the pocket-book market, while, in 1952, the House Select Committee on Current Pornographic Materials concluded: 'Some of the most offensive infractions of the moral code were found to be contained in low-cost, paper-bound publications known as "pocket-size books" . . . which . . . have denigrated into media for the artful appeals to sensuality, immorality, filth, perversion, and degeneracy.'"[19] Committees such as this one were formed to target adult novels because they represented the underbelly of U.S. sexuality and by extension the human impulses that needed to be contained to control subversion in the name of national security. Note that the senator's language equates "moral perverts" with "alien-minded radicals," implying that deviant morality derives specifically from sexual perversion and that these qualities stem from the "alien" presence hidden within American society, a move that collapses the difference between foreigners, Soviet sympathizers, and sexual outsiders. Note also that the House Select Committee is concerned not with the poor quality of exploitative literature but instead with the "artful appeals" that might convince those on the normative side of the sexual binary to defect to the side of perversion or, perhaps more frighteningly, be caught somewhere in an ambiguous middle space, where established surveillance practices might be ineffective. This concern implies that pulp held a significant amount of power to subvert narratives of normativity, and it also speaks to the assumed parallels between homosexual "recruiters" and artful undercover agents, making lesbian pulp an imperative target for containment. The constellation of state-sponsored marginalization, popular denigration and fetishization, and the impossible choice of living in the closet and suspect or out of the closet and ruined made this moment in history particularly fraught for lesbians.

On the Covers: Gothic Containment Crypts

Women in the Shadows, First Person 3rd Sex, The Odd Kind, Edge of Twilight, The Third Street, Twilight Lovers, Sex in the Shadows, The Third Sex, The Path Between, Odd Girl Out . . . the titles of lesbian pulp novels signal themselves with repetitive and derivative language, offering savvy readers clues to the lesbian content inside with words such as *odd, third, shadows*, and especially *twilight* recycled repeatedly.[20] The copy on the cover of *We Walk Alone through Lesbos Lonely Groves* describes the "love that dwells in twilight"; *I Prefer Girls* offers a "strange story of twilight love, jealousy and hatred"; and *Strange Friends* promises to whisper the "unspoken secret of a twilight love."[21] Neither night nor day, twilight figures an in-between state, as does the concept of the "third" in reference to those caught between lovers or between genders or between worlds.

The language of in-betweenness takes on new relevance in the context of Cold War containment culture, when those who crossed between the patriot/subversive binary were considered extremely dangerous.

The titles, cover images, and copy of lesbian pulp novels often utilize gothic conventions to emphasize the threatening aspect of those who lurk in margins of the normative, domestic sphere, by featuring darkness and highlighting "monstrous" sexual urges, sadomasochism, and incest. Publishers took great pains to craft cover art and copy that would signal the presence of homosexual content while indicating that the novels were, in fact, medical or morality tales designed to teach people about the "wrong" sexual path so that they might be guided toward the "right" one—a narrative trajectory reminiscent of those conservative eighteenth- and nineteenth-century Gothic novels that titillate through a "momentary subversion of order" followed by a comforting restoration of the status quo.[22] In a genre governed by profit margins, it is notable that publishers found gothic darkness to be so essential that they were willing to ignore common paperback printing conventions when homosexuality was a dominant theme of the text, a choice exemplified by the shadowy tones on covers such as *Stranger on Lesbos* and *Strange Breed*. Stryker explains that "most publishers avoided using black on paperback covers because it tended to show scratches and wear too easily. It was used primarily on gothic and horror story covers. The extensive use of black on pulp covers thus subtly suggested the psychological horror a straight mind might experience when confronted with bisexual ménages à trois or the prospect of homosexuality."[23] Black ink signaled the terror of crossing over into the realm of homosexuality, and twilight marked the moment of contact in which characters slipped, sometimes without warning, from their daylight world into the nighttime of perversion. Further, those who were confirmed lesbians in these texts generally spent their days closeted, working and surviving in straight society, and their nights in the bars and in the beds of their lovers, implying a double life akin to *The Monk*'s Ambrosio (a beloved monk by day and a sex-crazed Satan worshipper by night). This was a narrative that resonated with readers at a moment in which media and government were obsessed with subversive double agents, and gays and lesbians were linked with communists in the shared goal of undermining U.S. values. The gothic atmosphere of the covers suggested simultaneous fear, titillation, and condemnation in reaction to such un-American activities.[24] If unmarked lesbians were secretly infiltrating straight life by day, then straight Americans might be interacting with a double agent at any time, unable to tell that this "lesbian sicko" had brought a little bit of darkness into their world of light, casting shadows of doubt on all interactions and perhaps even tempting them into the twilight themselves.[25]

As in eighteenth- and nineteenth-century Gothic fiction, darkness in lesbian pulp also serves as a racial metaphor, specifically in its depiction of non-Western figures as exotic, fetishized Others, an orientation that centers a Western gaze through a specific fantasy of the East, which Edward Said theorizes as "Orientalism." In addition to introducing the concept of containment, Kennan's essay also emphasizes Russia's racial and cultural difference through an association with the "Orient." Nadel reads this conflation as marking Russia as the "West's Other, potentially a part of the Oriental harem." As such, Russia functions as the other side of a sexualized binary—both "perverse seductress" and potential "rival suitor"—attempting to tempt American defection and infiltrate those countries that the United States would like to claim for democracy. Nadel notes that this narrative "raises questions about Russia's orientation," so the Orientalized darkness associated with Russia becomes legible as a sexual threat—one that blurs notions of appropriate sexuality and gender roles while simultaneously nodding toward the specter of miscegenation.[26]

Lesbian pulp, a genre almost exclusively centered around white, middle- or working-class story lines and characters, frequently extracts race itself from the texts by eliding raced bodies with racialized metaphors of darkness and foreignness, thus representing the threat of homosexuality as perverse rival suitor and, like the Soviets, a threat to U.S. domesticity and national security. While lesbians of color and interracial lesbian couples exist within the pages of some rare lesbian pulp novels, lesbian pulp

Cover 1 (front):

CREST BOOK

s355

35¢

STRANGER ON LESBOS

The searching
novel of a lonely
young wife faced
with the temptations
of unnatural love

VALERIE TAYLOR author of
WHISPER THEIR LOVE and THE GIRLS IN 3-B

Cover 2 (back):

FRANCES HAD BEEN LEFT ALONE TOO OFTEN

Bill's occupation with business, his insensitivity, his indifference had drained their marriage of meaning and warmth.

Yet it never occurred to her to think of divorce—or to have an affair with another man. It was easier to shut herself off from all desire, all feeling.

It was like being dead. But it was safe.

Now Bake with her dark, knowing eyes, her tense young body, so alive, so full of passion and hunger, had changed all that.

FAWCETT WORLD LIBRARY

Cover 3 (front):

STRANGE BREED

By ALDO LUCCHESI
(an original novel)

A Touching
Story Of That
Breed Of Women
Who Receive
From Each
Other What
They Cannot
Receive
From Men

MIDWOOD
k 50¢

Cover 4 (back):

"Lesbianism, or female homosexuality, is quite widespread throughout the world . . ."

Dr. Edward Podolsky
State University of New York Medical College

"During treatment sessions with a homosexual person one becomes aware of how isolated, alone and apart from the mainstream of human activities this person finds herself . . ."

Dr. Nathan Blackman
Director, Psychiatric Division
Malcolm Bliss Hospital, St. Louis, Mo.

"Lesbians should be neither pitied nor ridiculed. They deserve only understanding and sympathy—especially from men. For, if there were fewer brutal, bungling, sexually inept and self-centered men, there would be far fewer Lesbians. Fantastic numbers of women become Lesbians because they seek—and obtain—from other women the gentleness, tenderness and loving affection they have never received from men . . ."

Dr. J. S. Guttenplan
The Psychoanalytical Assistance Foundation
Los Angeles, California

printed in U.S.A.

covers feature almost no people of color. In fact, Stryker notes that the cover art for *Cloak of Evil* and *Duet in Darkness*, by author Rea Michaels, "are among the only representations of lesbians of color in the entire lesbian paperback genre."[27] Instead, racial blackness is replaced with the markers of otherness that resonate with Cold War notions of an Orientalized threat and that map directly onto conceptions of the Cold War as a "politico-cultural *surrogate* for race war," in which "biological racism was repudiated, yet the idea of an enemy population inferior in its subhuman political organization was retained."[28] Shadowy, nondescript darkness allowed the texts to signify racialized difference while avoiding the material realities of race and miscegenation that might distract from the rhetorical function of darkness as a stand-in for the alien threat.

The "alien" lesbian depicted on pulp covers is often masculine, dark, and swarthy with an unusual or foreign-sounding name. Consider Bake, the tempter in *Stranger on Lesbos* who is worldly with "dark, knowing eyes." The back cover of *The Scorpion* by Anna Elisabet Weirauch explains that the "young, sensitive Myra meets and is conquered by Olga's worldliness" until the two women can do nothing but "live in the twilight zone of sex." In addition to the worldly Olga, names that ring of Eastern Europe and other foreign locales abound, such as Magda, Draga, and Hilda from *The One Between* (1962), *Queer Affair* (1957), and *Forbidden* (1952), respectively.[29] Further, cover art often features a dark, usually short-haired woman (usually wearing pants) who occupies the role of masculine seducer in relation to the frequently unhappy-looking feminine woman.

The covers featured here are just a sampling of many that contain the short-haired "butch," looking tough, knowing, and seductive. Although the women read as white, race is replaced by markers of otherness, including dark hair and eyes, as appears on the covers of *The One Between* and

1. (*opposite top*) *Stranger on Lesbos* (Valerie Taylor). Courtesy of ONE Archives at the USC Libraries.

2. (*opposite bottom*) *Strange Breed* (Aldo Lucchesi) cover art (Paul Rader). Courtesy of ONE Archives at the USC Libraries.

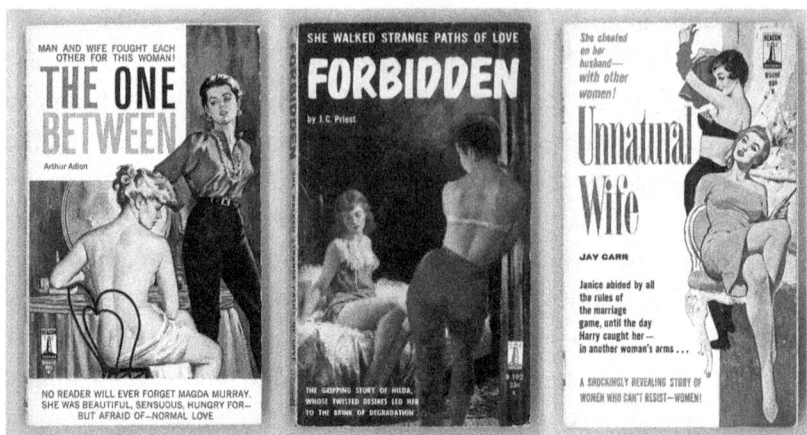

3. *The One Between* (Arthur Adlon), *Forbidden* (J. C. Priest), and *Unnatural Wife* (Jay Carr). Courtesy of ONE Archives at the USC Libraries.

Unnatural Wife.[30] *Forbidden* features a short-haired woman with her back to viewers, obscuring her eye color but featuring prominently the fact that she is wearing pants. Though these cover images are not so clearly gothic as those printed in black, red, and yellow, the dynamics of the couples in each mirror what Tania Modleski calls the "Shadow-Male" of Gothic fiction. Eighteenth-century Gothic texts marketed to women reflect the readers' paranoid "tendency to classify men into two extreme categories" of the "Super-Male and the Shadow-Male, the former almost always the apparent villain but the real hero, the latter usually a kind, considerate, gentle male who turns out to be vicious, insane, and/or murderous."[31] The seductive butch figures on these covers serve as sly "Shadow-Males" who tempt vulnerable women into their world and who are frequently revealed as insane and vicious—a gothic version of the foreign undercover agent who passes in the U.S. mainstream only to recruit vulnerable citizens to serve a dark, Orientalized Soviet power. Of course, it is impossible to ignore the eroticization of the exotic here, with two out of three of these images featuring the dark woman in some state of undress, speaking to the multiple functions of lesbian pulp in general. While there was a large following of lesbian readers to whom the gothic shadow figure might appeal, the texts were overtly designed for male voyeuristic pleasure or moralizing about the evils of lesbian sexuality, and these competing purposes play out in the sexualized exotic-yet-suspicious and vaguely racialized threat of the women featured on the covers.

Indeed, Orientalism itself is a mainstay of Gothic fiction. William Beckford's Gothic novel, *The History of Caliph Vathek* (1787), utilizes Orientalism both as a "signal of ethnic and cultural barriers and as a vehicle of desire."[32] The Orient in eighteenth-century Gothic fiction functions as a marker of the exotic, exciting, and threatening. For example, Charlotte Dacre's *Zofloya, or The Moor* depicts ominous power paired with sexual desirability, with the magical and seductive Moor revealing himself in the end as the ultimate inhumanly frightening (yet deliciously tempting) other, Satan. While Zofloya's body is partially determined by his blackness, it is the combination of racism, Orientalism, and desire that marks him as a dangerous and powerful presence, tempting those who encounter him (namely Victoria) to perform increasingly evil and sexually perverse acts. Said notes that European culture "gained in strength and identity by setting itself off against the Orient as a sort of surrogate and even underground self," and in the juxtaposition between the socially visible self and the "underground self" one can see the roots of that duality narrative so heavily utilized in containment culture—a narrative that also serves as a "Western style for dominating, restructuring, and having authority over the Orient."[33] The eroticized Orientalism on the covers of lesbian pulp not only evokes the conservative gothic approach to representations of nonnormative sexuality but also recirculates Cold War narratives through language historically used to maintain colonial power structures.

Lesbian pulp covers represent lesbian sexuality as a twilight world hovering between night and day, public and private, black and white, surface and undercurrent, and their Orientalist depictions of twilight and shadows function as containment crypts that locate, name, and control that realm that resists binary categorization. In addition to the between space of the twilight world, one of the most prominent examples of containment crypts appearing on lesbian pulp covers is figured in the designation of "third"—third sex, third way, third street, third theme.[34] This odd number appears again and again. "Third," as a marker of contested space located between two opposing forces, circulated in Cold War discourse through the "Third World," a concept that originated in the early 1950s to refer to the "global majority who had been downtrodden and enslaved through colonialism" and who now "refus[ed] to be ruled by the superpowers and their ideologies . . . [and searched] for alternatives both to capitalism and Communism, a 'third way' . . . for the newly liberated states."[35] The superpowers of the Cold War created the Third World by establishing these recently decolonized states as battlegrounds for political and economic dominance under the guise of spreading democratic or communist ideology. The United States established widespread interventionist policies that claimed, through a reworked imperialist narrative, to have the "duty" to inspire, maintain, and protect democratic ideals from that oozing spread of communism that threatened to infect vulnerable countries around the world. The United States viewed Third World countries as locations of potential and threat, requiring vigilance and control because of their imagined susceptibility to Soviet seductions, but also equally susceptible to U.S. interventions on behalf of democracy. This perspective on the Soviet threat in the Third World mirrors the positioning of lesbian sexuality throughout pulp covers as threatening, subversive, and unruly. They seduce vulnerable, impressionable women to slip into the third space of the "twilight zone of sex," a containment crypt that serves as an ideological battleground on the pulp covers.

Artemis Smith's novel, *The Third Sex*, presents a tale of a front marriage between Joan, a woman who could find the "satisfactions of love" only with other women, and Marc, her lover's brother, who had a "twisted fondness" for other men. This is an anxiety-provoking situation within the context of containment culture because the marriage creates the illusion of heterosexuality, allowing two sexual others to infiltrate and undermine the heteroexclusive domestic sphere. Joan and Marc move between worlds and utilize dominant social conventions as screens for their "curse." During

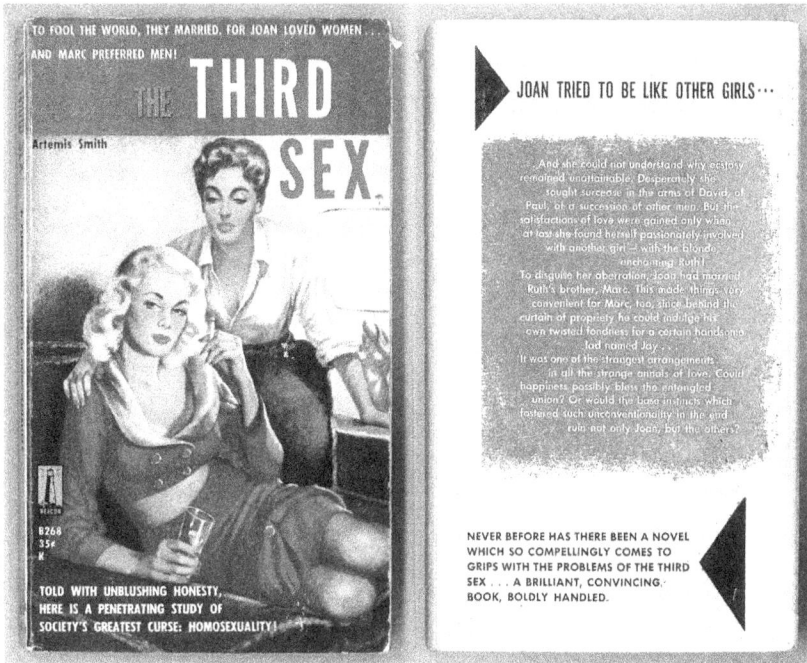

On the cover:

TO FOOL THE WORLD, THEY MARRIED. FOR JOAN LOVED WOMEN...
AND MARC PREFERRED MEN!

THE THIRD SEX

Artemis Smith

TOLD WITH UNBLUSHING HONESTY, HERE IS A PENETRATING STUDY OF SOCIETY'S GREATEST CURSE: HOMOSEXUALITY!

JOAN TRIED TO BE LIKE OTHER GIRLS...

And she could not understand why ecstasy remained unattainable. Desperately she sought surcease in the arms of David, of Paul, of a succession of other men. But the satisfactions of love were gained only when at last she found herself passionately involved with another girl — with the blonde, enchanting Ruth!
To disguise her aberration, Joan had married Ruth's brother, Marc. This made things very convenient for Marc, too, since behind the curtain of propriety he could indulge his own twisted fondness for a certain handsome lad named Jay...
It was one of the strangest arrangements in all the strange annals of love. Could happiness possibly bless the entangled union? Or would the base instincts which fastened such unconventionality in the end ruin not only Joan, but the others?

NEVER BEFORE HAS THERE BEEN A NOVEL WHICH SO COMPELLINGLY COMES TO GRIPS WITH THE PROBLEMS OF THE THIRD SEX . . . A BRILLIANT, CONVINCING BOOK, BOLDLY HANDLED.

4. *The Third Sex* (Artemis Smith). Courtesy of ONE Archives at the USC Libraries.

the Cold War period this type of passing was a terrifying prospect, as it threatened the heteronormative nuclear family structure that supposedly contained the spread of communism, so the crypt of the third sex names those subjects that might slip under the radar and threaten to distort social institutions such as marriage.

The pathologizing aspect of the third sex appears as another strategy of isolation and containment on pulp covers. *The Third Sex*, a novel that is clearly a specimen of popular fiction, is instead cast as a "penetrating study" that "compellingly comes to grips with the problems of the third sex." In other words, the concept of the third sex allows the publisher to present this erotic and potentially subversive tale as a pseudoscientific study of that namable social problem, the third sex. Rather than allowing the characters and the story line to remain muddy and complex in terms of

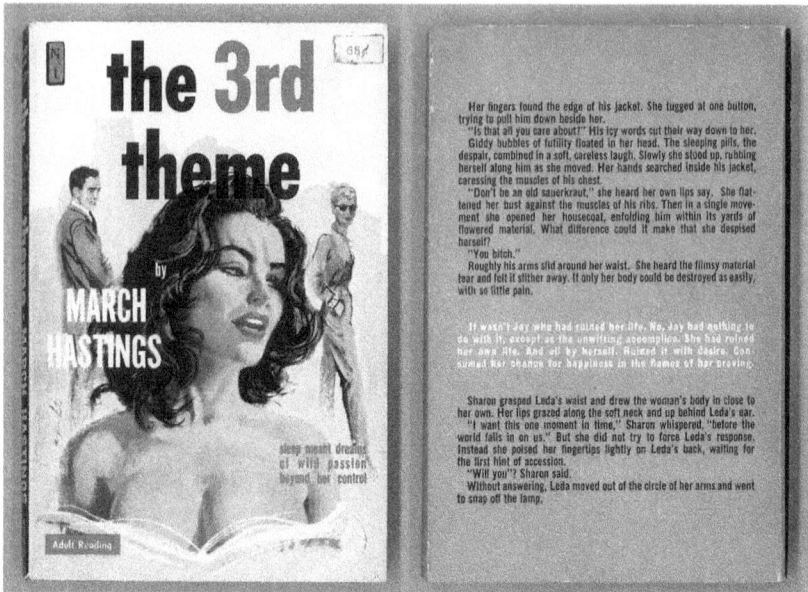

5. *The 3rd Theme* (March Hastings) cover art (Robert Bonfils). Courtesy of ONE Archives at the USC Libraries.

gender and sexuality, the cover text instead offers a space of containment, effectively codifying and cauterizing queer identity.

The 3rd Theme, by March Hastings, also attempts to situate sexual fluidity within a space of containment. The cover copy, in this case, does not assume a scientific or psychological tone. Instead this text, clearly labeled as "Adult Reading," focuses on the sexual drama of the story line, placing the image of a tormented-looking, yet exotically sexy, woman in between a man in a gray suit and a blond woman in a light-green pantsuit. The back cover consists exclusively of text from the novel itself, but the publisher has not refrained entirely from shaping the reader's understanding of this love triangle. The text is divided into three portions: the first portion of black text describes a narrative of straight sex and self-loathing, the second portion of black text describes the moments preceding a lesbian sexual encounter, and the third portion is written in white and sandwiched between the two sections of black text. The white section describes not a sex scene but an interior monologue, reflecting on how the "she" of this story had "ruined her own life . . . with desire." The editorial arrangement of the text effectively places her between the two poles of a sexual binary. The notion of thirds is implied throughout the cover design, and it is the queer woman who is caught between—in an unhappy space from which she is powerless to escape. Without this containment the unhappy protagonist might slip between worlds free from scrutiny, and the readers would be denied a venue for voyeuristically observing the erotic spectacle of her sexuality.

The Third Street does, spatially, what The Third Sex attempts to do with its pseudoscientific naming and what The 3rd Theme does with erotic titillation.[36] This text speaks of a street on which "no questions were asked" and "where few men were ever seen"—in other words, the realm of lesbians. The back copy implies that "gay street" contains a range of writhing, tormented souls seeking companionship and sexual satisfaction in a world set apart from the rest of society. Their "world of exotic evil" exists as a kind of catchall space for any one with "secret hungers" that are "condemned by society" but may not be easily categorized within the heterosexual/homosexual binary. Explicitly, this copy is probably meant to simply describe a street in Greenwich Village, or some other urban bohemian space in which queer folks congregate, but despite the fact that there are probably more than three streets in this urban neighborhood, it is labeled as the "third street" and characterized as an exotic, yet slightly terrifying, menagerie of freakishness, pathology, and sexual desperation. The third, here as with the previous texts, functions as a label that attempts to contain and control queerness, isolating it as a spectacle and fetishizing its exoticism. Those who walk the street at night might easily pass as "normal" during the day, so spatially local-izing that threat in a position between two presumably nongay streets creates a sense that these subjects are knowable, locatable, and even exploitable—their subversive power removed once they are trapped in the containment crypt.

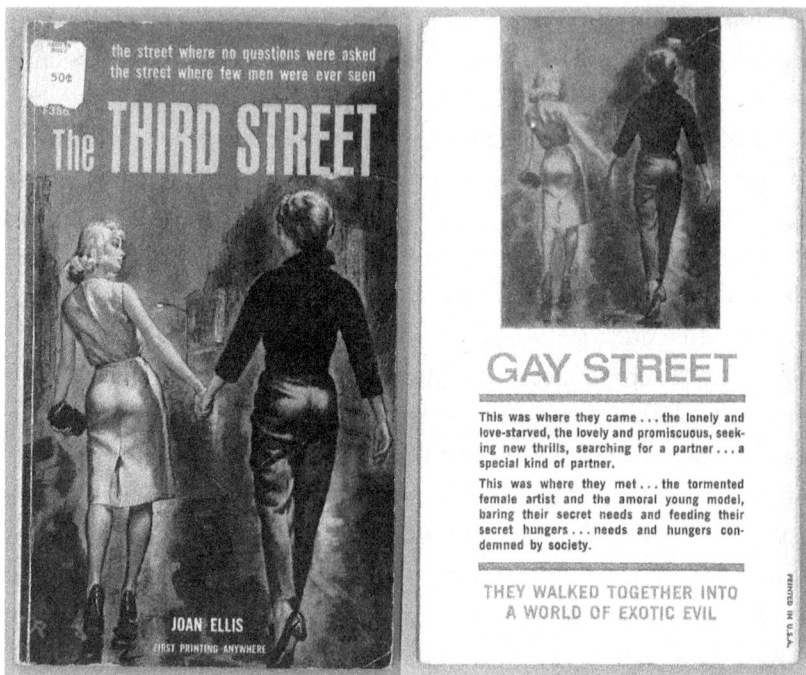

6. *The Third Street* (Joan Ellis) cover art (Paul Rader). Courtesy of ONE Archives at the USC Libraries.

The relentless negative messages of these covers were certainly microaggressive; however, they also provided hints to queer readers that they might find affirming content inside. Readers might not even consciously register the pathologizing, political, racial, and fetishizing function of the cover art and copy, but there is no doubt that the negative messages were internalized by a host of queer folks despite the common turn to pulp for representation. The implied surveillance, judgement, and control on the covers make these cultural artifacts a powerful vehicle for creating that slippery microaggressive experience in which one senses but doubts the slight that has occurred. Because of the slippery content and dual purposes of cover-art containment crypts, pulp functioned as a Cold War–era social tool that contributed to widespread queer oppression and created insidious trauma.

Under the Covers: Containment Crypts as Gothic Queer Culture

Although containment crypts functioned to name and control those confined there, their existence, along with the lesbian pulp texts themselves, also created a virtual subcultural location in which lesbians found representation and recognized themselves as members of a community. Lillian Faderman describes the traumatizing isolation many lesbians struggled with in the 1950s and 1960s: "Not only were American lesbians without a history such as helped to guide other minority groups, but they were also without a geography: there were no lesbian ghettos where they could be assured of meeting others like themselves and being accepted precisely for that attribute that the outside world shunned." But pulp novels' propagandistic cover art and copy that controlled and fetishized through containment crypts provided just such a space and began to create a shared history for lesbians around the country. Pulp's homophobic cover art and copy made the lesbian content visible and created a virtual space in which lesbians could recognize and learn about one another. Faderman acknowledges that "were it not for the publicity that was inevitably attendant on persecution, some women, even by the 1950s, might not have realized that there were so many who shared their desires and aspirations, that various lesbian subcultures existed, that lesbianism could be a way of life," but she does not recognize that this very persecution played out on the covers and in the pages of pulp fiction and created a "ghetto" space within which lesbians could form a subculture.[37]

This paradox could not have escaped the lesbian pulp writers at the time. While the content of the texts themselves vary widely, with many novels decidedly exploitative and designed for straight male audiences, at least "fifteen lesbian authors during the golden age produced over a hundred paperbacks in which lesbianism was presented in as favorable a light as publishers would allow."[38] Ann Bannon, Randy Salem, Vin Packer, March Hastings, Patricia Highsmith, Artemis Smith, Rea Michaels, and Paula Christian were lesbian authors whose sensitive and thoughtful approaches to sexuality belie the cautionary, sensational nature of the cover art and copy. Often the only narrative caveat that a publisher insisted on was that any novel about lesbian romance must end badly. This usually consisted of one of several options: suicide, insanity, or the character's realization that she was never actually in love with her same-sex romantic interest (usually after finding a more appropriate and desirable heteroromantic interest). The creation of nonexploitative lesbian pulp was restricted by many elements of the publication process—from publishers' capitalistic concerns to the desire for pornographic appeal and fears of censorship. Lesbian pulp authors rarely, if ever, had any say about the titles, covers, or endings of the novels, but within these limits, many were able to craft impressively sensitive, if flawed, portrayals of lesbian love and desire. If they were clever enough, the interior of the novel could offer hungry lesbian readers glimpses of the possibilities that the world held, even if those visions were consistently tempered by the dictates of publishers, censors, and market forces.

The prevalence of lesbian romances that take place within confined spaces and limiting heterosexual institutions speaks to the authors' use of containment discourse to surreptitiously circulate images and stories of lesbian love and desire. Tereska Torres's novel *Women's Barracks* (1950) is considered the first lesbian pulp novel to become widely popular, its story taking place primarily within the confinement of the London barracks for the Free French Soldiers during World War II. After its unexpected success, publishers were eager to find manuscripts with similar elements—confined, women-only spaces being one of the most prominent. Vin Packer famously describes the events leading up to the publication of *Spring Fire*, one of the most iconic lesbian pulps, in her introduction to the 2004 reprint of the novel. Following the success of *Women's Barracks*, Dick Carroll, editor for the newly created Gold Metal Books, commissioned a novel from his secretary, Marijane Meaker (Vin Packer). She said she wanted to write about a lesbian romance in boarding school. Carroll said that she would have to set the novel in a college sorority, rather than a boarding school, and that the story would have to have an unhappy ending. When she completed her novel, *Sorority Girl*, Carroll changed the title to *Spring Fire*, saying, "we have to jazz up the title and wrap it in a sexy cover. We have to! This is a business." As Packer describes it, the cover featured "two females who looked a lot like hookers, sitting in their slips on a bed," presumably to entice male readers, and its story implied that lesbianism could be located within confined spaces that caused young, confused women to make desperate choices.[39] This allowed readers and censors to explain away the presence of "real" lesbians by placing them in a containment crypt, to study the causes of their behavior, and finally to dismiss their existence entirely by the end (for one of the women turns out to be "normal" and the other turns out to be mentally ill).

In spite of the lurid cover, the misleading title, and the unhappy ending, Packer notes that "the fan mail came from women all over the United States" because "lesbian readers were able to look past the cover: to find themselves between the pages," even if many aspects of the text actually contributed to the insidious trauma of lesbian marginalization.[40] Following the success of *Women's Barracks* and *Spring Fire* came a slew of lesbian pulp set within confined spaces. There were sorority narratives such as Susan Sherman's *Give Me Myself* (1963) and Bannon's *Odd Girl Out* (1957), and there were also a large number of narratives set in prison such as Sara Harris's *The Wayward Ones* (1952), Reed Marr's *Women without Men* (1957), and Kay Johnson's *My Name Is Rusty* (1958).[41] Overtly, these containment crypt narratives made the publishers and censors feel more comfortable that lesbianism was characterized as knowable, locatable, and ultimately situational, but it was also true that the presence of the confined space signaled lesbian readers that the text might provide a virtual lesbian space—one in which lesbians could find representation and community, even if it was cast in oppressive terms.

Perhaps some of the most iconic and successful examples of lesbian pulp novels written by a lesbian are the five texts of Bannon's Beebo Brinker Chronicles: *Odd Girl Out* (1957), *I Am a Woman* (1959), *Women in the Shadows* (1959), *Journey to a Woman* (1960), and *Beebo Brinker* (1962).[42] Bannon's novels were not immune to alluding to the odd and shadowy, yet these texts play with the conventions that confined so many lesbian authors of this period, working cleverly with the stereotypes of the day and the requirements of the unhappy ending.

In 1955, when Ann Weldy sat down to write her first novel under the pen name Ann Bannon, she was a young homemaker living in the suburbs of Philadelphia. Though she had almost no practical experience as a lesbian, she had read two lesbian novels—Radclyffe Hall's *The Well of Loneliness* and Packer's *Spring Fire*.[43] Her proximity to New York City also allowed Bannon to take short trips to Greenwich Village to visit the gay bars, observe lesbians, and bask in the bohemian freedom she found there, even if she was not daring enough to leave her husband and children for the life that inspired her novels. After reaching out to Packer for help, Bannon wrote the novel that would eventually be published as *Odd Girl Out*, the first installment in the Beebo Brinker Chronicles. In the years following its publication, Bannon would receive hundreds of letters from women around the country, reaching out for guidance and connection in the face of extreme isolation and hopelessness. Bannon wrote that the women who contacted her "lived in a world where they thought themselves to be painfully unique. The bottom line was, they imagined themselves doomed to solitude in their yearnings for the rest of their lives and sadly, deservedly so, since they had no positive role models to contradict such self-prejudice."[44] Her novels provided a spark of recognition for those women who felt so unusual and so utterly alone.

Through her novels Bannon was able to expose a specific segment of lesbian life—the middle- and working-class, white, urban lesbians who pilgrimaged to Greenwich Village in New York City to find themselves (and one another). Bannon's novels echo the containment-inflected gothicism that alienates and marginalizes lesbians, but beneath the covers of her iconic novels Bannon inverts and redeploys gothic containment narratives by offering queered perspectives on gay and lesbian bars, domesticity, and marriage.[45] *Odd Girl Out* takes place in a sorority and introduces readers to Laura, a recurring character, who falls in love and has an affair with her roommate, Beth. On the verge of running off to New York with Laura, Beth decides to marry a man instead, leaving Laura to find her way home to her abusive father in Chicago. The remaining novels in the series, however, take place primarily in Greenwich Village, and they too play with the notion of the confined spaces evoked by containment discourse, with the lesbian bar replacing the sorority house.

As many have noted, the gay and lesbian bar scene was central to queer life in the 1950s and 1960s.[46] Even though one always ran the risk of being arrested during a police raid, people flocked to the bars because, as Faderman explains, "to many young and working-class lesbians the bars were a principal stage where they could act out the roles and relationships that elsewhere they had to pretend did not exist. The bars were their home turf." Lesbian bars, in a more tangible form than the pulp novels themselves, served as a kind of "ghetto" space, the existence of which Faderman initially denies. She later acknowledges, however, that the lesbians in the bar scene functioned as pioneers by "creat[ing] a lesbian geography despite slim resources and particularly unsympathetic times." The language of Faderman's historical study itself reflects an internalization of the containment discourse used in homophobic cover copy, describing the bars as "dark, secret, a nighttime place, located usually in dismal areas."[47] These "dismal" places also circulate throughout Bannon's novels as locations both overwhelmingly intimidating and desperately attractive to green lesbians, who often did not even have vocabulary for what they were seeing there. Lesbian bars play a larger role in the two novels that describe their protagonists' discovery of the scene in Greenwich Village: Laura in *I Am a Woman* and Beebo in the final novel of the series, the prequel *Beebo Brinker*. The bars, as they function in all these novels, are dark, frightening, and fascinating subterranean spaces. As "third spaces," the bars house those sexual and gender nonconformists who fall outside of the normative sphere and are rumored to lure new recruits into deviance. Bars also represent the development of an underground community in response to containment culture, and, as such, they take shape as literal underground spaces—basement bars segregated from straight society with passages that are tight and confined but that lead to discovery, sexual freedom, and identity formation. The depiction of these subterranean, crypt-like spaces as containers for both identity and community formation rather than as the disgusting and desperate realm of perverts, as the cover copy would imply, becomes representative of a distinctly gothic geography created by the very containment designed to stamp out lesbianism.

Beebo Brinker is the final book of the series and tells the story of Beebo's arrival in Greenwich Village and her discovery of the bar scene that later becomes her stomping ground. Beebo learns about her own desires and about lesbians in general by haunting underground gay and lesbian bars—primarily, the Colophon, Julian's, and the Cellar. The first time Beebo enters the Colophon, a "basement bar" with "more girls, more sizes, types, and ages, than Beebo had ever seen collected together in one place," she is excited and extremely anxious. When she sees women dancing together for the first time, she is "startled by it, afraid of it. And yet so passionately moved that she caught her breath."[48] This cramped subterranean space becomes a kind of Kristevan "vortex of summons and repulsion," as it forces Beebo to address her simultaneous fear and desire while reflecting containment's paranoid understanding of an oozing, fluid communism—seductive and foreign, fascinating and frightening.[49] In this abject underground space and on the verge of entering the "twilight" world of lesbian identity, Beebo suddenly perceives the basement bar as a gothic threat—evoking the trope of the frighteningly sexualized chase first established in Horace Walpole's *Castle of Otranto* when, in a scene charged with erotic fear, Manfred chases Isabella through the underground passages of the crumbling family estate. After watching the dancing couples for a moment, Beebo is suddenly panic-stricken: "At that point she murmured, 'Oh, God!' and turned to flee. She felt the way she had in childhood dreams when she was being chased by some vague terrible menace, and she had to move slowly and tortuously, with great effort, as through a wall of water, while the monster gained on her from behind." Beebo's sudden repulsion from the space is followed by her realization that the monster gaining on her was her own "fearful desire," echoing the language describing the seductive and alien lesbian women of pulp cover art who tempt "normal" U.S. women into the excesses of queer sexuality.[50]

Bannon brings in the language and imagery of homophobic containment crypts, but by turning to abject gothicism, she is able to craft from the Colophon a space of becoming and emergence out of the discourse designed to control and contain queer sexuality. The complexities of this negotiation play out in the overwhelming and conflicted emotions that Beebo first experiences in the underground bar. Eventually, however, the Colophon and the other underground lesbian bars of the Village scene become a kind of home for Beebo rather than a monstrous, threatening space. This occurs gradually, as she is drawn again and again to those dark passages that once repelled her. As she tries, and fails, to ignore "the one place she wanted to visit: the Colophon," Beebo learns to enjoy the scene that initially repulsed her because of its associations with desperate, shameful sexuality, noting later that she "liked to watch the girls move around the floor together, now that the initial revolt had worn off."[51] Bannon reframes the bar-as-containment crypt by depicting Beebo's shifting relationship to the space as she uses it to come to terms with own desires and to initiate practices that will satisfy them.

To Beebo and the other characters in the chronicles, the space of the bar becomes such a strong lesbian community that it even serves as a kind of lesbian phone book for those whose marginal status has erased them from conventional records and institutions. Julian Carter explains that lesbians' marginalized status as single wage earners frequently erased them from public record in a society in which "65 percent of white women had married by age twenty-four" (1954) and "95 percent of all adults in North America were or had been married" (1960).[52] The chronicles almost casually depict the characters' inability to gain and retain steady employment or residence due to their gender expression (Beebo's employment, for example, is limited to jobs in which she is able to wear pants), workplace discrimination, and the instability of a nightlife-centric lifestyle that often involves alcoholism. Instead of searching in the phone book or at the workplace, the characters in the chronicles simply enter the contained space of the Village bars to locate one another and, generally, they succeed. In *Journey to a Woman*, for example, Beth travels unannounced from Pasadena to New York City to find Laura, her college love, whom she has not seen in nine years. Despite the fact that she had not been to New York since she was a child, Beth knows about the lesbian bar scene because of the lesbian pulp she had been reading by author Nina Spicer. She contacts Nina, who then escorts her to the bars. After only a week or two, Beth easily tracks down Laura simply by asking around at the bars, speaking to the tightness of that community and its ability to function as a surrogate record based on oral and spatial contact.

As in *Beebo Brinker*, *I Am a Woman* prominently features the Greenwich Village bars as spaces of initial discomfort that eventually foster identity formation and community networking. The novel chronicles Laura's escape to New York City from her abusive father and her lesbian identity developed through the bar scene. More specifically, *I Am a Woman* inverts the Orientalist narrative that these bars are gathering spaces for the primitive, the foreign, the "alien-minded radicals and moral perverts" that had come to represent Soviet subversion. When Laura arrives in New York City, she already understands herself as a lesbian (although she does not yet have the vocabulary to express this), but she is still uninitiated into the Village scene. Jack Mann, a recurring gay character with whom she has been set up on a blind double date with straight couple Marcie and Burr, escorts her to the Cellar, a basement bar that "sounded sinister" to Laura. Once she realizes that she has been taken to a lesbian bar, she becomes "acutely uncomfortable," thinking "it was as if she were a child of civilization, reared among the savages, who suddenly found herself among the civilized. She recognized them as her own. And yet she had adopted the habits of another race and she was embarrassed and lost with her own kind."[53] Laura uses the Cold War practice of displacing material race and racism with a "racism of interiority that constructs its target populations with reference to their creeds, thoughts, and loyalties rather than their blood, color, and physiognomy."[54] But the portrayal of the lesbian as a racialized figure that occurs in so much of the pulp cover art is ironically reversed in Laura's introduction to lesbian bar culture. In the world outside lesbians are cast as perverse, shadowy and inhuman, but within this space Laura's lesbian identity becomes aligned, not with the savages, but instead with the "civilization" of lesbian culture. In conversation with Jack, Marcie, and Burr, Laura becomes enraged that they are talking about the bar patrons "as if they were a bunch of animals."[55] Here Bannon queers containment dualities that depend on the crypt of the subterranean bar, for once Laura realizes that she is in a lesbian bar and is given a vocabulary with which to name what she sees, she subverts the gay/straight hierarchy by casting her new lesbian community as a "civilization" among the heterosexual "savages" with whom she has been associating. It is only within the confined space of the bar that there is a strong enough sense of safety and community for Laura to make this inversion and comfortably identify as a member.

Bannon's strategy of inversion and redeployment extends beyond the bar scene to heteronormative spaces as well. To the uninitiated lesbians in Bannon's novels, the bar scene seems frightening and grotesque, but these initial associations are quickly disrupted by the possibilities for identity formation and community networking located there. Normative domestic spaces and institutions however, do not fare as well. After running away from her father's home at the beginning of the novel, Laura is desperately in need of an apartment and a job in New York City, and she is put in touch with Marcie, who is looking for a roommate. When she goes to meet with Marcie about the apartment, she arrives before Marcie gets home and observes the decaying apartment building as if it were a kind of eerie gothic castle: "Laura entered the vestibule. It looked like the reception hall in a medieval fort. The only light came from a small bare bulb on a desk in one corner. The whole hall was full of heavy shadows. . . . She swung slowly around on her heels to look at the hall while she waited. It gave her the shivers." As she enters the building, it is vaguely threatening in its shadowy gothicism, and, as she continues to explore the space in which she will live, she observes even more gothic elements, including a stone griffin on the roof and "pitiful groaning" coming from the pipes.[56]

The sinister nature of this apartment is never recuperated in the way the lesbian bar space consistently is. Instead, the "shivers" the building elicits from Laura stem from the very real threat that she faces as a lesbian entering into a heterodomestic sphere at the height of containment culture—here she is not protected by a close-knit community but is exposed to the traumatizing strategies so frequently used to censure "subversive" queerness when it is discovered within the ranks of the "normal." As Laura gets closer to Marcie, she begins to fall in love with this free-spirited, but straight, woman. Even though Laura believes she is subtly seducing Marcie without fully revealing herself as a lesbian, Marcie recognizes Laura's attraction to her and makes a bet with Burr, her ex-husband and current lover, that she can get Laura to make a pass at her. Marcie and Burr engage in this thoughtless game, operated from a position of heterosexual privilege, without realizing that their actions might be traumatizing and even dangerous to Laura. They also do not initially realize that this game might tempt Marcie to step into the "twilight" of lesbianism and never come back to her straight relationship, a possibility that eventually occurs to Burr and prompts him to violently threaten Laura and promise to report her criminal lesbianism to the authorities. By casting the apartment as a gothic castle, Bannon reverses the narrative of queer horror that plays out on the covers of pulp novels. The truly frightening space for a lesbian is that which is protected by the cult of domesticity and in which her existence is an impossibility. Laura has infiltrated that space and is threatened by violence—both physical and legal—to root out her subversive presence and protect the sacred domestic sphere from the "contagion" of queerness. The deployment of gothic horror depends on common assumptions of the gothic as undesirable, but Bannon displaces that narrative from its usual associations and instead casts the heterodomestic sphere as the truly frightening gothic space that does not offer any potential for lesbian becoming, only for censure and violence.

Bannon continues this reversal of gothicism-as-containment narrative in her portrayal of Laura's relationship with her father. Laura feels emotionally enslaved by her abusive father, and during their frequent arguments she often "trembled in terror, expecting him to brutalize her."[57] Laura's relationship with her father eventually mirrors the ultimate in gothic erotic chases—the interaction of Manfred and Isabella in *The Castle of Otranto*.[58] The extreme and hysterical fear that Laura experiences in this passage evokes George Haggerty's description of the "hallmark of gothic fiction": "the sexual anxiety of a victimized female, the incestuous desire of a libidinous male, the use of the actual physical features of the castle to represent political and sexual entrapment, and an atmosphere deftly rendered to produce terror and gloom."[59] In *I Am a Woman*, Laura runs away to New York City to flee her father's abuse, but she later encounters him when he is in the city attending a conference. Laura is drawn again and again to his hotel to watch him from a distance in a kind of repetition compulsion that forces her to engage with the perpetrator of her childhood trauma. During one of these visits, Laura sees him return her gaze in the hotel lobby and call out her name. When she makes eye contact with her father, "her eyes went huge with fear and she gasped and turned and ran as if the devil were after her. She ran headlong, panicky, her heart huge and desperate, struggling to get out of her throat. She ran with all her strength and with an unreasoning terror whipping her heels."[60]

On a later occasion Laura unknowingly wanders back to her father's hotel, drawn to the place as she had been on many other nights. The building itself becomes anthropomorphized when she realizes where she is, "as if the hotel had been sneaking up on her while she marked time on the sidewalk." In this moment the hotel itself comes to represent the threat of her father's paralyzing power over her. The gothic terror of incestuous desire, however, is unspoken until a later scene in which she confronts her father in his hotel room, and he admits to her, by violently kissing her, that he was cruel to her because he secretly desired her as a replacement for his dead wife. Laura's reaction to this revelation is to strike him with an ashtray and, once again, flee—running "in a terrible panic to the elevators" and jabbing at the call button "over and over again hysterically."[61] This scene offers all the hallmarks of the gothic chase; however, it is set in the space of a respectable hotel and in the context of a familial father-daughter relationship rather than in the "evil" spaces populated by homosexual "perverts" in which we might expect to find gothicism in a pulp novel.

Again Bannon undermines containment culture's deployment of gothi-cism by placing its truly terrifying elements squarely within the realm of dominant culture rather than in the shadows of the lesbian "third space."

Bannon's challenge to the gothic binary becomes more complicated when, in *Women in the Shadows*, Bannon depicts marriage not as a gothic threat but instead as an institution that has the ability to save Laura from her unhappy relationship with Beebo and to help her rise above her own selfish immaturity. In this novel Jack and Laura agree to be married, pro-viding each other with financial and emotional stability as well as the ability to continue with their respective homosexual affairs from the safe shelter of their "normal" domestic arrangement. It takes nearly the entire novel for Jack to convince Laura that this is a good idea, arguing, "It's either that or retire into a rotten little prison with the rest of the gay people and spend your life feeling sorry for yourself. No thanks, not for me."[62] Nota-bly, Jack seems to have internalized the Cold War containment structures that associate the gay world with confined prison spaces and marriage with freedom, and Laura eventually agrees to marry him and even have his baby by artificial insemination. The safety that Jack and Laura gain as a married couple can be accessed only because their normative gender expression allows them to "pass" as a straight couple (unlike Beebo, whose masculine gender expression outs her as queer; or Tris, a light-skinned African American woman who passes as East Indian but is continually outed by her dark-skinned husband), and their class status allows them to move out of the Village to an uptown apartment. These markers of privilege seem somewhat invisible to Bannon, who implies that this gay marriage is the best and most mature choice for gay and lesbian people.

The shift from normative domesticity as threateningly gothic to mar-riage as the only escape from the "rotten little prison" of gay life is rather confusing in the context of the containment crypt reversals I have been describing in the Beebo Brinker Chronicles. Carter posits that this unex-pected turn to marriage is disidentificatory, pointing out that Jack and Laura's union is a "gay marriage," in which both parties remain firmly attached to their gay and lesbian identities while accessing the privilege granted by the institution, a heterosexual coupling by appearance but homonormative in practice.[63] Reading Bannon's treatment of marriage as disidentificatory is convincing, but I would add that she does so specifically through the complex reframing of Cold War containment crypt structures. The containment crypts on pulp cover art and copy confined nonnormative genders and sexualities to the dungeons of depravity hidden beneath the "bright" "chrome-plated surfaces" of middle-class, white, heteronormativity, to return to Stryker's formulation. Within the novels Bannon offers instead several formulations for working within the gothic structures of containment, thereby disrupting the fantasmatic binary rather than simply reversing it. By turning the gothic containment crypts into formative, womb-like places, injecting horror into normative domesticity, and queering those structures meant to exclude the gays and lesbians—namely marriage—Bannon plays the interior narratives of the Beebo Brinker Chronicles against the oppressive containment narratives that take shape on pulp covers.

Another Containment Crypt Cover, Read Queerly

A young blond woman, wearing only a delicate pink slip, backs up against a door in a dimly lit room, grasping its edge in fear with one hand and covering her bare chest with the other. Her eyes are wild, as she gazes back in terror at someone who seems to be pursuing her. The door, slightly ajar, reveals the object of her terror: another woman with dark hair, dark eyes, and a collared shirt stands just outside the door, peering in with a serious expression. She lurks there, a gothic pursuer threatening to enter the blond woman's boudoir at any moment. Though the copy states that both women depicted "were driven by twisted desires," the image on the cover of Sheldon Lord's *The Third Way* implies that the dark threat of sexual subversion lurks just outside the domestic space. If the dark-haired woman is allowed in, she may seduce the innocent woman inside, corrupting her purity and turning her into a "deviate." Notably, the domestic space promises both safety and isolation to the white, feminine woman, while signifying exclusion to the woman who represents gender and sexual nonconformity, her difference figured through her darkness and aggression. This cover perfectly represents the ethos of containment culture—closing the door will exclude the threat, contain its spread, and keep those inside safe. But when read queerly, the cover might also imply the promise of the containment crypt. Perhaps instead of running from the woman outside the door, our blond femme is opening the door to her, eyes wild with desire rather than terror. In this reading the gothic containment imagery of the vulnerable boudoir becomes a space of desire, contained by secrecy, yes, but also made possible through that secrecy. Though, as the copy states, they "hid their claws under their nail polish," that nail polish can be read as the tactic of double agents deployed to hide their inhuman perversions or as a protective performance thinly veiling a gloriously animalistic passion, easily read by other "deviates" within the containment crypt.

3 MONSTROSITY

Melancholia, Cannibalism, and HIV/AIDS

I say, we say:
We, mud people, snake people, tar people
We, bohemians walking on millennial thin ice
Our bodies pierced, tattooed, martyred, scarred
Our skin covered with hieroglyphs & flaming questions
We, the witches who transform trash into wearable art
We, Living Museum of Modern Oddities
& Sacred Monsters

GUILLERMO GÓMEZ-PEÑA, "The New Barbarians"

A monstrous form with excessive meaning haunted the United States in the 1980s and 1990s: the queer body and the HIV-positive body (often imagined as one and the same). The iconic 1990 *Life* magazine image of gay activist David Kirby on his deathbed introduced a powerful new public image of the abject, AIDS-ravaged body.[1] As knowledge about the virus slowly unfurled, media portrayal of the bodies decaying from an unfamiliar and uncontrolled disease became a kind of spectacle of horror. Even when presented in the guise of sympathy, as in the case of Kirby's photo, the excesses of the wasted queer body were offered up to the public as the endpoint of queer identity—a monstrous confluence of nonnormative desire, threat, infection, abjection, and death.

A number of grassroots activist and caretaking organizations such as ACT UP and the Gay Men's Health Crisis arose in response to the AIDS crisis, and the government's unwillingness to recognize the severity of the situation pushed the LGBT community to support one another. In a 2015 article in *Gay Star News*, a lesbian reflecting on the era explained that "there is a somewhat mystifying (to me) separatist attitude between some gay men and lesbians, especially back then," adding, "this tragic time really brought us together."[2] Despite the community efforts to create support system for the dying, AIDS was often deeply isolating. Author Edmund White recalls that, when he was diagnosed, "mothers didn't want me picking up their babies. People didn't want to kiss you on the cheek. People certainly didn't want to have sex with you, especially other gay people. It was very isolating and demeaning."[3] The complex reality of those communities most affected by HIV and AIDS meant that isolation, fear, and stigma existed alongside unprecedented community support systems, political activism, and care.

But the public perception of the disease, as reflected in mainstream media, was almost exclusively dire. *Time* magazine's 1985 account of "AIDS hysteria" reads like a passage from Mary Shelley's *Frankenstein*, in which all of humanity shuns Frankenstein's creature, denying him companionship and care. When a sixteen-year-old prison inmate tested positive for HIV, they forced him to eat off of disposable plates, "which, along with his bed linen, were incinerated after being handled with gloves and double-bagged." When an AIDS crisis center tried to find a home for HIV-positive clients, the real estate agent kicked the center's representative out of his car, even though the representative was not HIV positive. No housing could be obtained without keeping the clients' HIV status secret. A longtime member of a bridge club was ostracized by his old friends and forced to wear surgical gloves when playing cards. In hospitals patients weren't spared from isolation and neglect; they were "sometimes left unwashed, lying in their excrement, their food trays stacked outside the door."[4] Beyond mere isolation the mid-1980s saw a spike in violence against those with HIV/AIDS and the people who cared for them, including bomb and death threats, acid attacks, and arson. The hysteria often left those with HIV/AIDS homeless, friendless, and reviled—described by *Time* as "pitiful nomads" and certainly akin to Shelley's ostracized creature, whose fellow beings "spurn and hate" him, leaving him to wander the earth "miserably alone."[5]

Today the horrors of the AIDS crisis seem to be fading from our collective memory, as people are able to live with the virus using effective antiretroviral therapy and to live with less fear of infection with the advent of pre- and postexposure prophylactic (PrEP and PEP) drugs. But there is still no cure, and living with the virus requires access to resources foreclosed to many. At the October 2013 opening of *Why We Fight: Remembering AIDS Activism* at the New York Public Library, ACT UP New York staged a "die-in." Activists scattered their bodies on the floor of the exhibition space, many holding signs proclaiming, "AIDS IS NOT HISTORY." The die-in featured the activist strategy made famous during the height of the AIDS crisis to acknowledge the past while focusing attention on the present and the future of HIV and AIDS. The protesters expressed their concern that the archival exhibit entombed the AIDS crisis in the historical past, a serious issue for those still engaged in battling the virus and decreasing public awareness about its ongoing global impact.

Dying from AIDS-related illness, witnessing the suffering of friends and loved ones, and experiencing violence related to one's serostatus—all are experiences that might be considered overtly traumatic. Additionally, the traumas of HIV/AIDS have been and continue to be permeated with less obvious traumas, insidious and ongoing "violence to the soul and spirit" from the loss of community, government inaction, victim blaming, laws restricting access to services (medical, funereal, tattooing, piercing) and limiting blood donation, slut shaming, health-care costs, and cultural amnesia, to name a few.[6] Many have implied that HIV-positive folks were monsters who deserved the disease—a conservative use of monstrosity that further reinforced the traumas of isolation and dehumanization.

Though the circumstances have changed drastically, the impact of HIV/AIDS on queer communities, both then and now, is a source of accumulated and unacknowledged insidious trauma. Indeed, survival itself can become an ongoing trial, as people live to see the loss of a generation of peers and the decimation of a community paired with survival guilt and a seemingly unaware and uninterested millennial generation born after the first effective antiretroviral therapy emerged. The insidious trauma around HIV/AIDS drives expression as people work to account for their experiences, and this expression often involves gothicism in part because gothicism forces us to pause in the horror rather than run from it or fast-forward through the crisis to find some comforting resolution. Monstrosity as a gothic metaphor of hybridity and excess reflected those dehumanizing narratives used against people with HIV and AIDS during the crisis, but gothic metaphors also have the potential to productively reframe these oppressive narratives. In the context of the so-called post-AIDS moment, gothicism forces history to remain open and challenges the ongoing insidious traumas that arise when people continue to be infected, to go into debt from exorbitantly priced drug treatments, and to die from a virus that is largely dismissed as no longer a crisis.[7]

This chapter reads Gil Cuadros's mixed-genre *City of God* (1994), a text written at the height of the AIDS crisis, as a piece of gothic AIDS literature that reflects the widespread association of queerness with monstrosity and offers a Frankensteinian model for queer subjects in the face of overwhelming loss. The chapter then turns to the post-AIDS era, focusing on the work of queer performance artist, Ron Athey, who tested positive for HIV in 1986 and continues a successful performance art career today. Athey's work evokes vampiric monstrosity in its disruption of bodily boundaries and often features needle penetration and flowing blood. Both Cuadros and Athey deploy the monstrous, leaky queer body and the perceived threat of ingestion and infection, offering a kind of cannibalistic monstrosity as a gothic strategy to address the ongoing conditions of HIV/AIDS. As gothic queer cultural production, their work suggests new modes of identity and community that—through excess and temporal hybridity—acknowledge both overt and insidious traumas and remain focused on the material realities of HIV and AIDS in the face of widespread indifference.

Gothic Monsters

Gothic monstrosity has resonated with readers for centuries, and it continues to offer contemporary writers and artists a rich rhetoric for responding to the impact of HIV/AIDS on queer subjects. Gothic monsters elicit fear because they collapse distinctions between self and other and challenge the assumption that the body is discrete and controllable. Monsters exhibit a characteristic "refusal to participate in the classificatory 'order of things,'" and their "chameleonic nature" makes the monster a "symbol of multiplicity and indeed invites multiple interpretations."[8] As metaphors, monsters can represent a number of cultural meanings at once—quite simply, the monster figures the excesses of culture by representing those on the margins while solidifying those in the center and embodying simultaneous fear and desire.[9]

Supernatural occurrences in eighteenth- and nineteenth-century Gothic fiction were sometimes explained away as the hysterical manifestations of the hero's fearful and suggestible mind. The corpse in the hidden garret turns out to be a wax figure; the creaking in the attic is a madwoman, not a ghost. The genuinely supernatural figures in Gothic fiction are often the devil incarnate, shapeshifting to manipulate a character's secret desires, or ghosts of ancestors returning to foretell a prophesy or take revenge on those who wronged them in life. Though literal monsters do not appear pervasively in Gothic texts, the mention of Gothic monstrosity brings to mind two unforgettable figures—Frankenstein's creature and Count Dracula.

In the case of Frankenstein's creature, specifically, its multiplicity arises from its origin as the amalgamation of parts harvested from the "unhallowed damps of the grave" and the "living animal."[10] The creature is constructed from human and animal, man and woman, and most likely from the deceased of several different races and classes. He defies a solid, orderly subjectivity because of this and is the embodiment of excess, containing meaning beyond his mere material existence. Frankenstein's creature is not killed in the course of the narrative, and he lives on in popular culture in myriad forms because of this excess. He can "never be vanquished," because he cannot be fully and coherently known, and he will always be the scapegoat for a culture, representing the thing that needs to be marginalized and contained.[11]

The vampire, whose most famous iteration is Bram Stoker's Dracula, is not literally pieced together from remains found in the charnel house as is Frankenstein's creature, though vampires do straddle multiple categories as simultaneously living and dead and human and animal shape-shifters.[12] In a more abstract way, vampires are indeed composed of multiple creatures, since they drink the blood of living humans and animals to survive. Therefore vampiric monstrosity is cannibalistic. Maggie Kilgour explains that cannibalistic incorporation creates an uncomfortable disruption of boundaries because it "depends upon and enforces an absolute division between inside and outside; but in the act itself that opposition disappears, dissolving the structure it appears to produce." Cannibalism demands and then collapses the distinction between eater and eaten, as the ingested creature becomes part of the eater. Or, as Kilgour likes to remind her readers, "you are what you eat."[13] In the colonial use of the cannibal label as justification for the occupation of indigenous territories, the cannibal "presents a disturbing fiction of otherness because it both *constructs and consumes* the very possibility of radical difference."[14] Vampires as cannibals represent a foreignness that collapses under the very framework of its otherness, thereby fundamentally disrupting identity, order, and stability.[15] The hybridity of the cannibal-vampire creates a figure that, like trauma itself, shatters linguistic binaries, collapsing such linguistically based concepts as self and other and thereby collapsing meaning.

Indeed, out of cannibalistic incorporation arises the inability to distinguish between binary opposites such as inside and outside, and the resulting uncanniness is "one of the terrors of the Gothic."[16] Perhaps because of its hybridity and traumatic resonance, cannibalism makes an appearance in Gothic texts beyond the vampire, such as Charles Maturin's *Melmoth the Wanderer*, which includes a tale in which two lovers, attempting to run away together, are instead locked away in a chamber deep within the subterranean vaults of a convent—the desperate young man eventually attempting to eat his lover by biting into the flesh of her shoulder. As quintessential monsters, both Frankenstein's creature and Dracula are "disturbing hybrids whose externally incoherent bodies resist attempts to include them in any systematic structuration. And so the monster is dangerous, a form suspended between forms that threatens to smash distinctions."[17] Gothic monstrosity has a particular resonance with those on the margins partially because of this characteristic hybridity and excess, and its "disturbing" qualities provide writers and artists with a rich strategy for addressing the traumatic reverberations of HIV/AIDS within queer communities.

Conquering Immortality

Gil Cuadros was a Chicano writer with AIDS, writing about AIDS, during the 1990s—a time when so many were battling a disease that seemed insurmountable and that linked the queer community with death in the minds of the mainstream. He grew up in an eastern suburb of Los Angeles, and later lived and eventually died in Los Angeles, and the city itself takes a prominent role in the text, often infusing his work with that nostalgia, pride, and melancholy that can accompany an affective connection to place. During his life the public was only beginning to become aware of the depth and quality of his work, which won a Brody Literature Fellowship and a PEN Center USA/West grant. But he published only a handful of stories and poems and a single book, *City of God*, before his death from AIDS-related causes in 1996. Now his writing is nearly lost, with *City of God* the only published text that is readily available and with limited critical engagement in the sphere of queer Chicano literary criticism.[18]

As a Chicano writer, as a Los Angeles writer, as a queer writer, as an AIDS writer, and as a writer who exceeds all these categories, Cuadros allowed the frightening reality of mortality to enter his work while somehow entertaining the vague and often evanescent possibility of immortality, resulting in a nuanced and complicated body of writing. The gothicism that infuses his writing allows him to access the idea of immortality not by some miraculous intervention but instead by resting in the excess and indeterminacy of a gothic mode that refuses closure. *City of God* begins with a death. In the opening short story, "Indulgences," the narrator's grandfather has just died, and he and his family are traveling to Merced, California, for the funeral. The last item in the book is the poem "Conquering Immortality"—a reflection on the imminence of death and decay for a man whose body is ravaged by AIDS-related illnesses. Arguably, one could view Cuadros's body of work as a production by a man who has a fatalistic obsession with death in a culture where being gay and HIV positive promises only limits and endings, and, indeed, readers of *City of God* cannot escape the overwhelming presence of death that pervades the text. These days the threat of HIV and AIDS has become more muted in our minds, and it seems hard for many to remember what a crisis it was. Queer culture has moved from being a marginalized and feared entity to one increasingly assimilated into the neoliberal cultural and economic machinery.[19] While the LGBT community was once limited by its entombment within the cultural imagination as always already dying, it is now becoming solidified as simply another consumer demographic, insofar as the public imagination equates "LGBT" with white, cisgender, gay men with financial resources to spare. *City of God* is an important text to recover in this moment, not because Cuadros offers some prescient vision of future queerness but because his text offers an unflinching reminder of an increasingly remote past.

Cuadros's adoption of monstrosity, death, decay, and loss can be read as a model of a gothic queer subject deploying the darkness of gothicism to acknowledge the horrors of undeniable trauma but also to powerfully reimagine what it means to be in a place of hopelessness and alienation. Whether the queer community is associated with death as a result of the AIDS epidemic (literal death) or as a result of assimilation (cultural death), queer subjects have faced problematic limits both during Cuadros's life and today. Queers of color, specifically, face erasure on multiple fronts, as many imagine that raced bodies and queer bodies cannot coexist within a single subject. Chicano theorists have often addressed this, and other, cultural impossibilities through the critical psychological lens of melancholia.[20] I argue that in *City of God* melancholia does not only help process and commemorate loss but functions as a trope that is expressly gothic. Through a gothic preoccupation with death and repurposing of monstrosity, *City of God* resists erasure and presents the possibility of a vibrant, subversive queerness in the face of physical and cultural mortality.

Gothic AIDS Literature

Like the popular Gothic novels written and published in the eighteenth and nineteenth centuries, *City of God* certainly responds to cultural anxieties about queerness and the unknown, and Cuadros reappropriates the monstrous and threatening queer body to reimagine the queer subject in the face of death. A disorienting and frightening multiplicity of meaning coupled with charged sexuality serve as the backbone of the gothic literary aesthetic. Often both fear and desire are projected onto gothic forms and tropes that embody the "excess of meaning" that the monster represents.[21] *City of God*, as gothic AIDS literature, not only deploys these classically gothic tropes but also overflows with excessive meaning in both its form and its exploration of emotions, relationality, disease, sexuality, race, class, death, abuse, and love. Through an elegantly reserved presentation of these weighty subjects, Cuadros at times challenges meaning, evokes fear, and dives headlong into desire, creating a text infused with gothicism.[22]

Cuadros presents queer desire throughout his short stories and poems; however, this desire is always paired with the readers' knowledge that this is a book written in the shadow of HIV and AIDS, a virus overdetermined by misunderstanding and fear. As Simon Watney points out, "the notion of homosexuality as a contagious condition" was a deep and abiding social belief during the height of the crisis, leading to a public fearfulness in response to contact with the LGBT community.[23] In addition to the notion that one can become a homosexual through contact with other homosexuals, many public figures, such as U.S. senator Jesse Helms, overtly linked AIDS with promiscuity, citing perversion, immorality, and "warped" sexuality as roots of the disease, even stating to Congress that "every AIDS case can be traced back to a homosexual act."[24] This kind of language circulating in government and media often implied that AIDS was "*intrinsically* sexual."[25] To counter that implication many public groups attempted to take measures to desexualize AIDS, such as ACT UP's 1987 installation, *Let the Record Show . . .* , which implied that government inaction was responsible for the disease's spread, not sexual immorality. Douglas Crimp explains that, while debate on these issues was complex, often the public messages attempting to desexualize AIDS existed in part *because* they were responding to the common assumption that AIDS was the "gay plague" brought on by sexual perversion.[26]

Knowledge about HIV and AIDS was further obscured within Latinx communities. In his 1990 reflection on being an "HIV-positive Chicano gay man," artist Ray Navarro explains, "to be 'gay' was not a reasonable option for me as a teenager. Gays were supposed to be white men with buzzed hair who lived in West Hollywood, not Chicanos. When I sought out my preferred way of expressing myself sexually it was under conditions of extreme secrecy." There were no words for his sexuality, he explains, except the insulting *puto*, and this mis- and missing information meant that HIV education within Latinx communities was slow and incomplete, leading to increased rates of infection exacerbated by poverty, lack of access to health care, insurance discrimination, immigration implications, and the exclusion of Latinx patients from clinical drug trials. Navarro concludes that "the AIDS crisis is part of the larger social agenda of an insensitive government" that disproportionately impacted Latinx communities in the height of the crisis.[27]

Even AIDS activist groups such as ACT UP targeted predominantly white communities with educational campaigns. The Los Angeles chapter of ACT UP, for example, focused on West Hollywood and lacked diversity in its leadership, meaning it largely failed to effectively reach communities of color with its messages about AIDS awareness and safe-sex practices.[28]

A 1987 report on the impact of AIDS on minority communities claimed that the "social dynamics of race" leading to the perception of AIDS "as a disease of gay white men" played a direct role in the overrepresentation of blacks and Hispanics in rates of HIV infection and death from AIDS-related illnesses.[29] In *City of God*'s moment, desire is never simply desire because it is inflected by these misunderstandings and blind spots—desire here is accompanied by fear of that dangerous unknowable disease and the implication that any kind of nonheteronormative sexual contact implicates characters in their own infection.

In the story "Unprotected," for example, the narrator is bursting with desire as he and his friend enter a Westside Los Angeles bar called The Brick during their Hawaiian Daze party. Here the narrator's desire is animalistic, unfocused, and energetic: "I needed to do something, make something happen, and like a cat, I pawed at the great white shark, suspended by the smallest test line." Even in this playful moment, the narrator's desire for sexual agency places him in the metaphoric position of a cat in relation to the ominously threatening great white shark, notably restrained only by a precarious wire or string, implying the threat that exists in relation to the narrator's sexually motivated actions. He soon is picked up by a man at the bar, and when they get to the man's condo the readers become voyeurs, watching them have sex in the "spotless" bedroom with a "cream-colored wood [headboard] twisted like a Bernini pulpit" and a "ceiling sparkling with glitter." The room is romantic, clean, and dedicated to sensuality rather than gritty, seedy, or public, as this type of cruising might imply (the narrator himself notes that he thought this type of pickup "was a bit sleazy"). The animalistic sexual tension continues as the narrator explains that he "was like a scavenger, hands tearing the hair that grew over his shoulders, tugging at his prick, pointed upright and bent." This voyeuristic moment is explicit and erotic, but the eroticism is inflected by the knowledge that the narrator is HIV positive, and the man he is having sex with is not. When the narrator learns that the other man has tested negative, he feels resentful, revealing his internalized belief that infection is a kind of punishment for immoral sexual behavior by "thinking that he was some seedy person who escaped the curse. I saw him do these things, in my mind, things that are considered unsafe, almost sinful now." The couple's serodiscordance is constantly in the thoughts of the first-person narrator, a persistent reminder of the danger and risk involved in the erotic situation. Juxtaposed with the immaculate condo and bedroom is the narrator's sense that he is "infectious material . . . being transported in an orange-red garbage bag, getting tossed out by sallow-colored gloves."[30] He feels shameful and morally irresponsible for allowing an HIV-negative man to have unprotected sex with him.

The fear of infection and shame permeates the entire erotic encounter, causing an oscillation between erotic arousal and fear- and grief-induced flaccidity. Like the obvious class difference that fuels the encounter, the narrator's disclosure of his positive status seems to spark his partner's desire rather than turning him off. This is a moment that precedes the conscious subcultural reclamation of "bug chasing" and bareback "breeding" that Tim Dean has more recently theorized, but the presence of this risky intimacy further infuses the narrative with the discomfort of a potentially deadly, yet undeniably erotic, sexual act.[31] While contemporary bareback subculture favors condomless sex and fetishizes positive serostatus because of its potential for creating kinship, intimacy, and community, the practice of unprotected sex in this instance offers the erotic thrill of a taboo sexual act followed only by isolation and shame. This is not the kind of intentionally productive risk that Dean traces in contemporary bareback culture, but it is a moment in which the intimacy of unprotected flesh-on-flesh offers an overwhelmingly multivalent experience, in which death and desire bleed into each other. The risk that pervades this story is simultaneously threatening and sexy, a narrative excess that disrupts meaning.

Regardless of the thrilling rejection of caution in the heated moment, once the encounter is over the narrator's sense of fear and shame becomes a more palpable sense of disgust and repulsion, as he focuses on the bodily remnants that speak to his "sinful" sexual choice. Riding home on the bus in the morning, he becomes overwhelmed with the fear that the other riders "could smell the shit that was in my beard, see the sticky shine of cum over my body, and know what I had done that night."[32] The narrator feels marked as abject and infectious, and he is filled with shame as he imagines his own body as monstrous and overdetermined by the fluids that stain him and circulate within him. In the narrator's mind his body becomes a beacon of excess that is publicly readable through those abject substances that muddy the boundaries of subject and object, evoking the Kristevan "vortex of summons and repulsion" that places the one "haunted by it literally beside himself."[33] In this moment the narrator's sense of his own grotesqueness overwhelms the pleasure of his encounter, and the reader is taken along with him on a journey from the excitement of sexual intimacy to the disgust and repulsion that the narrator feels in relation to his internalized shame.

The presence of infection and death haunt this story, along with desire and excess, to create a gothic AIDS narrative. Indeed, the book as a whole oscillates between such extremes of desire and fear, including stories that pair young love with haunting loss and juxtaposing lusty poems with heart-wrenching verse about the frighteningly abject decay of a lover's body and mind. It works to evoke desire, yet because it operates in the shadow of the AIDS crisis, desire is always infused with the knowledge that each sexual encounter might be dangerous. Additionally, each new narrator or lover might be the next to die—indeed, may already be dead, since the chronology of the text is not strictly linear. The consistent undercurrent of death and decay lurking behind the corners and within the crevices of the narrative creates a work that is as gothic as a horror film or an eighteenth-century Gothic novel, tapping into readers' shared fear of annihilation.

In addition to its gothic content, the form of the text itself reflects the multiplicity that characterizes the monstrous body—it cannot be reduced to a single genre, a single meaning, a single narrative arc, or a single narrator. *City of God* encompasses both prose and poetry, and it defies any tidy definition in terms of its fictional or autobiographical nature. Rather than presenting the events in a chronological narrative form, Cuadros writes the first half of the book as a series of short stories with shifting narrators and points of view. While the reader might be inclined to assume that many of the narrators are versions of Cuadros himself due to biographical similarities, there is no identifiable continuity of narrative voice throughout the stories. The narrators remain unnamed or their name changes from story to story, their gender shifts, and their age changes in no discernable chronological manner. Then, more than halfway through the book, the genre changes from prose to poetry. The poetry also includes various personas who often appear to represent Cuadros himself, but this association is slippery, since it is based merely on biographical coincidence and the often-confessional nature of the poems.

Readers might dismiss Cuadros's disaggregated subject and play with genre as simply postmodern fragmentation and potentially subject to critique regarding postmodernist abstraction that diverts attention from the materiality of raced, classed, and gendered bodies. But Cuadros subverts this abstraction by deploying these generic tactics with the purpose of highlighting a monstrosity rooted in the body. In fact, the text itself becomes one of the several elements shattered in the course of *City of God* to create a text both monstrous and embodied, a choice that informs Cuadros's gothic vision of subjectivity. What looks to be postmodern abstraction ends up being a return to the materiality of suffering and loss. The biographical knowledge that Cuadros wrote this text while HIV positive and that he died in 1996, two years after its publication, contributes to the sense that the only consistency in the text is physical decay and death—concepts that defy meaning and push the limits of human understanding.

While the text itself functions as a kind of fractured monstrous body, the narrative voices in *City of God* also decompose as the text progresses. The opening story's narrator is very strongly linked to Cuadros—his name is Gilberto, his family is Latino, and he is a young gay man. *City of God* also begins with a narrative that portrays heteronormative patriarchal subjects reinforcing dominant culture through the violent exclusion of the sexually nonnormative. "Indulgences" recounts Gilberto's parents' nostalgia for the cozy Americana of their hometown, Merced, California. They "romanticized the red checkerboard-patterned water tower on J Street, the Purina feed store on K, the old, semi-demolished church that looked like Mexico, rough-hewn, gritty pink stone L Street," and "the time when blacks kept to their own side of town." Their memories were of a time when things were simple because they were normative—commercialism and religion dominated a landscape where racial borders were neatly demarcated. The family is clearly invested in policing heteronormative sexual borders as well. Gilberto, the first-person narrator, is thirteen in this story, and, rather than being interested in girls, he is becoming aware of his attraction to the boys who would punch him and call him a "fucking sissy" at school. In reaction to his apparent romantic apathy, he says his mother "begged me to find a girl soon, not to be so shy, said it was natural for me to like girls. She said she worries because she's a mother."[34] Her words reflect the family's desperation to maintain clear heteronormative behaviors and pursuits.

The strongest testament to the familial investment in heteronormativity occurs when the family scapegoats Gilberto's mother's cousin, Evelyn, for the death of Gilberto's grandfather. She was his caretaker, and when he passed away the family projected their grief and anxiety in the face of death on her body. She, like a gothic monster, becomes a screen on which the family projects multiple meanings—in their eyes she becomes everything that is outside of their heteronormative comfort zone. They would "tell each other what a tramp, a slut Evelyn had become. They'd snicker about how she slept with black men, white men. Papa should have put her away. Evelyn's Papa's angel. Evelyn's a lesbian." Here Evelyn becomes the symbol of a multiplicity of racial and sexual boundary crossings. The family is able to shore up its own normative status by projecting their anxieties on her body and then beating her "like a mob, women pulling her hair, kicking Evelyn in the stomach, the ass, her breast."[35] By destroying her body through physical violence, the family reinforces their own normative subjectivities at the expense of the destruction of her monstrous queer one.

In addition to being a coherent and traditional narrator, Gilberto is normative in the sense that he is aligned with his patriarchal heteronormative family in opposition to Evelyn. Despite his own emerging queerness, he and his brother sided with the family members beating Evelyn; they "jumped up and down in the back seat, acted as if we could feel the blows or were giving them, vocalized the sound of each good hit." After the attack on Evelyn, however, the narrator wonders "if my family would ever turn on me."[36] This is a moment of epiphany, in which he realizes that perhaps he, in his emerging queerness, is more like the monstrous Evelyn than like the rest of his family. Subsequently, the coherent narrative voice and structure begins to pull apart as the text disintegrates into a fractured multiplicity of fragmented subjects and stories—divorced from that coherent, heteronormative subject with which his text begins.

"Chivalry" has a first-person narrator who is well on his way toward a fractured, incoherent subjectivity—one that more closely mimics the pieces of Frankenstein's monster than the consistent, intelligible narrator who begins the text. Although the narrator appears to be a member of the same family from "Indulgences" (both he and Gilberto share a Grandma Lupe), he is unnamed, so it becomes more difficult to place him in relation to the original narrator or the author himself. The narrator begins the story by explaining how he frequently occupies the blurry threshold between life and death, detailing a wrist cutting at the age of nine and a "near-drowning the year before," in which he found his feet "tied in fishing line and algae at the lake's bottom." In a later story, called "Baptism," this very event occurs when the narrator, Angela, describes a near drowning in a lake, in which she suddenly feels her "foot tangle in some kind of line" until a "warm feeling of having nothing to worry about" comes over her.[37] Although the events align very closely, the narrators differ in gender and age. Through these similarities the reader is invited to make comparisons and to draw links between the stories, but this attempt is confounded by the increasingly fractured narrative voice in the text, as the coherent narrator who begins the book both breaks from and merges with other narrative voices.

City of God also places early queer sexual experiences in conversation with death and decay. When the narrator of "Chivalry" and his cousin David are looking at pornographic magazines together, the narrator describes his arousal as "the same buoyancy inside as if I were held underwater, a similar dizziness to losing blood," evoking that warm, carefree feeling described as the process of drowning in "Baptism." In the scene following the one in which the narrator is introduced to "dirty pictures," David also introduces him to another of his hobbies. He takes the narrator into a shed to show him "something special." Thinking that this secret was another stash of pornography, the narrator gets sexually aroused. He says, "my dick pressed against my zipper," as he reaches into a red clay pot to touch "something dry and porous." After his "fingers found holes to slip into," he looks more closely and recognizes that the objects he had been touching are partially decayed mouse and bird heads that his cousin had collected from the fields and saved in pots. The bird heads had "small feathers still attached" and "rotted eyes," and the mouse skulls were "sun bleached."[38] The final pot he reaches into is full of rattlesnake tails. The narrator's anticipation of further sexual exploration with his cousin arouses him, and the arousal is paired with the tactile discovery of the mouse and bird heads as fascinatingly disgusting objects of dismemberment and death, a culmination in which emerging queer sexuality becomes closely associated with decay and fragmentation.

Queer sexuality itself functions as a gothic element in its association with fear, desire, and death—there is the literal near death of the narrator, the dead animals that he encounters during his sexual awakening, and the increasing disruption of a coherent narrative subject that seems to be associated with the emergence of sexuality. Leo Bersani describes the association of sex, death, and shattered subjectivity when he talks about sex as a "masochistic *jouissance*" or a "self-shattering" that necessarily happens to the subject as a result of sexuality. The "*mystery* of sexuality," he argues, "is that we seek not only to get rid of this shattering tension but also to repeat, even to increase it."[39] Since the death of the coherent narrator results from a shattering into adult sexuality, it is coded as desirable in certain ways, since humans generally seek "to increase" the "shattering tension" of sexuality. This drive might be best described through the transgressive musings of Georges Bataille in "The Practice of Joy before Death," in which he depicts an ecstasy suffused with "inner violence." Though he associates it with mystical religious experiences, Bataille locates in the transcendent moment a sensual experience ("those who would be afraid of nude girls or whisky would have little to do with 'joy before death'") leading to the *"loss of self."* A vortex of conflicting and mutually heightening sensations leads to a simultaneous ecstatic joy and the annihilation of the self rooted in a violently erotic corporeality. Bataille imagines this as "the gift of an infinite suffering, of blood and open bodies, in the image of an ejaculation cutting down the one it jolts and abandoning him to an exhaustion charged with nausea."[40] The narrator's sexual awakening evokes this threatening and erotic swirl of sensations in which pleasure and death collapse to shatter or annihilate the self, once again bringing together fear and desire to trouble the assumption that the narrator is a knowable, unified subject.

Cuadros dismantles his narrator by bringing together death, decay, and sexuality. This is a reversal of the type of narrative trajectory, the bildungsroman for example, that drives toward character development, wholeness, and coherence. Instead, the text moves from a more coherent whole toward excess and fragmentation. It is as if we begin with the whole corpses that Victor Frankenstein then pulls apart before our eyes to build his monster, as the narrators are dismembered to rebuild a subject constructed from the remaining multiple and disparate pieces.

Patchwork Monstrosity

Drawing attention to the materiality of queer Chicano subjectivity in the midst of a very real medical, social, and political crisis, the narrative moves from fragmentation and self-shattering to the combination and rearrangement of those shards into a new kind of patchwork subjectivity, offering the possibility of existence within and beyond the promise of death for those who are HIV positive and for queer communities. In "Mourning and Melancholia" Freud frames melancholia as a pathological response to loss in which subjects cannot properly detach their cathexis from the lost object. Instead, they incorporate the lost object into the ego, causing an "*identification* of the ego with the abandoned object," and in this way the object does not need to be given up because it can be eternally entombed within the ego of the melancholic. He associates this incorporation with the "oral or cannibalistic phase of libidinal development," since the ego wants to incorporate the object into itself "by devouring it."[41] The incorporation of lost objects as specifically oral or cannibalistic is quite fitting in a book that is gothic in form and monstrous in content, and it cannot be denied that the text deals with loss on many levels—lost lovers and friends, lost health, lost freedom (especially the perceived sexual freedom of the pre-AIDS era, as evidenced in "Unprotected").

The book's numerous images of burial and consumption are symbols of cannibalistic melancholic incorporation—a paradoxical adoption of melancholia as productive and reconstitutive rather than pathological for a queer subject whose only resources seem to stem from overwhelming loss. "My Aztlan: White Place" begins with an image of loss and burial, as the narrator, an unnamed HIV-positive Chicano man, drives down the San Bernardino Freeway to locate the place where he imagines his childhood home is "buried, near the call box, under the fast lane." He returns to this site of his buried home after having "watched my lover and friends melt away, their hands held in mine. The last of their body's heat: fuel to move me along, to my own impending death," but, in addition to this loss, the narrator mourns the loss of "my ancient home, my family." These losses are multiple—lost friends and lovers, lost family bonds, lost mythical homeland and cultural heritage, and the loss of his own future. Tied together in the narrator's mind, all of them are contained and buried with the image of his childhood home. The loss of his own coherent subjectivity is present in this narrative as well when he says, "I can feel my body becoming tar, limbs divide, north and south. My house smells of earth and it rumbles from the traffic above. White clay sifts through the ceiling. My bones shine in the dark."[42] Not only does this image conflate the burial of the house with the burial of the narrator himself, but it also attests to the narrator's fragmentation and decay. The line "My bones shine in the dark" is reminiscent of the dismembered, sun-bleached mouse heads from "Chivalry" that shone white in the dim light of the shed.

The burial, however, does not do away with these losses because, as melancholic incorporation, burial retains the losses deep within the narrator's psyche. Instead, this burial allows him to revisit the lost people and places whenever he chooses, and, as a result, the images evoke a kind of grief-infused nostalgia rather than utter, hopeless loss. Here Cuadros queers melancholia by pointing out the possibility for an ongoing attachment to loss that accepts the pathology assigned to melancholia. If the narrator had progressed appropriately through the stages of grief, as a mourner rather than a melancholic, he would have had to detach from his losses and move on. Since persistent loss is one of the only resources available to our narrator in the midst of an epidemic, he embraces melancholia as a means of existing both with pathology and with unrestricted access to the losses he has buried within his psyche.

This melancholic burial is a cannibalistic move, and, indeed, images of consumption infiltrate this text. In "My Aztlan" the narrator explains how the virus that had infected his lover's brain is now infecting his own—apparently the same infection that infiltrates his lover's brain and leaves it "half-eaten" in the "Quilt Series" poems in the book's second half. Cannibalistic consumption also appears in various instances as erotic references to being "eaten alive," having "parts of my body chewed," and swallowing semen. The image of semen brings together the tropes of cannibalism, burial, and sexuality to reflect on the narrator's response to the frequently oppositional pull of race and sexual identity. As the narrator increasingly exhibits signs that the virus is taking hold, his mother refuses to "think about the white man who infected" him, because the "milky white fluid" of his lover's semen infiltrates his "body's space, breaks into the secret bonding of her sex, my father's sex, and the marriage of their cells."[43] Here the cannibalistic swallowing of semen is a kind of burial within the narrator's body, an ingestion of his (lost) lover. It is also an ingestion of whiteness that complicates the narrator's racial and sexual identity, threatening his mother's understanding of discrete subjectivity—her refusal to acknowledge his lover an erasure of her son's queer identity in the service of maintaining the racial and sexual demarcations that structure her world.

As the narrator recalls the relationship with his lover, he points to the challenges of being a queer person of color. When his lover was alive, the narrator "became white, too," buried under the assumption that queerness equals whiteness and rendered invisible by the exoticizing impulses of his lover's friends. Anne Anlin Cheng reads this type of racialized erasure as melancholic. Dominant culture incorporates racialized others while denying them full access to that culture, thereby sustaining itself "through the ghostly emptiness of a lost other." This creates "deep-seated, intangible, psychical complications for people living with a ruling episteme that privileges what they can never be." But, she clarifies, "this does *not* at all mean that the minority subject does not develop other relations to that injunctive idea which can be self-affirming or sustaining."[44] The narrator will never have access to the privileges of whiteness, but his melancholic strategies for functioning within cultural norms that value what he "can never be" mean that he develops other ways of surviving. Rather than resenting his burial and erasure at the hands of his white lover and friends, the narrator instead "beat[s] off to their memories," recalling being "buried under their bodies' weight."[45] He accesses this complex memory of sexual freedom and racial erasure for a moment of pleasure in the midst of his grief and isolation, and with this burial he addresses his nuanced and unresolved experience of being an HIV-positive, queer person of color.

If melancholic incorporation is a means of retaining loss through burial, then this narrative emphasis on cannibalism and burial allows the narrator to retain and reimagine his identity as a complex web of identification and counteridentification with dominant narratives of race and sexuality. Dean claims that today HIV itself can be considered "a particular form of memory, one that offers an effective way of maintaining certain relations with the dead," and the memory of ingesting semen in

"My Aztlan," perhaps the genesis of the narrator's seroconversion, represents the "imperishable connection" of the virus as a link to the past lovers whom he refuses to forget.[46] This melancholic response comes into focus a form of disidentification—a process "informed by the structure of feeling that is melancholia," according to José Esteban Muñoz.[47] The images of consumption and burial signal a kind of melancholic relation to multivalent loss that has the potential to restructure limiting dominant ideologies of race and sexuality because it allows the narrator to "mingle the power of the past with the decay of the present," creating new possibilities for identification.[48]

Melancholic incorporation as a strategy of disidentification opens up a space for queerness as a kind of recycled identity, one that fuses together the bits and pieces of dominant narratives (and resistance to those narratives). Judith Butler describes the melancholic process as "the congealment of a history of loss, the sedimentation of relations of substitution over time, the resolution of a tropological function into the ontological effect of the self."[49] The ego is constituted by the "sedimentation of objects loved and lost"—both those who have died and those from whom object-choice is redirected in accordance with normative expectations around gender and sexuality.[50] It is in this notion of sedimentation that loss itself has the potential to produce a new hybrid ego that includes many lost objects brought together into an unstable, multiple subject. I would like, however, to imagine this newly formed ego not as a sedimentation but as a patchwork of lost objects, like Frankenstein's monster, pieced together from multiple sources. Both gothic monsters and the patchwork melancholic ego exceed meaning because of their multiplicity, and both allow for a kind of immortality—the melancholic ego retains the lost object indefinitely, and the monster escapes our grasp and cannot be destroyed due to its slippery and shifting meanings. In *City of God* melancholic incorporation is a way of suturing together the pieces of the dismantled narrative and subject. The result is an ego that is monstrous in its patchwork existence, created by what was lost and what still remains. In this way Cuadros presents a version of what Emma Pérez calls the "decolonial imaginary," a "rupturing space" that offers an alternative to the singular history written by the oppressors and one that, importantly, honors "multiple experiences."⁵¹ In the multiplicity of his monstrous narrative and patchwork narrator, Cuadros envisions a past that cannot be solidified into a singular narrative and settles in the ruptured space of Pérez's decolonial imaginary. Because of its resistance to solidification and annihilation, Cuadros's monstrosity rests in the disruption at the center of his gothic narrative, honoring the traumas expressed there.

The final poem in *City of God*, "Conquering Immortality," begins with an image of the Egyptian Theatre, once extravagantly grand, now decaying on Hollywood Boulevard, and its former glory is compared to the queer community before it was ravaged by the AIDS crisis, when "we only used first names / on their quilts." The quilt image calls to mind a community impacted by loss and a consciousness made of many parts. The narrator compares himself to the "derelict theater," but there is hope in this depiction of decay and neglect. Though the theater may eventually be "bulldozed in haste / this sacred space can never die out." In spite of the theater's impending destruction, there remains a kind of immortality through traumatic fragmentation and melancholic burial. This concept is punctuated by the story of Osiris, who was dismembered and scattered throughout Egypt by his brother Seth. The dismembered pieces were brought back together to form a new type of subject—he "became the god of the dead." Like the theater, like the narrator's decaying body, and like *City of God* itself, Osiris is pulled apart, but he is reconstituted in a new form that lives on. In the poem the theater becomes the devourer, swallowing the dead and dying and preserving them for eternity in its "sacred space." It is also a place of racialized queer desire; the narrator reminisces about a sexual encounter with a black man in the public restroom of the theater in a kind of queer temporality that remembers the ecstasies of the past while looking toward the future, or the "dream of immortality" with which he ends the poem. The narrator finds this immortality through gothic queer melancholia as the poem (and the book itself) ends with an image of the narrator being "enfolded in this theater's / tomb-like darkness."[52] He seems to finally come to terms with his impending death and allows himself to be incorporated into the community as one of the lost—like a patch added to the AIDS quilt and like a limb sutured to the monstrous body of Frankenstein's creature. This final poem is a culmination of the book's gothic gesture toward a queer patchwork subjectivity as it encompasses the concepts of monstrosity, decay, loss, desire, burial, and immortality.

Gothic Queer Monstrosity in the Flesh

Death haunts the queer community in two ways: the threatened death of a community as a result of HIV and AIDS (an issue perhaps more salient in the 1980s and 1990s) and the death of queerness as a subversive mode of existence that resists the normalizing effects of capitalist culture. This cultural death comes from what Muñoz calls "gay pragmatism"—akin to Lisa Duggan's "homonormativity" and David Eng's "queer liberalism"—a neoliberal identity that seeks "a life integrated within North American capitalist culture."[53] The contemporary LGBT movement has certainly trended toward integration through assimilative politics around marriage equality led by large lobbying groups such as the Human Rights Campaign. The Toronto and New York City Black Lives Matter chapters' critiques of the annual PRIDE celebrations as white, capitalist, and homonormative reflect a division in the movement between those invested in assimilation and those who challenge the intersecting structures of oppression that continue to marginalize the most vulnerable members of the community.[54]

The sense of unity experienced by many in the height of the AIDS crisis has seemingly devolved into a unified trend toward capitalist assimilation, which performs a glittery but insubstantial form of inclusivity (think T-shirts emblazoned with "love is love") and in fact depends on and reinforces the marginalization of a portion of the community for the sake of the mainstreaming of others. The infection that once mythically united the LGBT community in grief and anger is not gone, however. In the United States in 2015, 1.1 million people were living with HIV, and 39,513 people were newly diagnosed with HIV.[55] The Centers for Disease Control and

Prevention makes a point to remind visitors to its website that people continue to die from HIV and AIDS.[56] While the current moment may not face the specter of overwhelming death that loomed over Cuadros and his contemporaries, the lingering threat of HIV now circulates in conjunction with expanded neoliberal assimilationism, creating a different, more insidious, trauma lurking under the rainbow surfaces of the contemporary LGBT movement. To resist this assimilationist trend while acknowledging its histories, Muñoz suggests that the queer community embrace a utopian ideology that disrupts "any ossified understanding of the human" by adopting an economy of desire in which "past pleasures stave off the affective perils of the present while they enable a desire that is queer futurity's core."[57] In other words, Muñoz locates queer possibility as a reinterpretation of what it means to be "human," and this mode of existence in excess of humanity may very well look like gothic queer monstrosity.

Performance artist Ron Athey channels the overt and insidious trauma of living with HIV both during the crisis and today with a body of work that uses his own queer, HIV-positive body as a primary medium. Through leakiness and excess, Athey's performing body—both monstrous and queer—provides an interrogation of corporeal integrity that raises questions about what it means to be human and serves as a bridge linking traumatic histories and futures, offering a gothic queer temporal orientation that "strain[s] to activate the no-longer-conscious" while extending a "glance toward that which is forward-dawning."[58] His performances incorporate spectacle, religious ritual and iconography, and sadomasochism, and they return again and again to the rupture or penetration of flesh—he pierces his skin with needles, bleeds on glass panes, injects his testicles with saline or staples them together, hooks the flesh of his eyelids open, and inserts items into his spectacularly tattooed anus. Athey insists on the "realness" of his work, or a "sense of being anchored, something with weight: not fantastical in origin, and definitely not strategic or polite," adding that the "live anal penetration in a non-sexual setting" and "real infected blood" in his performances are "blatantly not fakery."[59] In other words, he does not mimic bloodletting with imitation blood or imply penetration with magic tricks—these acts and substances are exactly what they appear to be. The insistent display of real body horror centers not only the "breach in the body" but also a breach of the subject that threatens to disrupt assumptions about the unified self, a nod to the multiplicity of the gothic monster.[60]

Athey was raised in a fanatically religious Pentecostal household by an aunt and grandmother fixated on suffering, faith healing, the "Gift of Tongues," and miraculous stigmata. By the time "Ronnie Lee" was nine years old, he was speaking in tongues and going into ecstatic states, recognized by the community as having a special calling, but by fifteen he saw these practices as delusional and abandoned them. To rid himself of the "Gifts of the Spirit," Athey turned to Valium, self-administered "Christ aversion therapy" (giving himself an electrical shock anytime Christ entered his thoughts), and an increased interest in science.[61] Athey began performing in 1981 as part of the group Premature Ejaculation, a "post-punk, proto-Goth collaboration" with his lover Rozz Williams, who was the original singer of pioneering gothic rock band Christian Death and a successful gothic solo artist afterward. Athey took a hiatus from performance during a period of drug use in the mid- to late 1980s, at which time he discovered that he was HIV positive.[62] In the early 1990s he reemerged on the performance scene with performances that explicitly addressed the AIDS crisis and queer identity. The *Torture Trilogy* (1992–95), for example, included three performances focused on the "desperation for healing in the time of AIDS."[63] Athey explains that his images are loaded with the "spectre of AIDS," including performances that present his body as a "living corpse" or a "living 'dead' body."[64] Indeed, metaphors of the undead and the monstrous circulate throughout the description and criticism of Athey's work, reflecting not only the monstrous excesses of Athey's oozing, queer form but also the relationship between his work and the traumas of HIV/AIDS.[65]

Athey is still alive today, his flesh seemingly incorruptible, as he has miraculously emerged from what he calls a "time of plague" and has incorporated the virus into his vision of existence in a new "post-AIDS" era.[66]

Later work, such as *Incorruptible Flesh: Dissociative Sparkle*, continues to respond to HIV/AIDS but with new relationalities in which illness is "not an interior enemy to be fought or expelled, but an alteration necessitating new understandings of freedom."[67] Athey uses the term *post-AIDS* with "irreverent insistence," meaning the "next phase of the development of the epidemic" and a "subsequent period of political engagement with a disease whose terms of experience have shifted, at least in much of the West, without being 'cured' or overcome."[68] Even while using the term *post-AIDS* (which to some implies that HIV/AIDS is no longer a threat), Athey's "time of AIDS" is certainly not relegated to history—it encompasses then, now, and the future, until people have access to a cure.

His work received national attention and conservative political outrage as it became caught up in the "culture wars," a period of heightened censorship in the 1980s and 1990s. Though Athey's performances are invested in "realness," the permeability of his body in concert with his known HIV status made Athey into a scapegoat during the AIDS crisis, as journalists and politicians projected fantasies of contagion and threat onto his body, often inventing narratives about his performances that misrepresented the actual events. After the fashion of the classic Gothic monster, in the 1990s Athey became a fantasy screen for a multitude of fears and anxieties and a figure to be expelled to reify the bounds of decent humanity.

He is perhaps most well known for the controversy surrounding *4 Scenes in a Harsh Life*, the second installment in his *Torture Trilogy*, performed as part of the Walker Art Center's Minneapolis LGBT Film Festival in 1994. The performance included a series of short vignettes from *4 Scenes*, but the vignette that threw Athey into the national conversation was "The Human Printing Press":

Athey made 12 cuts on [fellow performer Divinity] Fudge's back, using a scalpel: three crisp sets of parallel triple lines, and a broad triangle. With each deep cut of Athey's blade, Fudge's body heaves slightly under its pressure. Each gash reveals a bank of white fat, highlighted by the shining brown of skin; the white pockets slowly brim with blood, which streams down the centre of Fudge's back. Athey works quickly, blotting the wounds with absorbent square towels. Using butterfly clips, Pigpen and Tolentino attach the prints to a series of taut lines that pass through the audience. After the tenth or so, the prints sharpen, showing a more precise print of the 12 wounds in their four geometric formations, a repeated blunt logo of Fudge's mute endurance, passing from the factory floor of Athey's dutiful exertions.[69]

After the series of vignettes were completed, the hundred-person audience stayed for a twenty-minute discussion of the performance, at which Athey responded to audience questions and comments. Following the performance the *Minneapolis Star Tribune* published the sensational and anxiety-ridden article "Bloody Performance Draws Criticism," in which journalist Mary Abbe (who, Johnson notes, did not attend the performance) calls Athey a "knife-wielding performer . . . known to be HIV-positive" and inaccurately describes audience members knocking over chairs in a panicked attempt to get out from under the hanging towels.[70]

News of the performance traveled all the way to Congress, prompting Republican senator Jesse Helms to use Athey's work in a polemic attack on the National Endowment for the Arts (NEA). Helms zeroed in on Athey, along with several other artists including Joel-Peter Witkin, Robert Mapplethorpe, and Andres Serrano, in an attempt to reinstate a version of the Helms Amendment (which had been defeated in 1990). The amendment forbade NEA funding for art or activity involving "human mutilation or invasive bodily procedures on human beings, dead or alive" or "the drawing or letting of blood."[71] Helms was determined to cut federal funding to the NEA, and to do so he found a convenient scapegoat in Athey, an artist whose work he could depict as unquestionably distasteful, obviously disgusting, and clearly without artistic merit.

In a July 25, 1994, Senate speech, Helms merely describes the performance in sensationalist terms and, without any logical argumentation, simply *assumes* that the public would find his description of the performance to be disgusting and abhorrent:

> That is his picture, a very handsome man, if you like that kind of man. But let's talk about him. He appeared as a part of the Minneapolis Walker Art Center celebration of the "Fifth Annual Minneapolis Lesbian, Gay, Bisexual, and Transgender Film Festival," and I don't need to identify it further. It was a homosexual film event which the NEA supports annually with your money. Now here's how Mr. Athey's performance went. He informed his audience that he has the AIDS virus. Then he begins his bloody performance, but he tells them nothing about the HIV status of the other performers, whom he later slashes and slices on the stage. . . . The broader issue, I think, is the sober realization that for the past two decades an unmistakable decadence has saturated American society. A furious assault on the traditional sensibilities of the American people has taken its toll. So many have become afraid to stand up and declare the difference between right and wrong, what is uplifting and what is destructive, and what is noble and what is degrading. No wonder, no wonder Mr. President [gesturing toward Athey's picture on an easel], there has been a cultural breakdown. Is it not time for billions of Americans, the people more than one president have referred to as the great silent majority, to go on the offensive to regain the control of their social and cultural institutions?[72]

In this speech Helms takes for granted that the public will find the mere existence of a "homosexual film event" to be unworthy of federal funding and that the public will agree with his assumptions about what constitutes "traditional sensibilities" and the difference between "right and wrong," "uplifting" and "destructive," and "noble" and "degrading." He also takes for granted that they will share his disdain for the "artistry" that he consistently and sarcastically mocks, and that the public he addresses already exists in a definable way, calling them the "taxpayers" and the "great silent majority."[73]

Helms uses Athey as a screen for all that is marginal, uncontrolled, perverse, and infected—a monster through which Helms can define a fantastmatic public that is by extension centered, unified, normal, and uninfected, or, perhaps more important, uninfect-*able*. The misrecognition and misrepresentation of the art and its reception is at odds with the intentional realness of the spectacle and serves to construct a "dominant public," as Michael Warner defines it—unified in its invincibility and that takes its "discourse pragmatics and their lifeworlds for granted, misrecognizing the indefinite scope of their expansive address as universality or normalcy."[74] This kind of taking for granted and misrecognition becomes obvious in the way Helms presents Athey's work, not only constructing a dominant public but utilizing a rhetoric of disgust to imagine a universal, sanitized public bolstered against the fluidity, permeability, and infection that Athey represents.

By publicly excreting, Athey queers the public-private divide, a violation that Warner explains "can produce a sharp feeling of revulsion" and is often met with "disgust" and "abhorrence."[75] Athey brings interiority onto the public stage and violates taboos around the shame of bodily excretions—it is not only the fluids that produce disgust but also the publicness of their flow. Etiquette dictates that the excretion of bodily fluids as well as any intimate, sexualized acts of penetration (kinky and vanilla alike) should be hidden from public view, ideally behind a locked door deep within a private dwelling. Indeed, the public staging of a kind of interracial intimacy in *4 Scenes* (Athey is white and Divinity Fudge is black) enters directly into conversations at the time about the very legality of same-sex sexual conduct, as the 1986 *Bowers v. Hardwick* Supreme Court ruling had upheld the conviction of a man who, in a consensual sexual encounter in the privacy of his home, violated the Georgia state sodomy law. The 2003 *Lawrence v. Texas* Supreme Court ruling would later strike down the conviction of a man who also engaged in consensual sodomy, with an emphasis not on the sex act but on his right to privacy.[76]

At a pivotal moment between these landmark court cases, *4 Scenes* stages a sexualized act (the penetration of one man by another) in a public forum, openly challenging the federally supported sodomy laws of its time but also challenging the logic that would ultimately be used to strike down those sodomy laws. All combined, *4 Scenes* staged an aggressive disruption of bourgeois respectability by highlighting its subsumed racial politics and its assumptions around the separation of the public and private spheres. Though conversations around Athey's place in the "culture wars" frequently discuss HIV and homosexuality, they fail to theorize the way race might have factored into the "disgust" factor that Helms responds to and depends on to communicate his message. Though his argument may have been about morality and decency on its surface, it functioned as a paranoid, homophobic, and racist reaction to the specter of AIDS, the monstrous bodies housing the virus, and its threat of permeating those communities that do not "deserve" the disease.

Indeed, permeation is at the heart of Athey's work. Athey's performative leakiness (both his own and that of his fellow performers) forces the audience members to consider their own permeability as well. In the frenzy of the AIDS crisis, there were wildly circulating fears about transmission, and Athey's queer and bloody art embodied threats of vulnerability and infection. The blood itself becomes threatening, however, only if the audience imagines they are somehow exposed to the virus, a kind of penetrative fantasy. Helms exploits these fears to achieve his political goals, implying that Athey's art must be contained because it threatens a "public" that is, in comparison, not infected, not vulnerable, and discretely solid—a classic use of monster as a scapegoat for the expulsion of difference and the reification of the human.

Athey became a scapegoat precisely because his disruption of systemic structures such as inside/outside, public/private, us/them, and human/inhuman exposes these distinctions as constructions, not inviolable truths. René Girard notes that the scapegoat *seems* to represent a fear of difference, but it in fact points out the "potential for the system to differ from its own difference," thereby threatening the system itself and becoming "monstrous." "Difference that exists outside the system," he adds, "is terrifying because it reveals the truth of the system, its relativity, its fragility, and its mortality." Helms's mischaracterization of Athey's performance testifies to his attempt to project cultural anxieties on the work to abject Athey and the community that he represents. Girard reminds us, however, that "persecutors are never obsessed by difference but rather by its unutterable contrary, the lack of difference."[77] In *4 Scenes* the skin, a container supposedly limning a coherent self, is broken and so are audience assumptions about separateness. Athey collapses difference and by extension the system itself by refusing to be contained by corporeal limits, making him a scapegoat turned monstrous. The threat of Athey's work lies in the fantasy that Athey's leakiness and permeability would, in turn, penetrate the audience members, leading them to become leaky and infected themselves, or not so different from Athey after all.

This threat is not simply monstrous but specifically vampiric. Like the scapegoat and the monster more generally, the vampire defines the norm through its otherness, but in the process it collapses the very difference it is supposed to demarcate, because the vampire "belongs to death, yet it does not respect the boundaries that should keep it dead—that is, inactive and away from the living."[78] The project of assigning monstrosity to Athey and others who were HIV positive works to marginalize queer and HIV-positive folks by linking them with death, a slippery form of oppression that in the shadow of the overt traumas of AIDS presented as microaggressive and difficult to process. Athey's gothic queer cultural production, however, returns from the grave and redeploys the incoherency of the vampire to disrupt and collapse the boundaries constructed to maintain divisions between "normal" and "monster."

The Penetrative Reciprocity of the Vampire

Athey's work, overdetermined by the traumas of HIV/AIDS and its losses, is certainly melancholic. As in *City of God*, death is always present in Athey's work, whether centralized or just out of frame. Though Cuadros reimagines the queer subject as a patchwork monster, reconstituting the ego through loss in a Frankensteinian manner, Athey's queer monstrosity works with incorporation in more material ways. The items that he takes into himself are balanced only by the substances that he expels, and this exchange does not reconstitute the ego but instead dissolves it. Athey uses the materiality of blood and the pricks of needles to evoke a different kind of queer monstrosity, one inflected by the exchanges of vampirism.

In Bram Stoker's *Dracula*, the count not only drinks the blood of others but forces others, specifically Mina, the "model representative of womanhood upon whom England's future symbolically depends," to drink of him.[79] Dracula has been sneaking into Mina's room to drink her blood over several nights; one night, in a climactic scene, Van Helsing breaks into Mina's room to find her husband, Jonathan, passed out on the bed while Mina is drinking blood from a self-inflicted wound in Dracula's chest. Dracula states that this blood drinking makes Mina "flesh of my flesh; blood of my blood; kin of my kin," and the blood exchange gives Dracula and Mina a telepathic connection with each other. She is able to see and hear what Dracula is doing, and it is implied that he enjoys a mutual privilege of interiority with Mina. The exchange of fluids muddies the separation between them. The holes in Mina's neck mirror the hole in Dracula's breast, and blood from both oozes onto Mina's nightdress in one indistinguishable blot, marking her as changed and "unclean."[80]

Athey's 2009 *Self-Obliteration #1, Ecstatic* performs a similar reciprocal exchange, as Athey spills his own blood and in turn "prick[s] the spectator and remind[s] her of her own holes."[81] The effect is both political and relational.[82] While the fear surrounding his work partially involves the potential for literal incorporation of bodily fluids, Athey's work also penetrates the audience *affectively*, confronting them with the complexities of their own feelings, assumptions, and reactions and drawing attention to the precariousness of identity and the interdependence of existence. Amelia Jones describes how the work "pricks us to make us feel, to make us reattach to our own hurt and our own socially embedded place in the world."[83] The vampiric exchange of punctures and fluids is not a literal threat but a reminder that the idea of physical disruption can challenge marginalizing assumptions of otherness, thereby serving as a political and social intervention.

The reciprocal "pricking" that Jones alludes to sometimes causes physical reactions from audience members, as I observed when I attended a live performance of *Self-Obliteration #1, Ecstatic* at *You Belong to Me*, an evening of performance art curated by Jennifer Doyle and hosted by the University of California–Riverside's Sweeney Art Gallery in 2009. Though all the performances that evening were powerful, *Self-Obliteration #1* had a distinct effect on the audience. We were ushered to a dim room with a raised wooden platform in its center. The floor around the platform was taped off to keep the audience at a distance, and attendants wearing latex gloves and looking distinctly medical stood at intervals to enforce the boundary. Deep, amelodic digital feedback music filled the performance space, as Athey climbed, naked and wearing a long blond wig, onto the platform to pose on his hands and knees. He proceeded to slowly and firmly brush this wig over his face, allowing the brush to slam against the platform at the end of each stroke. After an extended period of brushing, he removed the wig by pulling out a series of large needles, revealing, to my surprise, that the wig had been attached directly to his scalp. The purpose of the gloved attendants and taped off performance space suddenly came in to focus as protective measures when Athey tipped his body in a kind of downward-facing-dog stance to allow the blood to flow onto a glass pane placed underneath him. He then performed complex choreography with the bloodied glass, passing it over his body and smearing the blood between himself and the glass. He finally placed the pane in a groove at the end of the platform, precariously perching it there while he repeated the procedure with a second pane. In this particular performance, Julie Tolentino performed a live "archive" (*The Sky Remains the Same*) by precisely mirroring Athey's actions on the platform so that both plodded through the subsequent iteration of the choreography simultaneously.

This performance refuses to allow AIDS to be relegated to the past, instead insisting on leaving that wound open (even erotically so) in its denial of closure. When discussing *Self-Obliteration #1*, Athey explains that the glass aspect of the performance came from an earlier work, *Incor-*

ruptible Flesh (Perpetual Wound): "Identifying myself, the decomposing post-AIDS survivor, with the eternally gaping and unhealing wound of Philoctetes, the glass was used as a barrier to press my nasty gash against the fresh wound I inflicted on your body, as a young Neoptolemus figure run through a *Pink Narcissus* filter. This is followed by an action on the floor where I shuffle two sheets of bloody glass over my supine body: a sick frenzy, then holding a pose, and back to display as a living corpse."[84] In *Self-Obliteration #1* Athey shuffles the glass over his bloody, wounded body, but he does not literally inflict a "fresh wound" on another. Instead, the audience is allowed to imaginatively stand in place of the other body, and Tolentino's reenactment in the second half implies that Athey's "nasty gash" is transferrable to others. Tolentino's mirrored actions become indistinguishable from Athey's, as she penetrates her own scalp with needles and proceeds through the bloody choreography, implying a ripple effect that threatens to engulf the audience members as well.

At the start of the performance I attended, the audience cozied up to the taped line, but by the end it had thinned out drastically. Fantasies of crashing glass and spraying blood certainly flitted through my mind when Athey and Tolentino gingerly placed the large panes of glass, blotted with still-dripping blood, in the plywood grooves at the ends of the platform, and I noticed that most of my fellow viewers had backed away significantly, perhaps imagining a similar scenario. As the remaining audience members filtered out of the space at the end of the performance, I noticed several people seated on the floor and leaning against the walls, obviously a bit queasy from the spectacle. The audiences' obvious lightheadedness certainly had to do with the sight of blood, but I would argue that their visceral response stemmed to an even greater degree from the affective pricking that occurs in the piece, as they become aware of both Athey's holes and their own. The threat of dissolution is overwhelming.

Like the interchange between Dracula and Mina, in which their fluid exchange allows them to exceed the limitations of their individual minds, the imagined two-way exchange of blood in Athey's performance collapses the divide between performer and audience. By perforating his skin, the

7. Ron Athey, *Self-Obliteration*, performance still. Image by Christophe Chemin. Donau Festival, Krems, Austria. Courtesy of the artist.

imagined border between inside and outside, and releasing his blood from containment, Athey forces the audience to address the permeability of their own sense of separate corporeal space. The title, *Self-Obliteration*, not only refers to Athey's body but also implies the obliteration, or at least the challenging, of the audience members' sense of discrete selfhood. Rather than allowing an audience to safely disconnect from the affective experience of his performance, the audience's imagined permeation forces them to consider their sense of self and identity as fluid and changeable—an uncomfortable epiphany that may push viewers to feel fear, disgust, or the sense of being, in Mina's words, "unclean." This disruption may also "prick" the viewers into a more ethical consciousness, as Jones points out, as they become more aware of their "socially embedded place in the world."[85]

As I mentioned earlier, vampiric monstrosity is cannibalistic and thereby works to disrupt difference and confound identity, even as it has been used to establish difference. In *Imperial Leather* Anne McClintock points out that not only did the imperialist labeling of indigenous peoples as cannibals serve to justify genocide and conquest, but the word *cannibal* also stood in as a boundary marker of the known, a place of vulnerability and potential engulfment. At the edges of the mapped world, cartographers imagined a cannibalistic and monstrous realm: "The failure of European knowledge appears in the margins and gaps of these maps in the form of cannibals, mermaids, and monsters, threshold figures eloquent of the resurgent relations between gender, race, and imperialism."[86] By labeling newly encountered people as cannibals, colonizers justified murder, enslavement, theft, and conquest and marked their fear of cultures and practices that challenged or exploded their entrenched worldviews.[87] The sodomite, just as monstrous as the cannibal, justified murder without question because both marked a collapse of the structures created to establish and maintain hierarchies through difference—for cannibals the eater becomes the eaten, and with penetration the sodomite collapses the imagined difference between self and other. In a passage that might uncannily describe an Athey performance, Jonathan Goldberg analyzes a colonial description of sodomites: "The 'well-proportioned' bodies of these men are 'deformed'; orifices have been opened and distended in ways they should not be. The male body is violated, pierced. And these practices are continued in self-mutilations that stop just short of the ultimate violation of life."[88] The vampire is both cannibal and metaphorical sodomite, ingesting the other through penetration and becoming the other through reciprocal penetration.[89] Vampires, cannibals, and sodomites all break open the imagined boundaries of the human form and create distinctions only to have those distinctions collapse into themselves.

In his disruption of boundaries, Athey forces a kind of receptive witnessing, a traumatic experience that returns to haunt the viewer and that engages in penetrative reciprocity, like the exchange of blood between the vampire and prey. This is the orientation of Carla Freccero's "queer spectrality" and one inspired by cannibalism.[90] For Freccero penetrative reciprocity "suggests an alternate path to the Western melancholic's incorporation of the lost other and its permanent, if uneasy, entombment within the crypt of history."[91] Athey, however, opens up a new relationship with melancholia that resists this relegation to past by modeling a receptive witnessing experience with his queer, leaky body. He materializes the possibility that the melancholic incorporation might in fact ooze back out of the opened flesh, a return that (like a haunting) holds our mouths to the breast of the lost other and asks us to drink in their return. The losses written on and in Athey's body refuse to stay entombed there, and he facilitates their return in a constant exchange of ingestion and excretion.

In *Incorruptible Flesh (Dissociative Sparkle)* (2006), Athey places his own body on a metaphoric spit, positioned as simultaneous subject and object of a cannibalistic ritual. Adrian Heathfield describes the performance, as witnessed in a small gallery in New York City:

> He sees Athey located at the centre, lying naked on a high table or bed constructed of narrow steel poles. . . . Hovering at the side there is a female figure dressed in black, an attendant of sorts, who subtly motions welcome. . . . The "bed" frame has a tubular "headboard" that functions as a lashing point for taut cords attached to metal hooks piercing Athey's cheeks and eyebrows, pulling his flesh back and apart into a startling grimace. . . . Athey's buttocks are sunken in the middle of the frame where, at an upward angle, a greased blue aluminum baseball bat is fixed and consequently lodged deep in Athey's rectum. The slender handle juts out. Pinioned and penetrated. . . . Sitting atop the intrusion, Athey's testicles and penis are bulbous balloons: inflated to a preposterous limit they present as animal or desexed genitalia. . . . A delicate vein of translucent liquid is trailing down the handle of the baseball bat and gently puddling on the polished wooden floor.[92]

Like dismembered bodies roasting on the spits of cannibals in the etchings celebrating the sixteenth-century colonization of the Americas, Athey rests before the audience, penetrated and castrated.[93] At the same time that he has incorporated the baseball bat, a kind of sodomical ingestion, Athey's body drips, stretches, and bloats outside of its bounds. He is both eater and eaten at once, hungrily taking items into his body and simultaneously expelling others, thereby taking penetrative reciprocity to a different register. Heathfield likens this exchange to "a dialogue between the present and the past, between the surviving and the lost. Here what it means to 'carry' (a virus, a memory, another body) and what it means to carry on (to bear the unbearable) are at stake." Athey's holiness stages this dialogue in very material ways. His evocation of the cannibal's spit and the annihilation of the self that occurs with the vampire's bite offer a different kind of melancholia, "a kind of re-nurturing of lost lives in the present; not 'properly' nostalgic or melancholic, but attendant to the past in ways that make it live again, differently."[94] As both powerful creator and passive receptacle, Athey offers up his body to demonstrate how melancholia can, in fact, allow for the receptive witnessing of the past by refusing solidification and entombment and remaining open to the return of that which has been ingested.

Athey's work is infused with loss and death, fear and shame, glory and sparkle, but it is also quite explicitly about trauma. He explains that he centralizes the anus because of its association with repulsion (a misogynist and homophobic fear of penetration), pathology (the shame of one's sexual proclivities being labeled "sick"), and disease (the imagined portal for HIV): "There is a homophobic repulsion at the idea of the rectum as a receptacle for sex. . . . There's also the pathology of shit-eaters, a direct link to cannibalism. But more importantly, in our time, this particular hole garners more phobias for its symbolic potency as a receptacle for disease."[95] All these associations point to the shame and trauma around queerness and HIV, compounding the accumulated losses of the "plague years" with the anxiety of a society that judges and condemns. The illness and losses around the AIDS crisis were traumatic, and the homophobic fear and blame placed on the queer community have been integrated into the popular imagination in subtle and blatant ways, creating ongoing insidious trauma as well. Kilgour writes that "the image of cannibalism is frequently connected with the failure of words as a medium, suggesting that people who cannot *talk* to each other *bite* each other."[96] Like trauma, cannibalism is incomprehensible and uncanny because it creates a fractured space in which one encounters a failure of language—perhaps why the term *unspeakable* is frequently applied to both cannibalism and trauma. Athey stages a cannibalistic metaphor to acknowledge both a history of traumatic loss and ongoing insidious trauma. In exploding the human with his leaky and monstrous body, Athey opens a temporal bridge that honors the losses of the AIDS crisis without entombing them as historical objects and that recognizes the ongoing reality of living with HIV and living on the queer margins.

Both Cuadros and Athey represent gothic queer monstrosity—Frankensteinian and vampiric—as modes of subjectivity that access past losses to continue to exist in a traumatic present and an unknown future. Cuadros offers melancholia as a means of fusing past losses and present reality to create a hybrid notion of time, place, and identity. Similarly, Athey defies any "ossified understanding of the human" by disrupting coherent subjectivity and creating a monstrous, excessive body that materializes the give-and-take of a melancholic approach imbued with both penetrations and excretions. Although monsters are generally cast as inhuman, frightening, and grotesque, the monstrosity outlined here is a queer mode of being that defies the eradication that the AIDS crisis promised the queer community, one that queers melancholia to resist limiting narratives of race, sexuality, and temporality and one that embraces desire and disgust to move beyond solidified and limiting notions of the human as merely an assimilated consumer, a pawn in neoliberal ideology. This move is particularly important today—as pre- and postexposure prophylaxes allow a new relation to safer-sex practices and what it means to be queer and sexual in a "post-AIDS" moment and as the AIDS crisis becomes increasingly archived and memorialized as the distant past. It is precisely their gothicism that allows Cuadros and Athey to embrace seemingly limitless death, decay, and negativity as a means of creating a queer temporality bridging past, present, and future.

While eighteenth- and nineteenth-century Gothic monstrosity was largely intended to limit and contain the transgressive body, monstrosity is paradoxically "mobile, permeable, infinitely interpretable" because of its excessive meaning and its defiance of categories and boundaries, making it an optimal mode for responding to trauma that also fractures meaning and exceeds language.[97] Cuadros dismembers heteronormative narratives of identity and quilts the monstrous out of the pieces, while Athey offers up his own infected, leaky body to aggressively disrupt assumptions about the discrete self, instead proposing penetrative reciprocity as a vampiric mode of being that shatters the subject and allows the traumatic past to ooze into the present. Both offer gothic queer rhetorics and aesthetics that acknowledge the traumas of the past and present, overt and insidious, while reimagining queer possibilities in the face of neoliberal assimilation.

4   SADOMASOCHISM

Strategic Discomfort in Trans* and Queer of Color Performance Art

Sadomasochistic practice and the debates surrounding
it . . . reminded us that dominance, submission, and
violence, real or imagined, are often integral parts of
queer sexual practice.

ROBERT F. REID-PHARR, *Black Gay Man*

In *Life* magazine's June 26, 1964, article "Homosexuality in America," journalist Paul Welch characterizes San Francisco's "s&m" scene as "another
far-out fringe of the 'gay' world" and describes the Tool Box, San Francisco's first successful leather bar: "Inside the bar, the accent is on leather
and sadistic symbolism. The walls are covered with masculine-looking
men in black leather jackets."[1] The opening spread features an image
of the bar, dense and crowded with men, their leather jackets and caps
haloed by an overexposed doorway leading into the vibrant, but shadowy,
cruising ground. As the ethnographic *Life* magazine study intuits from
its admittedly external gaze, the s&m community holds a central place
in the history of queer culture in the United States.

Gayle Rubin's "The Catacombs: A Temple of the Butthole" offers
another glimpse of sadomasochism and queer culture's intersection. A

world-famous party venue for fisting and sadomasochism in the 1970s, the Catacombs offered a nominal nod to those morbid subterranean passages so prevalent in eighteenth- and nineteenth-century Gothic fiction. It even featured a "Bridal Suite" and a "dungeon," spaces that have steadfastly graced the pages of Gothic novels. Rubin explains that the Catacombs began as a sex club that hosted gay male fisting parties and later integrated s/M, early lesbian s/M parties, and some of the first "mixed gender/mixed-orientation s/M" events.[2] In addition to its world-famous parties, the Catacombs eventually "took on a role as a community center for the local s/M population."[3] Sadomasochism may not be the exclusive province of queer folks, but development of sadomasochism as a visible community structure is inextricable from gay and lesbian activism and culture.

Although the Catacombs ultimately became a "casualty not only of AIDS but of the misguided witch hunts of AIDS hysteria," and the Tool Box has now been replaced by a Whole Foods Market, San Francisco's "south of Market" (SOMA) district continues to be associated with the queer leather scene, partially because it hosts the annual Folsom Street Fair, the "world's biggest leather event."[4] Black leather, masks, uniforms, crops, corsets, ropes, boots, chaps, harnesses, chains, glistening naked flesh, public sex, and all imaginable kinks dominate thirteen city blocks each September for the Folsom Street Fair and its myriad ancillary activities. This iconic festival emerged not simply as an annual gathering for like-minded kinky folks in the bondage/discipline, dominance/submission, sadism/masochism (BDSM) community, but it also owes its existence to community-based political organizing against the city's development policy regarding the so-called blighted SOMA area that predominantly housed working families and "unattached single males" from the port industries. The fair came to be what it is today through a two-pronged drive: to fight against the gentrification-driven "cleansing" of the area and to support a thriving and visible queer kink community.[5]

Life's midcentury exposé on the "secret world" of homosexuality, the Catacombs, and the Folsom Street Fair are only a few regional examples of how sadomasochism in its many shifting forms has been a central element of queer community building in the shadows of a hostile dominant culture. Sadomasochism is fundamentally tactile, visual, and performative, with the elaborately detailed leather, vinyl, and metal accoutrements of sadomasochistic fetish gear; the role-playing and careful construction of sadomasochistic scenes; and the theatrical nature of both public and private sadomasochistic events. Practitioners often revel in the dark and shadowy, emphasizing power play and performances of cruelty, torture, and humiliation. Proponents are quick to point out, however, that the subculture is built around "safe, sane, and consensual" play that stages carefully designed scenes of erotic power, dominance, and submission.[6] Rubin describes the Catacombs, for example, not as a violent or frightening scene but as a "sexually organized environment where people treated each other with mutual respect, and where they were lovingly sexual."[7] BDSM's carefully designed fantasies offer visually rich and passionately enacted scenes of dominance and submission, slavery, and abject humiliation, but the practice requires a structure of trust, attention, and care. Participants recreate and denaturalize social hierarchies by enacting (and finding pleasure in) the charged historical, racial, and gender dynamics that often oppress them in their daily lives. Jeffrey Weeks calls these radical practices the "eroticization of power itself" performed in the "theatre of sex."[8] Sadomasochistic practices support imaginative and subversive sexualities and kinship structures and offer a platform for community building and social action that rethinks normative hierarchies.

This chapter argues that sadomasochism also offers a mode for rethinking normative temporality that collapses the weight of the future into the present, a strategy queer artists have adopted as a gothic rhetoric and ethical orientation responding to insidious trauma. When trauma is insidious—a result of persistent and repeated microaggressions and naturalized structural inequalities—the horrors of that lived reality are often invisible to those occupying positions of privilege. Some queer folks have responded to that invalidation through sadomasochistic practice, using the materiality of the physical body to speak to insidious trauma and to elicit engaged affective responses from others. Sadomasochism creates a productive space that uses elements of pain and deferral as political and aesthetic resources and offers a form of empowerment through the painful and uncomfortable deferral of pleasure paired with the hopeful anticipation of a future pleasure that may never arrive. As a model for political consciousness, sadomasochism shatters complacency in the soothing trajectory of progress—that supposedly inevitable march toward equality—and refocuses on the current moment in all of its pleasures and pains. But an emphasis on the painful present is not merely indulgent or hedonistic; it means that one cannot relax into smug assuredness that social justice will simply arrive in due time. As a state of indefinite and anticipatory deferral, the sadomasochistic present is in constant negotiation with all possible futures. The responsibility falls on the public now to remain always unsettled, vigilant, and adaptive both by recognizing complicity in present violence (and the futures tied to it) and by finding pleasures in what is available now.

In this chapter I focus specifically on queer visual and performance artists M. Lamar, Cassils, and Zackary Drucker to argue that they deploy gothic sadomasochism through the complex negotiation of power and strategic discomfort to force a change in the social myths that silently structure violence against queers of color and gender nonconformists.[9] While I claim that the works I examine here have the *potential* to lead to organized and collective activism, my goal is to show that their important intervention involves upsetting audience members' self-perception. People invested in an understanding of themselves as well intentioned and liberal-minded are often blind to their participation in everyday forms of aggression and to their implicit support of structural oppression. By disrupting the comfortable self-satisfaction of their audience, these queer artists offer a challenging but compelling mechanism for social change in response to both overt and insidious violence.

Slippery Sadomasochism

Sadomasochism's almost supernatural ability to shapeshift, to perplex, to undermine assumptions, and to reconstruct structures of oppression make it not only an apt element of gothicism but also a viable mode of queerness that redeploys the themes and aesthetics found in eighteenth- and nineteenth-century Gothic texts. Sadism and masochism are highly ritualized embodiments of pain, pleasure, and power. The concepts most famously trace back to the erotic fiction of the Marquis de Sade (*120 Days of Sodom*; *Justine*) and Leopold von Sacher-Masoch (*Venus in Furs*), but they also find expression in sexually charged differential power relations at play in British Gothic novels such as Charlotte Dacre's *Zofloya* and Matthew Lewis's *The Monk* and are taken up by nineteenth- and twentieth-century sexologists such as Richard von Krafft-Ebing (*Psychopathia Sexualis*) and Sigmund Freud (*Three Essays*; "Economic Problem of Masochism"). *The Monk*'s Ambrosio, for example, is masochistic in that he is driven to sexually possess only those who will ensure a painful deferral of his sexual satisfaction. He first desires Rosario, a woman who has disguised herself as a young monk. For Ambrosio she is a forbidden sexual object because of her ambiguous gender and his vows of chastity, and this promise of deferral fuels his desire. But as soon as he discovers that she will not resist consummation, he becomes quickly bored and disgusted by her presence. Moving on, Ambrosio jumps to the next object who promises to resist his sexual advances, Antonia, a woman who is not only characterized by innocence and chastity but who is also his sister. Through his shifting desires Ambrosio creates sexual scenarios in which he must struggle for sexual satisfaction and in which he is almost guaranteed a kind of masochistic deferral of that satisfaction. Ambrosio's actions, however, are not solely masochistic, since Ambrosio does everything in his means to gain sexual dominance over Antonia, even dabbling in spells and potions to have nonconsensual access to Antonia's body and eventually succeeding in his plans to rape her. Here his masochistic leanings come into focus as sadistic, pointing out the messy and not always legible nature of sexual power in the Gothic novel. While the play of sexualized power in these texts is not the consensual sadomasochistic fantasy play that we might recognize in the leather bars and BDSM clubs today, George

Haggerty explains that Gothic novels exhibit eroticized power that is "crudely" sadomasochistic since "desire is expressed as the exercise of (or resistance to) power. But that power itself is charged with a sexual force—a sexuality—that determines the action and gives it shape. By the same token, powerlessness has a similar valence and performs a similar function."[10] Erotically charged power circulates within Gothic narratives in unexpected ways, and contemporary sadomasochism speaks to this history through a playful engagement in artifice and ritual that often resists rigid binary and hierarchical dynamics through the deliberately aestheticized refashioning of those same hierarchies. Leo Bersani notes that this kind of engagement with eroticized power can be productive, emphasizing *"the possibility of exploiting the shattering effects of sexuality in order to maintain the tensions of an eroticized, de-narrativized, and mobile consciousness."*[11] One of the unifying elements of discourse around sadomasochism is its unexpected resistance to presumptive structures of hierarchical power or easy binaristic divisions along with its powerful potential for social and relational change, whether for good or for bad.[12]

Sadomasochism plays not only with its own apparent framework but also with notions of normalcy and perversion. If, as Freud claims, sadomasochism is the "most common and the most significant of all" sexual perversions, then how does this redefine our understanding of the normal?[13] If, as Bersani argues, all sexuality is masochistic, then perversity, it seems, creeps into the most vanilla of bedrooms. Sadism and masochism as concepts are slippery and deceptively complex, and as "perversions" they have the potential to serve as a "disruptive force" that "subverts many of the binary oppositions upon which the social order rests" and challenges the hierarchies written into that order.[14] They evoke power structures and then paradoxically defy them by recreating those very structures in the space of the sadomasochistic fantasy scene.

Sadomasochistic practice has come under attack precisely for its reenactments of hierarchical power dynamics, especially those dynamics that mirror sociological gender, race, and class hegemonies.[15] Elizabeth Freeman writes at length about sadomasochism's perceived dangers, especially when sadomasochistic role-playing invokes collective traumatic histories such as the transatlantic slave trade. Critics argue that sadomasochistic role-playing simply "repeats the historical violence it cites" by reenacting power relationships inspired by the Holocaust or chattel slavery, for example.[16] Freeman argues, however, that historiographic sadomasochism can function as a kind of "erotic time machine," in which the body serves as an access point for an encounter with the past by moving the "players back and forth between some kind of horrific *then* in the past and some kind of redemptive *now* in the present."[17] As Gilles Deleuze notes, masochism offers contingent pleasure based on the disavowal and deferral of pleasure. The centrality of deferral leads Freeman to conclude that sadomasochism disrupts temporality by denaturalizing an individual's sense of time. As a physicalization of history, sadomasochism makes traumatic pasts visual and visceral, leading to a present in which participatory bodies experience both now and then at once. In other words, Freeman describes sadomasochism's potential to create a temporality that opens up the bodily experience of the past.

I argue that gothic sadomasochism opens up bodily experience of queer insidious trauma and its specific temporalities that overlap with but also differ from the temporalities of historical event-based trauma that Freeman describes. In the art I examine here, the artists use gothic sadomasochism to create shared sensation in the performance space that forces the recognition of the often-ignored material effects of insidious trauma. Amber Musser points to the ability of sensation to access a "level beyond the discursive," which is precisely where the experience of trauma lies and where the failure of its expression is located. The extradiscursive nature of masochistic sensation also points to the connections between sensation, affect, and politics, she adds, making the social structures that produce certain sensations visible or, more precisely, *felt*.[18] The artists' replication of traumatic sensation—the creation of those feelings associated with the microaggression and insidious trauma caused by structures of oppression—takes audience members out of discursive and identitarian modes and delineates the structural causes of that sensation. Gothic sadomasochism is particularly suited to recreating the unresolved sensations associated with ongoing, insidious trauma, and the reproduction of these sensations in the performance space expresses traumatic temporality in a socially rooted manner. In the context of live performance, gothic sadomasochism asks audience members to reflect on their place in various structures of oppression without resorting to identity politics that might polarize and shut down rather than activate.

Dissonance and Discomfort

M. Lamar is a visual artist, performer, composer, singer, and filmmaker. He calls himself a "devil-worshipping free black man in the blues tradition" and a "goth kid" invested in "goth, metal, and punk subcultures."[19] He also calls himself a "Yale dropout," having left the Yale School of Art's sculpture program to pursue his musical career.[20] As a "practicing homosexual" who is "outside orientation," he explains, "I've chosen to reject *gay* as a term for myself. I'm interested in the behavior of sexuality. I think of gay culture as having always been tied to white culture." Instead, he identifies as "*Negrogoth*—a term [he] created that allows [him] to exist in a nebulous space."[21] Like his "nebulous" identity, Lamar's work also reflects the hazily complex forces shaping black masculinity and sexuality, and he labels the aesthetic of his art and music infused with gothic horror, romance, and sadomasochism "Negrogothic." M. Lamar is popularly known for his relation to Laverne Cox, transgender actor and activist and Lamar's twin sister. Lamar played Cox's pretransition character in a 2013 episode of *Orange Is the New Black*, a choice that he says he is "not proud of" because the series places a white character's narrative at its center.[22] Lamar's multigeneric and avant-garde visual art, music, and live performances invoke the miseries and horrors that swirl around black histories in the United States and offer up a stark contrast to such mainstream media investments. His pieces examine the historical trauma of slavery, sexual exploitation, and lynching while asserting the inextricability of those pasts from the present moment. Lamar's work does not allow audience members to brush off the miseries it depicts in favor of focusing on more comfortable narratives. Instead, it dwells in those miseries, creating an uncomfortable affective space that honors past horrors while challenging present-day complicity in the ongoing structures that made those horrors and their legacies possible.

Slavery, Jim Crow, and structural racism have caused generations of overt trauma for people of color, but recent assumptions that U.S. society is somehow "postrace" or "colorblind" points to a kind of large-scale gaslighting that ignores the violence of those histories and their lingering impacts. Even in the aftermath of several highly publicized murders of black men by police officers (Michael Brown, Eric Garner, Freddie Gray, Alton Sterling, Philando Castile, and others), many in the United States refuse to see the structures and legacies that make these atrocities possible. In a *New York Times* op-ed addressed to white America, Michael Eric Dyson explains the damaging effects of the refusal to acknowledge widespread racism fueling present-day violence: "You will never understand the helplessness we feel in watching these events unfold, violently, time and again, as shaky images tell a story more sobering than your eyes are willing to believe: that black life can mean so little . . . that the police are part of an undeclared war against blackness. You can never admit that this is true. In fact, you deem the idea so preposterous and insulting that you call the black people who believe it racists themselves."[23]

The myopic and defensive insistence on redirecting conversations about racialized violence to issues of individual innocence and guilt and personal insult reflects the frustrating insidiousness of institutionalized racism in the United States today. Without acknowledgment of the ongoing impact of slavery and the white supremacist laws and policies that have accumulated in this country since the Reconstruction, the deep-seated roots of violence against people of color will continue to be obscured. Lamar points to this kind of willful blindness and to the way traumatic pasts impact present lived experiences for blacks today. In an interview with the *Observer*'s Emily Nathan, he explicitly links a lack of historical awareness with reductive and uninformed contemporary conversations about race and gender:

If people don't even know about these histories, then how can we possibly have a sophisticated discussion about why the police officers that shot Mike Brown imagined him as some Hulk figure? That construction of black masculine identity as this monstrous thing, as this overly sexualized thing within the white imagination is real: the thing that allows a police officer to violently shoot down a black man is the same kind of thing that allows someone having phone sex with me to imagine me as a thuggish black man, asking me to rape and rob them. I'm really concerned about the extent to which black people have internalized this kind of "niggerization."

Lamar goes on to explain that his work both politically responds to racist histories and provides an opportunity for him to personally process his subjective existence in relation to the history and politics of white, heteropatriarchal supremacy: "I am a black male and I have this black male body and I'm having sex and working through this stuff, so it just really behooves me to unpack it, simply for the quality of my own life. And maybe this work isn't going to change the world politically—but it's certainly changed my life, in terms of just being able to *deal*, emotionally."[24] Lamar's Negrogothic aesthetic is part of his project to bridge the personal and the social and to assert the traumas of his particular experience in relation to both past and present.

Lamar's uncomfortable shows are not simply about the horrors of the past. He is quick to point out that he has "always been obsessed with this romance and this horror: I mean, I'm living through it."[25] Indeed, the horrors of living as a queer person of color in the United States offer daily reminders that the racist past is not truly past. Class and race privilege, however, allow many to remain blissfully unaware of the ongoing horrors of racism. As the media coverage around the Black Lives Matter movement has highlighted, many white folks become defensive and refuse to see the connection between individual racist acts and the historical and structural context that supports them, even when confronted with circumstances that point toward large-scale institutional oppression. It is this refusal to see that compounds the horror; denying that individual experiences of trauma are created from racist structures functions as a particular kind of microaggression called "microinvalidation," or such refusals and erasures that "exclude, negate, or nullify the realities of individuals of oppressed groups." Microinvalidations function alongside microassaults ("explicit derogations") and microinsults ("rudeness and insensitivity" that "demean a person's heritage or identity") to form a trio of microaggressions that shape the experiences of people of color and members of LGBT communities.[26] Repeated microinvalidations accumulate to form insidious traumatic experiences that function alongside the overt traumas Lamar references.

Lamar refuses to let audience members easily dismiss the continuing structures and influences of racist institutions and practices, and he also refuses to create art that "heals" those wounds. There is no sense of closure in his work. The videos, photographs, and sculptures settle into, even revel in, the horrors they depict, and when the music ends its eerie strains linger in the minds of the audience members as they stumble, dazed, out of the performance space. The ever-open traumatic wound is part of the pleasure and pain in Lamar's work and part of his political intervention. Ann Kaplan notes that "if the wound of trauma remains open, its pain may be worked through in the process of its being 'translated' via art," but part of the discomfort around the experience of Lamar's art and music involves an open wound that refuses to be "worked through."[27] Freud, too, considers the therapeutic function of the "repetition compulsion," noting that those who experience trauma might repeat the traumatic experience—by passively repeating scenes of the trauma or by "reveng[ing] himself on a substitute"—in part to gain mastery over the traumatic stimulus.[28] Lamar does gain mastery, in a sadomasochistic sense, but it is not mastery over the traumatic event itself as a means of processing or moving beyond trauma. Instead, Lamar asserts pain as perpetual and ongoing, mastering audience members, forcing them to confront and acknowledge its existence, and refusing them the comfort of any psychic defense through invalidation or denial: "I'm not interested in making people feel comfortable. I'm into scaring people! My work is about a certain level of discomfort. It's about a level of confrontation with regards to white supremacy in this country and my awareness of that."[29]

In 2014 I attended M. Lamar's first New York solo exhibition, *Negrogothic, a Manifesto: The Aesthetics of M. Lamar*, which included video installations, large-scale photographic prints, sculptural props, and live performance.[30] The sculptural props punctuated the open space; a nine-foot-tall penis guillotine with a small crotch-level hole dominated the exhibition, along with a pillory set next to a pile of books, which included G. W. F. Hegel's *Phenomenology of Spirit* and Toni Morrison's *Beloved*. On the brick-and-plaster walls of the gallery hung small flat-screen televisions playing videos on a loop interspersed between large-format black and white photographs. Lamar's video installations included music composed and performed by the artist in his signature countertenor voice with dissonant musical elements and genre blending, including opera, doom metal, and blues. Projected directly onto the back wall of the gallery was the centerpiece of the exhibit, *Surveillance Punishment and the Black Psyche, Part Two, Overseer*, a portion of a feature-length musical film-in-progress.

Lamar's dark, sadomasochistic aesthetic offers a complex commentary on lingering traumatic pasts, the links between these pasts and present-day constructions of black masculinity and sexuality, and the possibilities for playing with horror and misery as ingredients for simultaneous suffering and pleasure. Lamar explains his intentional deployment of a gothic aesthetic as a means of accessing the horrors of history: "People talk about the gothic novel as this blend of romance and horror, but in the context of my work, the horror is actually not fictional."[31] Kilgour describes eighteenth-century Gothicism's "crudely" Romantic values as "an interest in the bizarre, eccentric, wild, savage, lawless, and transgressive," and Lauren Goodlad and Michael Bibby explain that contemporary goth subculture offers an uncanny version of bourgeois Romanticism through its "fetishized representations of past bourgeois social formations. Hence, like Freud's seminal concept, goth is both *heimlich* and *unheimlich*."[32]

Lamar's exhibit uncannily circulates these Romantic values partially through sadomasochism, depicting savagely sexualized power within a nostalgic dreamscape and highlighting transgression by confronting the dangers of sadomasochistic reenactment. He intentionally juxtaposes the Romantic elements of gothicism and sadomasochistic eroticism with the horrors of black history to heighten the viewers' experience of the work, thereby "mak[ing] black horror really explicit."[33] The highlighting of blackness through a goth aesthetic is particularly uncanny, since the contemporary goth look generally involves excessive whiteness (often achieved with white facial makeup).[34] But Lamar defamiliarizes the goth aesthetic through an assertive blackness, or "negrogothness," thereby highlighting the intersection of race, gender, sexuality, and gothic horror. In *Surveillance Punishment and the Black Psyche* and the photographic stills taken from the film such as the Mapplethorpe's Whip series, Lamar makes horror explicit through classic sadomasochistic props and postures—whips, hoods, torture devices, kneeling submission. The sadomasochistic image becomes gothic in its depiction of real historical horror paired with a sexualized nostalgia in the scenes of racialized master-slave relations, cotton picking, whips, and anal penetration, a transgression that can feel disorienting, wild, and lawless. Sadomasochism's potential to viscerally connect participants with a traumatic ancestral past, as Freeman argues, does not make the scenes any more comfortable for audiences confronted with the sexualized racial dynamics present.

Lamar plays with the temporal possibilities associated with sadomasochism as a way to acknowledge past and present violence, challenge white supremacy, and explore the pleasures and pains associated with sexualities emerging from such violent contexts. *Surveillance Punishment and the Black Psyche* offers a dream/nightmare-scape that collapses history and fiction, past and present, and violence and pleasure. The exhibition press release describes the film as a "fictional narrative loosely based on Willie Francis, a sixteen-year-old black boy who was sentenced to death (and executed twice) in Louisiana in 1947 for killing Andrew Thomas, his pharmacist boss, rumored to be Francis' lover."[35] After hearing about this story,

Lamar "attempted to research the possibilities of the history of homosexuality on plantations. Finding little to no information on the subject, Lamar decided to create a fictional realm of historical desire in his video."[36] In the absence of a literal historical narrative, Lamar offers an abstract film of disjointed scenes focused on "repositioning the ghostly figure of the black male 'Overseer.'"[37] In one scene Lamar, as the overseer in a dark, hooded cloak, slowly walks among stark cotton plants shrouded in fog, whip in hand. In another the overseer mounts the penis guillotine, as several naked white men kneel below. He inserts the crotch-level whip into the guillotine, and a hooded white figure pulls the cord, severing the whip-phallus and causing it to fall into a waiting basket of cotton. Later the overseer saunters along another line of naked white men bent over in submission and slowly inserts the handle end of a whip into each receptive anus. Once all the whips are inserted, he holds them in his hand like tails or leashes, standing connected to and ultimately in control of the prostrate figures before him. The gothic queer aesthetic of the show—permeated by sadomasochistic power, darkness, doom, and horror—puts viewers in contact with the violent (and largely invisible) history of black sexual subjection, forcing viewers to encounter the then and now of histories that they might rather forget while simultaneously implicating them in the future of race relations. The video creates a temporal bridge between slavery, Jim Crow, and today, and it uses structures of punishment and pleasure to do so.

The link between the history of slavery and unacknowledged present-day racism is also present in Lamar's explicit response to Robert Mapplethorpe's work. The anally inserted whips that appear throughout the exhibition, perhaps most prominently depicted in the Mapplethorpe's Whip photographs, evoke Mapplethorpe's "Self-Portrait with Whip" (1978), and the sexualized nudes call to mind Mapplethorpe's famous black male nudes in The Black Book (1986). Kobena Mercer reads Mapplethorpe's photographs of black men as a "cultural artifact" that not only reflects the photographer's desire to possess and objectify his subjects but that also "says something about certain ways in which white people 'look' at black people and how, in this way of looking, black male sexuality is

8. M. Lamar, *Mapplethorpe's Whip VII*, still from *Surveillance Punishment and the Black Psyche, Part Two, Overseer*. Courtesy of the artist.

perceived as something different, excessive, Other."[38] Lamar redeploys Mapplethorpe's tropes (the fetishistic gaze, the phallic whip, the receptive asshole) but infuses them with historical signifiers (the cotton plant, the hooded cape, the castrating guillotine) and a gothic atmosphere (brooding shadows, misty landscapes, a mysterious cloaked figure). Lamar himself plays the romantically mysterious overseer to a group of submissive white men. Though the raced power dynamics seem to be reversed, Lamar's whip-phallus nods to the white fetishization of the black physique while the castrating apparatus, operated by a hooded white figure, reminds the viewer that the fetishized black penis is simultaneously desirable and threatening. Who is dominant and who is submissive in his series? Is Lamar's overseer, in fact, forcing the hooded white man to commit the symbolic castration for his own debased pleasure? Why does the overseer pick the cotton himself; the very same cotton that cushions the whip's fall as it drops from the guillotine? Where does fantasy end and torture begin?

By recreating and remixing Mapplethorpe's whip motif in the context of gothic sadomasochism and the history of slavery and Jim Crow, Lamar draws attention to the ties between that history and the hypersexualized constructions of black masculinity that resonate in contemporary culture.[39] According to Emily Colucci, Lamar is "admittedly obsessed" with Mapplethorpe's sadomasochistic and eroticized images of black bodies. Lamar sees the trope of the whip as one rooted in black subjection and argues that Mapplethorpe's "use of the whip echoes him as a person who is deeply invested in white supremacist notions of blackness."[40] The Mapplethorpe's Whip series uses the whip to figure the collapse between neat distinctions of pain and pleasure as well as a collapse between racist histories and their links to normalized assumptions about race, gender, and sexuality today. This temporal collapse between past and present forces viewers to encounter their own potential present-day complicity in racialized narratives that have roots in violently racist histories.

While sadomasochism trades in participant pain and discomfort by definition, Lamar's musical, visual, and performance art creates *audience* discomfort as well by constructing an experience in which incompatible feelings and concepts operate simultaneously to dizzying effect. Lamar's gothic sadomasochism creates conceptual and aural dissonance, a typically sonic phenomenon implying unpleasant noise, instability, and the lack of harmony. His gothicism offers dissonance by depicting the horrors of history through a romantic lens, an echo of those eighteenth- and nineteenth-century novels that set their Gothic romances during the Inquisition.[41] His deployment of the whip recirculates racist narratives with an erotic inflection, resulting in dissonant scenes of apparent violence performed for the sake of pleasure. Jennifer Doyle argues that "difficult" art is difficult because it produces a "complexity of emotion" in an environment in which one is expected to maintain critical distance. Complex emotions create a kind of "noise" where "affect appears as an interface, as a rupture in which the viewer is thrown back onto, into a disoriented self."[42] Lamar's work creates affective "noise" through its depiction of dissonant emotional complexities and deploys dissonance literally in its musical elements as well. In an essay appearing on Lamar's official website, Brandon Peter Masterman explains that Lamar creates vocal dissonance in his musical performances with a "rapidly oscillating vibrato," "occasionally delaying or anticipating the arrival at a certain consonant pitch following a glissando in favor of a slightly sharp or flat one."[43] Indeed, Lamar's piercing vocalizations are intense—durational, repetitive, and incessant—with looped videos and extended live performances consisting of amelodic over and under pitch vocalizations. This trio of dissonances—erotic, historical, and musical—creates artistic noise, making the work difficult, uncomfortable, surreal, and disorienting.

In addition to creating discomfort through dissonance, Lamar creates audience discomfort through the intentional reflection of white complicity in the narratives being depicted, a mirroring of the audience gaze. Galleries are elite spaces generally populated by those with access to privilege—usually highly educated, politically oriented, often white people—and the audience gaze is central to M. Lamar's project. To this point Lamar states, "What's really in the foreground of images in the show is whiteness; white people looking at black people. . . . I think there's an amount of urgency for white people to start looking at things differently, to really interrogate their personality in terms of these long kinds of histories and these long narratives, which white people seem unwilling to do."[44] He highlights the whip-phallus featured in his work as a reflection of the "'big black cock' mythology," which is "an invention of the white imagination. It's a fantasy. I like the idea, in a surrealist way, of making the whip also this black penis that white people have invented. It's like, 'Here. This is your invention. It's your thing. Have it back.' I try to understand the black body in the white imagination." But he does not imagine his audience as exclusively white. He adds, "I think a lot of black men have internalized the gaze of whiteness. . . . Part of the point of *Surveillance Punishment and the Black Psyche* is to get inside this internalization of white supremacy. We usually refer to it as internalized racism."[45] In both cases Lamar uses scenes and metaphors of sexualized power to confront his viewers with weighty topics such as racist complicity, histories that many would prefer to forget, and the direct links between that history and the structure of society today.

The visceral presence of trauma and horror, the sonic and conceptual dissonance, and the confrontational reflection of internalized white supremacy circulate in the exhibition space, folding viewers into a sadomasochistic experience. Reviewers have described Lamar's work as "weighty" and "deeply mov[ing]" and as "public punishment" that "jolts and startles."[46] Lamar elaborates, "I would never call my shows 'fun'— they're always about mourning in some way. . . . Ultimately, they're not uplifting shows. They're just sort of depressing, which is fine, I think it's cathartic and necessary."[47] Of audience reaction, he adds, "Maybe they cry." Lamar's work takes viewers to their dark places, where pain circulates and pleasure is deferred. Indeed, audience reaction seems to support this claim. I attended a 2015 musical performance of the black-metal opera *Destruction* that took place in a dimly lit Gothic church in Brooklyn, at which the restroom was off-limits for the duration of the show, adding an additional level of audience discomfort. As people gathered on the steps of the church after the show concluded, I overheard a young woman complaining that the experience "gave me anxiety."

The discomfort structuring Lamar's art alters the audience members' interaction with it—taking it from object for consumption to lived experience. This controversial and potentially alienating move allows his work to avoid the problems associated with the call to activism through empathy. Saidiya Hartman critiques the call to empathy because it "fails to expand the space of the other but merely places the self in its stead."[48] Hartman explains that abolitionists asked white people to understand the horrors of chattel slavery by imagining themselves in the place of the suffering black body, a logic that assumes suffering can be experienced only by substituting the white body for the black one and implying that black suffering is not repugnant for its own sake. In this way empathy as an abolitionist strategy unintentionally buttressed the foundational assumptions about black objecthood that structured the institution of slavery. But Lamar's work—though perhaps a call to action—is not attempting to elicit empathy. Instead, he depicts horror, misery, and trauma in ways that do not ask audience members to *imagine* misery; to a certain degree they actually *experience* it. This forces the audience to encounter a queer of color critique that pushes against the liberal ideologies that occlude the violent intersections of race, gender, sexuality, and class highlighted in Lamar's art and performance. Roderick Ferguson envisions this kind of intersectional visualization as a productive rupture, something akin to traumatic fragmentation:

> We must see the gendered and eroticized elements of racial forma-tions as offering ruptured—i.e., critical—possibilities. Approaching them as sites of critique means that we must challenge the con-struction of those formations as monstrous and threatening to oth-ers who have no possibility of critical agency and instead engage nonheteronormative racial formations as the site of ruptures, cri-tiques, and alternatives. Racial formations, as they are constituted nonnormatively by gender and sexual differences, overdetermine national identity, contradicting its manifold promises of citizenship and property. This overdetermination could compel intersecting antiracist, feminist, class, and queer struggles to emerge.[49]

By recirculating racist historical narratives, creating sonic dissonance, confronting the audience members with their own mirrored gaze, and challenging the very basis of liberal ideology, Lamar's difficult art pushes the limits of audience comfort in ways that are sadistic, masochistic, and tough to pin down. The sadomasochistic temporal collapse forces viewers to consider their own *cognitive* dissonances, which include the slippage between liberal conceptions of the self, the complicities inher-ent in accepting and internalizing the structures of white supremacy, and the illusion that the past is truly past. This strategic production of discomfort is not simply indulgent or vindictive; instead, it is a political intervention. Doyle argues that difficult artists "turn to emotion, feelings, and affect as a means of not narcissistic escape but of social engagement" and that difficult affect gives art the power to shake viewers out of their complacency.[50] M. Lamar's gothic sadomasochism—its dissonances, its temporal hybridity, and its strategic creation of discomfort—visualizes the present as a moment of crisis arising from the horrors and miseries of history but also inextricably linked to the future.

The Horror of Complicity

Cassils and Zackary Drucker are two contemporary transgender artists whose performances inflict aggressive discomfort on themselves and a less direct but no less aggressive discomfort on the audience. While their aesthetic is not as overtly gothic as M. Lamar's Negrogothicism, they use similar sadomasochistic practices to address historical and ongoing violence and to recreate traumatic sensation in their performance spaces. Like Lamar's work, their deployment of discomfort is a gothic mechanism for responding to traumatic histories and experiences while shaking viewers out of complacency and forcing a recognition of complicity.

Cassils and Drucker respond to the insidious trauma of systemic impossibility by visibly foregrounding gender construction and fluidity in performances that center on the materiality of their gender-nonconforming bodies. As trans*-identifying artists, their inclusion within the mainstream art scene is a remarkable exception to the art world's traditionally narrow vision of the kinds of artists who belong within gallery or museum walls. For example, the *Huffington Post* named both artists in "10 Transgender Artists Who Are Changing the Landscape of Contemporary Art"; Cassils's 2013 first gallery solo exhibit received a favorable *Artforum* review; and Drucker's collaborative work with Rhys Ernst appeared in the 2014 Whitney Biennial.[51] Of course, Cassils and Drucker deserve their recent notoriety, but it may also be true that they serve a tokenizing role for galleries and museums that are facing greater scrutiny over their exclusionary practices. Further, it is important to note that both Cassils and Drucker benefit from the privileges of whiteness and access to education (both artists hold an MFA from the California Institute of the Arts). While galleries and museums begin to open their doors to gender-nonconforming artists, the art establishment as a whole remains a bastion of whiteness and privilege often populated by "well-intentioned" liberal elites who, Derald Wing Sue explains, are frequently the perpetrators of microaggressions.[52]

The presence of these artists in a world built on an ethos of exclusion depends on the interaction between the specific intersections of their lived experiences and the demands and limitations of the contemporary moment. Regardless of the forces that have placed them in the public eye, the burden of trans* representation falls on them, as it so often does for minorities, as they become the visual symbol of "progress" in the art world.[53] But their art challenges microaggressive assumptions about gender and disrupts the self-congratulatory narrative of progress through the sadomasochistic deployment of discomfort, a decidedly gothic mode of queer cultural intervention.

Because my argument depends partially on a reading of audience experience, I focus on performances that I have personally witnessed. I have seen Cassils's *Becoming an Image* twice: once in 2012 at the ONE National Gay and Lesbian Archives in Los Angeles as part of the large-scale arts initiative *Pacific Standard Time* and once in 2013 at Cassils's solo show, *Body of Work*, at the Ronald Feldman Gallery in New York City. I saw Zackary Drucker's *The Inability to Be Looked At and the Horror of Nothing to See* in 2009 at an evening of performance art, *You Belong to Me*, arranged by the University of California's Sweeney Art Gallery in Riverside. Though I have seen both Cassils and Drucker perform and display additional pieces in other contexts, these particular performances most strongly elicited the distinct audience reactions that I analyze in this chapter.

Cassils's *Becoming an Image* is uncomfortable to watch. At the ONE Archives performance I attended, ushers carefully guided the audience into a small space, cramped and completely dark. Because the space was so small, we had to enter in waves as the performance went on, so each new group was ushered in as a previous one left. In the larger gallery space of the New York show, we all filed into a lit room, and once all attendees were in place, the lights went out, leaving us to adjust to the total darkness in our places. In the center of the room sat a giant mound of clay, and when the performance began we heard heaving, slapping noises as Cassils pummeled and kicked the clay. The small space at the ONE Archives meant that no audience member was able to watch the performance in its entirety; however, it also meant that the discomfort was heightened, as we jostled past one another in the darkness of the confined space with no time to pause as our eyes adjusted to the darkness. The close room was humid and pungent with the sweat of exertion, and we were often so close to the action that sweat and droplets of clay sprayed on us. Periodically, the flash of a professional photographer's camera illuminated Cassils's body—often in midpunch or kick, covered in nude briefs, hands wrapped in gauzy bandages—giving us a momentary glimpse of the action occurring just feet in front of us and leaving a ghostly image lingering on the retina. Each time the camera flashed, Cassils's assaults had drastically altered the clay's shape. In the darkness I could sometimes feel the whoosh of Cassils's body as it moved past, and when the camera flashed my eye often lingered, not on Cassils and the clay but on the horrified faces of my fellow audience members. The grunting and panting increased as Cassils became more and more exhausted from the intense exercise. At the gallery show in which we were allowed to stay for the duration of the performance, at a certain point it became clear that the performer had suddenly exited the space when the lights came on, leaving only the clay remnant in the center of the room.

When I attended Zackary Drucker's *The Inability to Be Looked At and the Horror of Nothing to See*, it was part of a series of performances held in a multiroom space. Over the course of the evening, the audience members were ushered from room to room to discover a prearranged mise-en-scène from which the next piece emerged. As we were herded into yet another room toward the end of the evening, the audience came upon Drucker's body, clad only in bikini briefs, lying ball-gagged on a metal table strewn with tweezers. Drucker's prerecorded "disembodied" voice guided us through a series of meditations, instructing us to touch the body on the table and eventually asking us to use the tweezers to remove all the hair on the body—"Don't be afraid; the bitch can take it," the voice told the audience members, as those around me hesitated before moving forward to begin plucking. The voice used the second-person "you" to verbally assault and denigrate the listeners, replicating a self-critical inner mono-

9. Cassils, *Becoming an Image Performance Still No. 7*. National Theater Studio SPILL Festival, London, 2013. C-print, 22 x 30 inches, edition of 5. Photo: Cassils, by Manuel Vason. Courtesy of the artist and Ronald Feldman Gallery, New York.

logue and asking us to channel our personal misery into the hairs that many of us began to pluck out one by one with increasing boldness. The monologue seemed to have varying effects on the audience members, as it clearly tapped into their different experiences and self-perceptions, some laughing, some tensing, some tearing up. When the voice calmly stated, "This body is the receptacle for all of your guilt and shame and trauma," the initial hesitation of the people around me seemed to melt into eagerness as they formed orderly lines behind each set of tweezers, plucking a few hairs and then passing the instrument to the next pair of impatiently awaiting hands. I watched in awe as Drucker remained motionless on the sterile metal slab throughout the duration of the performance, despite offering her entire body for plucking, with serenely closed eyes and no opportunity to anticipate where the next pinch or pull would occur.

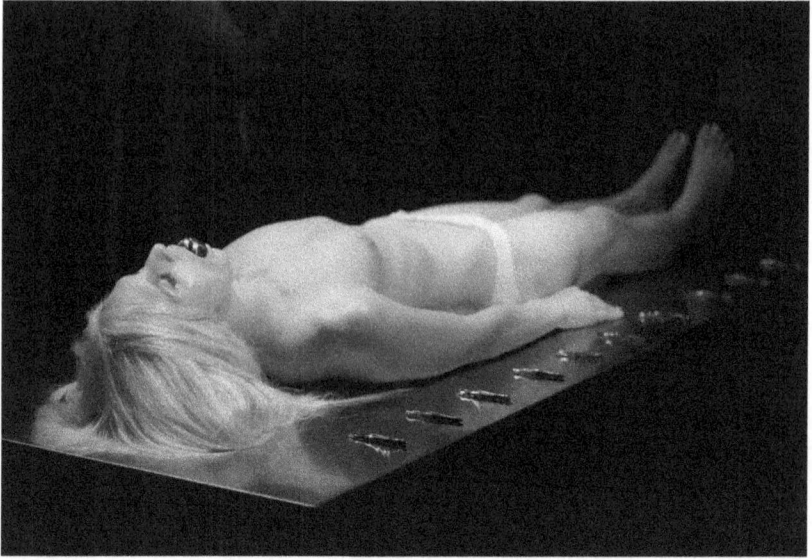

10. Zackary Drucker, *The Inability to Be Looked At and the Horror of Nothing to See*, 2009. Live performance, seventeen minutes. Courtesy of the artist and Luis De Jesus Los Angeles.

One of the violences Cassils and Drucker confront in their work is public ignorance and indifference regarding the complex manifestation of those myriad experiences, behaviors, and identities that fall under the category of transgender, or trans*, "an umbrella term for describing a range of gender-variant identities and communities within the United States" and which "most generally refers to any and all kinds of variation from gender norms and expectations."[54] The mainstream media frenzy surrounding trans* celebrities Laverne Cox and Caitlyn Jenner could potentially signal that the United States has arrived at what *Time* magazine calls the "transgender tipping point," a period of "radical increase in trans consciousness" and a moment in which Cox can claim that "more of us are living visibly and pursuing our dreams visibly."[55] Increased trans* representation in the media is an important shift, but public willingness to acknowledge Jenner and Cox depends partially on the fact that they do not challenge limiting social, medical, and legal expectations super-imposed on gender-variant bodies. These expectations involve a narrative of unidirectional transition from one's gender assigned at birth (assumed to be "natural" and "biological") to one's desired gender (assumed to be the "opposite" of this assigned gender). Julian Carter explains that the concept of "transition" as a "standardized trajectory of 'sex reassignment' in which people were shuttled from the psychiatrist, through the endo-crinologist, to the surgeon, to the judge . . . weighs especially heavily on people who lack the resources or the wish to conform to its polarized definitions of sexed embodiment, such as poor and/or uninsured people and those whose gender expression is not formed in relation to dominant white European American conventions."[56] With this formulation in mind, any gender location that does not settle on one end of the dualism or the other is often problematically assumed to simply be in the process of a standardized transition—not a gender based on fluidity or ambiguity but one that is as yet unfinished and therefore unrecognizable.

In addition to this misrecognition, trans* and nonbinary folks are often dehumanized through that conservative gothic trope used to shore up normativity—monstrosity. Susan Stryker articulates the dire (and cer-tainly gothic) consequences of unrecognizability: "Because most people have great difficulty recognizing the humanity of another person if they cannot recognize that person's gender, the gender-changing person can evoke in others a primordial fear of monstrosity, or loss of humanness. That gut-level fear can manifest itself as hatred, outrage, panic, or disgust, which may then translate into physical or emotional violence directed against the person who is perceived as not-quite human. Such people are often shunned and may be denied such basic needs as housing or employment."[57] Even though famous figures like Jenner and Cox offer a form of trans* visibility, their stories reinforce the standardized transition narrative of dysphoria, transition, and arrival and may even contribute to the violent dehumanization of those who are nonbinary, agender, gen-derfluid, or any number of other gender possibilities that fail, refuse, or exceed binary recognition.

Janet Mock—best-selling author and trans* activist—responds to the potential complacency that can arise from a few select trans* figures dominating media coverage. In her blog she reflects on the relationship between visibility and violence for the trans* community, pointing out the shocking rate at which trans* women were murdered in the United States in 2015.[58] She reminds her readers that although there is "much we should be applauding" as some trans* folks achieve media fame, we must resist tokenization to ensure the survival of those who are neglected and punished by political and institutional indifference and disdain.[59] Survival depends not only on visibility, she argues, but also on disrupting deeply held myth systems that explicitly encourage or implicitly support antitrans* violence. Mock asks readers to remember that violence against the trans* community has roots in multiple, intersecting forces, including both systemic erasure and institutional and interpersonal violence.

Systemic erasure may seem like a minor issue in relation to the overt violence perpetrated against trans* people, but small, persistent aggressions can significantly impact individuals and communities. When a person is forced to check a box on a form that does not account for their experience in the world, cannot use a public restroom without fear of violence or arrest, is unable to depend on police protection, or is excluded from "sex-segregated" services (such as residential drug-treatment facilities), it is an act of aggression against them. In *Normal Life* Dean Spade notes that U.S. laws and policies "produce systemic norms and regularities that make trans people's lives administratively impossible."[60] The consistent struggles of an "impossible" life combined with daily interpersonal and institutional microaggressions operate alongside more overt forms of violence used to police and oppress those who exist outside of a culture's mythical norm, which Audre Lorde defines as "white, thin, male, young, heterosexual, christian, and financially secure" and to which we should add cisgender, a term that indicates one's gender identity aligns with one's assigned gender. "It is with this mythical norm that the trappings of power reside in this society," Lorde explains, and those who fall outside of the norm suffer from their oppressed status in numerous unacknowledged ways, the accrual of which creates insidious trauma, an overlooked instrument of structural oppression.[61]

Like Lamar, Cassils and Drucker use gothic sadomasochism to denaturalize structures of oppression by recreating the affective and corporeal sensations of insidious trauma. The usefulness of a turn to sensation, Musser explains, is that it is "both individual and impersonal; it occupies a sphere of multiplicity without being tethered to identity."[62] Each audience member has a shared reference point—the art itself and its resonances with trauma—but the experience of the art is unique to each individual. Identities and their attendant privileges and hierarchies are often part of the structures that create traumatic oppression, so shifting audience focus to their own sensations in relation to the work opens up the art to a productive multiplicity, notably a primary characteristic of the gothic monstrosity I explore in chapter 3. But the turn to corporeality has its dangers, especially for trans* folks, for whom medicalized transition narratives and an obsessive focus on the state of the body often reduce them to their biology. Does the emphasis on corporeal spectacle simply reinforce trans* objectification? As with the formulation that Hartman outlines in her critique of the call to empathy, the audience certainly has the potential to inadvertently perpetuate the objectification and violence these artists invoke. Though Cassils and Drucker play with the danger of dehumanization by using the body as medium, like Lamar, they are not truly eliciting empathy. Cassils and Drucker account for audience complexity while avoiding the empathic trap by using sadomasochism to create microaggressive traumatic affect. Both performances create intense discomfort among audience members, and both artists inflict that discomfort on themselves in a give-and-take of physical and psychological pain. By recirculating internalized narratives about the natural versus the modified body, these difficult pieces of art challenge audience comfort and consent in ways that are complexly sadomasochistic. Remarkably, they produce an emotional experience that replicates some of the feelings associated with being the recipient of microaggression, thereby using sadomasochism to shatter their audience into a mobilized political consciousness.

While Cassils admits to a kind of violence in *Becoming an Image*, they insist that the violence is directed at the clay rather than at another human.[63] Cassils emphasizes their own athleticism and rigorous training in preparation, noting that they wanted a "sense of raw power and strength to be something that you take away" from the performance.[64] Though Cassils disavows the role of violence to a certain degree, they take on the role of master and aggressor by creating a scene in which they assert their physical strength and power, are fully aware of the parameters of the space, understand the length and scope of the action, and control the numbers and placement of the audience members. Cassils not only attempts to master their own body but also performs the role of master in relation to the relatively disempowered and submissive audience. Though audience members consent to their participation when entering the space, they cannot easily exit during the duration of the performance because of the densely packed, pitch-black room in which one could easily stumble into the "violence" being committed on the clay.

This was true in both of the performances I attended, though in different registers. In the tight space of the ONE Archives performance, the small room was at capacity, and there was a lot of movement as attendees were being ushered in and out of the active performance. The density of people, the proximity of the clay, and the chaos of moving around while partially blinded by the drastic change in lighting made agency and escape feel very difficult. In the New York gallery performance, the space was larger but still as tightly packed. Without the constant movement of folks in and out, an escape from the gallery would be more distracting, and there were fewer obvious paths since people were locked into place once the lights went out. The more formal environment of the gallery and the conventions of art spectatorship also implied a certain code of conduct in which viewers were expected to maintain a cool emotional distance. It is unseemly to be overcome with emotion when viewing artwork, and works that evoke that "noise" or "static" of emotion tend to make art critics and historians "nervous precisely because such work requires a turn against the discipline."[65] Exhibiting emotion in the art space would expose the overwhelmed viewer as a naive outsider, a consequence that might impact a viewer's choice to admit emotional defeat by exiting. Each situation created a uniquely claustrophobic aura, as the audience submitted to their captivity at the hands of the artist.

Some might get a thrill from this submissive role, and indeed the intersection of pleasure, power, and submission is complex in the sado-masochistic relationship. As proponents of "safe, sane, and consensual" BDSM proclaim, it is the masochist/submissive who designs the scene, who consents to the relationship, and who may end the scene at any time, using the designated "safe word." Further, as Deleuze points out, the contract is central to the creation of the fantasy, giving the masochist power to construct the terms of submission and ensuring the full consent of all participants. "The ultimate paradox," Deleuze explains about the masochistic contract, "is that such a contract should be initiated, and the power conferred by the victim himself."[66] In this sense the masochist is the one who holds the power. The discomfort in *Becoming an Image* may be located in the disruption of that dynamic, for although there is a certain degree of audience consent, there are several factors that wrench that power back from them. The most obvious one is the difficulty of a subtle exit. There is no agreed-on "safe word," and if one were to speak out in the otherwise silent space, that utterance may or may not actually have the power to end the scene. *Becoming an Image* gently defies understandings of consent and submissive power to simultaneously affect the audience while disempowering them, throwing Cassils into the role of sadist.

The dominant/submissive relationship between artist and audience, however, is fluid. Cassils explains, "there's something very interesting about the materiality of clay. . . . You're not just molding it, but the clay actually pushes back at you. So as I'm forming it, it is also forming me. . . . So there is this kind of reciprocity that is occurring."[67] Paradoxically, Cassils's performance of mastery depends on submission to the clay and the limits of the body. To prepare for *Becoming an Image*, Cassils follows an extremely rigorous dietary and training regimen, gaining twenty-three pounds of muscle in the twenty-three weeks preceding the performance to create a "larger and more menacing" body. Cassils combines this extreme reshaping of the body with a durational performance, in which they perform at maximum exertion, or "hyper-performance." It is sometimes only through exaggeration, Cassils explains, that you can "really point to the construction" of gendered bodies.[68] Cassils's self-consciously constructed body shares the spotlight with the clay mound, and the artist shapes both. The analogous shaping of the clay in the temporal present links the gendered construction of Cassils's body to the violence that plays a role in the continued shaping of gender-nonconforming bodies and spirits. In this way the performance asserts the visible presence of bodily construction as a form of violence inflicted on a passive mound, but also as a means of agential self-actualization. Cassils uses violence and aggression—something trans* people encounter all too often—as resources for art and political intervention. The rigorous training cycle and the "hyper-performance" of the durational work imply that Cassils takes a certain amount of pleasure in the tortured shaping of the fleshy clay of their own body, even if that pleasure lies in the satisfaction of communicating a political message about that very process.

While Cassils's performance appears to be sadistic at first glance, Drucker's certainly appears masochistic. The passive position of Drucker's body, the BDSM-inspired prop of the ball in her mouth, and the unflinching request to be plucked all contribute to the sense of masochism. Drucker takes on the masochist's burden of designing the scene in which she relinquishes power. Though the audience has a bit more agency in this performance (it is easier to exit the space or to not participate in the plucking, for example), that agency is slowly and subtly disrupted as the performance goes on. In the performance I attended, Drucker's disembodied voice, both affectless and soothing, lured the audience into a place of trust and relaxation and then subverted that sense of security. After leading a series of deep-breathing exercises, the voice encouraged audience members to dissolve any distinction between themselves and those around them through a series of actions and visualizations, ordering them to feel that they are "occupied by the flow of cosmic energy . . . cleansing your entire being."[69] The voice eventually instructed us to look at the body on the table with "eyes half closed and half open" and imagine that "you yourself are this body." After guiding us into this passive position, the voice then assaulted the audience with what we might imagine are the self-deprecating insults that circulate in the mind of the body with which we had just been asked to identify. As the voice instructed us to begin sadistically plucking hairs, we were also insulted: "Your world is collapsing into a scum-filled puddle of frothy lard, fat-ass thighs. You're never going to be rich enough or thin enough. You will never be desirable. Pluck faster." The people around me tittered nervously while continuing to follow the directions that clearly made them uncomfortable. Our role had slipped, almost imperceptibly, from submissive to sadistic as the audience took an active role in painfully reshaping the body before us.

By integrating the audience into the performance, Drucker makes visible the role that audience members play in constructing and enforcing the messages playing over the speakers. The audience is invited to identify with the negative internalized messages they hear about gendered beauty while at the same time inflicting a painful ritual on a passive body, potentially generating a sense of personal gender failure, guilt, and shame. Indeed, the narratives around gender failure that Drucker voices are not exclusive to people who identify as trans*. In his study of gender and violence in Romanticism, Nowell Marshall points out that the inability to perfectly attain idealized gender norms can cause a sense of failure and loss for both gender nonconformists and those cisgender folks who want desperately to conform to the gendered ideals assigned to them at birth. Marshall argues that (in Gothic fiction and beyond) gender failure can lead to "performative melancholia," or the depression and rage resulting in the loss and incorporation or disavowal of gender normativity as an ideal. In his reading of both Gothic novels and contemporary instances of gender failure, Marshall notes that performative melancholia often manifests through masochism and violence.[70] The narrative of gender failure and self-hatred circulating in Drucker's voiceover taps into the performative melancholia of the audience members, whether gender conforming or nonconforming, to generate a swirl of gothic sadomasochistic impulses.

In the sadomasochistic moment the audience is not allowed to relax into the role of passive spectator, comfortable in the knowledge that the artist will emerge from the space unscathed. Instead, the future of the body on the table is contingent on audience choices. The weight of that responsibility may be what "mov[es] some members of the audience to tears."[71] As with *Becoming an Image*, not only does the extreme nature of the performance represent the construction of gendered bodies, but its sadomasochism also creates an atmosphere of uncomfortable, weighty responsibility. Doran George points out that Drucker refuses the audience a comfortable position of "*anonymous* consumption of a transgender spectacle," adding that instead "through their collaborative act they are called upon to *embody* transphobia."[72] The confusing slipperiness of sadomasochism leaves viewers with a sense of guilt and unease. Microaggressions often leave a lingering, unsettled feeling that one has been insulted, but the "micro" nature of the aggression causes doubt and uncertainty rather than indignation. Was what I just experienced really racist, sexist, or ableist? Am I being too sensitive? Although the experience of this sensation is stripped of historical and institutional weight to a degree, both artists create this kind of lingering traumatic affect. This controversial move is a potentially productive deployment of eroticized power in that "crudely" sadomasochistic style present in Gothic fiction.

Traumatizing audience members is a volatile practice, and a lot depends on what kinds of bodies and histories occupy the space. Regardless of the generalizations one can make about audience demographics in these spaces, the reality is that audience is one of the least predictable elements of any performance or exhibit. As Kimberlé Crenshaw explained in 1989, social location is a complex matter, and certain aspects of privilege often intersect with aspects of oppression.[73] This means that audience members may have the privilege of access to education, for example, but they may also have experienced microaggressions or violence in relation to their race, gender, or ability. Even those who are invested in activism or who experience marginalization on some level are not exempt from internalizing bias and committing microaggressions. Remember, Sue argues, that some of the most damaging interactions come from those who "experience themselves as fair-minded and decent people who would never consciously discriminate."[74] Even those trans* folks invested in binary gender might critique or exclude others who identify as trans* but who are genderfluid, genderqueer, nonbinary, or agender or do not wish to take measures to "pass" as one gender or another. Ultimately, one never knows exactly who will be in the crowd or whether discomfort will open their eyes or drive them deeper into their oppressive behaviors, but the shared sensational and affective experience may very well instigate audience contemplation and action.

Admittedly, audience volatility is a danger of the sadomasochistic interventions of all three artists I discuss here. But the dangerousness of the sadomasochistic approach also gives it the power to shake privileged viewers out of complacency and denial. For audience members who have themselves experienced insidious trauma—whether rooted in gender, race, sexuality, or some other aspect of identity—the art can serve as validating representation of their experiences, but it can also remind those viewers that they too may be complicit in structures of oppression. While there is a potential for this strategy to backfire, there is certainly an equal potential for the creation of what Tiffany Ana López calls the "critical witness."[75] Critical witnesses are "activism-driven viewers" who are so moved by a difficult or disturbing performance that they are motivated to advocate for change. Critical witnesses, regardless of social location and experience, are moved to recognize their responsibility for all futures, not just their own, possibly leading to organized action. Kaplan, too, examines the ethics of witnessing trauma vicariously through literature or media. She explains that witnessing requires "understanding the structure of injustice—that an injustice has taken place—rather than focusing on a specific case." Individualized responses to systemic injustice often refocus arguments to individual actions and circumstances rather than examining the contexts that allow transantagonist or racist behaviors to occur. The type of witnessing that López and Kaplan identify challenges observers to move beyond the invalidating and unproductive focus on specificities. The resulting orientation has the potential to create a witness who "feels responsible for injustice in general. Witnessing involves wanting to change the kind of world where injustice, of whatever kind, is common."[76] While performances may not always succeed in creating a room full of critical witnesses, it is important to recognize the potential for such a creation. Regardless of how (or if) future collective activism takes shape, these gothic queer cultural productions are important because their sadomasochistic strategies challenge entrenched self-perceptions that can make audience members blind to their role in microaggression and insidious trauma.

A Gothic Queer Intervention

The very nature of a live performance—whether it is Lamar's concerts or Cassils's and Drucker's performance art—allows little protective distance between audience and art since the audience must consider the physicality of the performers' bodies and their own within a shared space. This dynamic has the unique potential to create productive trauma. In *Worlds of Hurt* Kalí Tal explains that traumatic events often cause personal and national myth systems to be "tragically shattered." A national, or collective, myth is "propagated in textbooks, official histories, popular culture documents, public schools and the like," while a personal myth is a "set of explanations and expectations generated by an individual to account for his or her circumstances and actions." Trauma, Tal claims, is a "transformative experience" because it shatters one's sense of reality, rendering many personal and national myths meaningless. To bear witness to this shattering is an "aggressive act" because "if survivors retain control over the interpretation of their trauma they can sometimes force a shift in the social and political structure."[77] In Tal's formulation, survival itself is both aggressive and activist.

Cassils's, Drucker's, and Lamar's lived experiences in imperialist, white supremacist, capitalist patriarchy (to echo bell hooks) make them survivors of microaggressive collective myths that marginalize, erase, and invalidate the complexities of their existence. They are not only survivors, however; they also use the aggression of survival to create critical witnesses who leave the space as survivors themselves. While Tal argues that linguistic communication cannot cause trauma—"*The personal myths of the reader are never 'tragically shattered' by reading. Only trauma can accomplish that kind of destruction*"—the unique space of live performance allows for the creation of that myth-shattering trauma.[78] Through the crudely sadomasochistic experience of discomfort, Lamar's, Cassils's, and Drucker's audience members can actually feel a degree of affective and corporeal traumatic sensation that mirrors the insidious trauma of pervasive institutional and interpersonal microaggression, regardless of whether they have personally encountered those microaggressions in their daily lives. As Judith Butler argues, trauma's disruptive effects can lead to a mode of activism freed from the fantasy that change must be grounded in "a single model of communication, a single model of reason, a single notion of the subject." Instead, it is the *breakdown* of this assumption that can lead to action: "For if I am confounded by you, then you are already of me, and I am nowhere without you. I cannot muster the 'we' except by finding the way in which I am tied to 'you,' by trying to translate but finding that my own language must break up and yield if I am to know you. You are what I gain through this disorientation and loss. This is how the human comes into being, again and again, as that which we have yet to know."[79] The artists' sadomasochistic strategies shatter viewers' personal and national myth systems, compelling them to reimagine the systemic structures that create trauma and reminding them of their complicity in those structures. That shattering also has the potential to collapse distance between viewer and performer, between viewer and viewer, and to open up a space of action in the wake of traumatic "disorientation and loss."

Gothic sadomasochism for these artists is both personal expression and political intervention. Lamar's Negrogothic aesthetic is a direct response to his survivor status and his drive to recenter the "post-traumatic stress disorder that's not talked about in black life." He explains, "I'd like to think there's a sense of great loss and mourning. We can't even mourn enough for the lost bodies, the lost spirits, the lost souls. . . . And in my Negrogothness, that will always be a huge part of my work."[80] Lamar's sadomasochistic aesthetic is "really specific and personal," but his personal expression allows him to "balanc[e] my own experience with the black experience in general" and to force new conversations about past traumas that are "not talked about."[81] Cassils notes that it is in the "spectacle" of the art that they locate the "social relationship." Cassils explains that *Becoming an Image* is about "the sort of violence, the undocumented violence, that's existing outside the lens of representation. So although I'm enacting a sort of violence on the sculpture, it's about the black . . . the dark spots, the spots that aren't illuminated in the performance."[82] To further emphasize the connection between the violence in *Becoming an Image* and the violence perpetrated against trans* folks, Cassils has cast the clay remnant into a bronze sculpture called *Resilience of the 20%*, a "monument to the resilience of queer communities" and a reference to the "sickening statistic: in 2012, murders of trans people increased by 20 percent worldwide." Cassils has also created the film *Monument Push*, documenting "a performance that mobilizes the bronze sculpture as a collective action" in which "members of the local LGBTQI+ community joined in pushing the one-ton monument to local sites of trauma, resilience, and survival, including a prison where LGBT youth of color are incarcerated."[83] Cassils's sadomasochistic political strategy uses assertive visuality to construct a hybrid temporality—making the complexities of the constructed body visible in the *present* while creating a clay remainder for *future* viewers that represents bodies *once* pummeled by interpersonal violence. Drucker, too, uses aggressive spectacle to address absence. As of August 2015, her personal website (which has since been redesigned and the text modified) noted that "her work is rooted in cultivating and investigating under-recognized aspects of transgender history." Drucker's sadomasochistic approach consciously "disarms audiences" by using "her body to elicit desire, judgment, and voyeuristic shame from her viewer."[84] Though Drucker's traumatic scene does not produce a lingering physical relic besides her plucked body, it sends viewers away haunted by choices made in the moment. Once again the sadomasochistic present shatters audience comfort and insists on the relationship between choices now and future consequences.

By pulling audience members into an uncomfortable affective register, Lamar, Cassils, and Drucker make visible the connections between absence and violence, survival and aggression, past and present, and aesthetics and politics. They create gothic queer culture to visualize and corporealize trans* and queer of color experiences that media, public institutions, and contemporary historical narratives have neglected, but they also extend their temporal reach into the future. Sadomasochism's deferral of pleasure and deployment of pain and discomfort visualizes the present as a crisis, a traumatic moment, in which individual and collective decisions impact all possible futures. As with the other instances of gothic queer culture that I have explored in these chapters, they linger in the gothic space of disruption and incoherency to refuse closure and focus on the ongoing traumatic present. Through gothic sadomasochism these queer and gender-nonconforming artists create a type of witnessing that potentially "involves a stance that has public meaning or importance and transcends individual empathic or vicarious suffering to produce community."[85] This community, forged through discomfort, is asked to recognize that the future and our role in it is always becoming, being shaped by our choices now. In that shaping lies an uncomfortable responsibility, a constant negotiation. It is a reminder that we cannot become complacent with a future that we imagine is on its way. Instead, it asks us to imagine what we would do if we suddenly landed, like the giant helmet of *Otranto*, in the middle of a Gothic novel to witness the horrors occurring there. How might we alter the narrative? Would our passivity be a kind of choice that allowed its horrors to proceed? What survives as the audience leaves the performance or gallery is not only a revision of gender or racialized history but also a political consciousness that requires constant ungrounding and a productive (even pleasurable) relationship with discomfort that combats both insidious trauma and liberal self-righteousness. In other words, this art plops us in the swirling center of gothicism, disallows easy escape or closure, forces us to encounter the traumatic wound, and perhaps dismembers our comfortable sense of self in the process. Through the deployment of gothic sadomasochism, Lamar, Cassils, and Drucker offer a militant cry that shatters violent structures now in anticipation of an open and contingent future that is forever deferred.

CONCLUSION
The Challenges of Neoliberalism

"God Hates Fangs"

True Blood TV series, opening credits

Haunting, live burial, monstrosity, sadomasochism—these gothic tropes emerged in eighteenth- and nineteenth-century Gothic fiction, and they continue to appear and reappear in cultural production, aiming to titillate, censure, and horrify. Gothicism is perhaps best characterized by its excess, bringing the disruptive, the unspeakable, into our field of vision. As much as those visions horrify, they also provide glimpses of promise in their mutation of reality. This is what makes the gothic something that visionaries turn to as well as those who would use its alternate realities as cautionary tales. No matter the motive, the gothic is always already queer since its monsters, ghosts, and transgressive desires expose a world outside of normative structures. This exposure is titillating, and its deviance has historically been exploited to bring people temporary excitement with a comforting return to normalcy, the queerness destroyed and order reestablished by the last page. Queers, however, have always been good at finding representation in cultural productions meant to punish and erase them. They also have been good at reappropriating and redeploying that which was meant to silence them. This has been a survival strategy, and it has meant that not only has the gothic always been queer but also that queerness has been gothic.

The persistent erasure, censure, and silencing of queer experiences and ways of being certainly do "violence to the soul and spirit," even though their effects may be subtler than the overt violence that has been (and continues to be) committed against those who resist normative scripts.[1] The implied and microaggressive messages policing nonnormative genders and sexualities accumulate over time to have real traumatogenic effects. This insidious trauma is constant and everywhere yet largely unacknowledged and invalidated, creating a cycle of insidious trauma in which the refusal to acknowledge experiences as traumatic serves as its own form of insidious trauma. Trauma by nature is difficult to communicate and understand—leading to its unspeakable quality—but trauma that is insidious is perhaps even more disruptive and fracturing because of its elusiveness. In spite of its resistance to narrativization, trauma demands to be spoken, and this leads to creative and sometimes unconscious attempts to communicate traumatic experience. I have argued that gothicism—a form and aesthetic that, like trauma, exceeds meaning and confounds explanatory strategies—has become a primary tactic for expressing the insidious traumas of queer existence, leading to gothic queer culture.

Gothicism, however, has always had the dual function of exposing queerness while policing it, and this function continues, as popular culture reappropriates the queer reappropriation of the gothic in an ongoing battle of purposes. To examine how gothicism continues to function as a battleground, I turn briefly to Charlaine Harris's Sookie Stackhouse series, the inspiration for HBO's *True Blood*. The novel *Dead until Dark* began a series of thirteen novels about a romance between spunky telepathic waitress, Sookie Stackhouse, and vampire Bill Compton. The Sookie Stackhouse novels were picked up as the television show *True Blood* that HBO ran for seven seasons (2008–14). The novels and the television show begin with a reference to vampires coming "out of the coffin" and integrating into human society.[2] It is set in rural Bon Temps, Louisiana, a small southern town struggling with internal conflict about the recent integration of vampires into mainstream society, resulting in discomfort, prejudice, and sometimes violent confrontation. For centuries vampires had to keep their identities secret by passing as human and indulging in their appetites below the radar of human detection, but as the series begins vampire rights groups are fighting for the right to live openly within human society. The development and mass distribution of a synthetic blood beverage (called "Tru-Blood" in the television series) facilitated this integration by allowing vampires to patronize human restaurants and bars and to satisfy their cravings without draining nonconsenting humans. But there are still plenty of consenting humans, or "fang-bangers," who frequent vampire bars and are erotically drawn to vampires, allowing "vamps" to drink their blood as part of a sexual encounter or as a separate (but still highly sexualized) activity. The series stages a struggle that very much reflects both the racial integration of the 1960s and the contemporary fight for LGBT rights. But even with its depiction of nonnormative sexualities, Harris's world of vampires and those who love (and fuck) them proves to be a neoliberal appropriation of gothic queer culture, signaling a return to the socially conservative function of gothicism, but under the guise of liberalism and progress.

Not only are the series' vampires exotic, forbidden, and slightly dangerous, but they are also hypersexualized in the eyes of humans, and this results in the development of several different factions in reaction to the subject of vampire integration. There are those with secret curiosities and desires who fetishize vampire subculture and either overtly invite sexual relationships with vampires or visit vampires on the down low. The second faction consists of politically conservative and religiously fanatical groups, such as the Fellowship of the Sun, who believe that vampires are evil, perverse, and inhuman, an argument that allows them to justify their call for vampire persecution and murder.[3] The final faction consists of those, like Sookie herself, who are both fascinated by and properly tolerant of mainstreaming vampires and who are vocal supporters of the right for vampires to be granted social acceptance, civil liberties, and equality under the law.[4] These factions map directly on to the ideological and political responses to LGBT communities in the age of marriage equality—people fetishize and consume gay culture (think of the mainstream popularity of television shows like *Queer Eye* or the trend to hold heterobachelorette parties at gay bars); religious and conservative political groups aim to discriminate and even harm members of LGBT communities (think of recent legislation attempting to limit trans* access to public facilities such as bathrooms); and liberals accept and even fight for LGBT assimilation through causes such as marriage equality and inclusion in the military.

Sookie's initial love interest, Bill Compton, is a self-proclaimed "mainstreaming" vampire, a home owner and upstanding citizen. His assimilationist lifestyle is in stark contrast with the "antisocial" vampires, who insist on following an alternative vampire code of ethics that emphasizes pleasure, indulgence, and violence with little regard for human life or human law. In *Dead until Dark* Sookie explains that several of the nonmainstreaming vampires had been making it "impossible for other vampires who wanted to mainstream" by "behaving outrageously, offensively." She rationalizes that the "freedom of being out of the coffin had gone to their heads. The right to legally exist had withdrawn all their constraints, all their prudence and caution." In other words, the vampires who are mainstreaming do their best to avoid doing the "antisocial stuff" that characterizes the underground vampire culture (or at least they use "prudence and caution" while doing it), and the implication is that the well-behaved vampires are the ones who deserve the benefits of liberal citizenship, while the resistant vampires do damage to the cause of integration and equal rights.[5]

The tension between "antisocial" and "mainstreaming" vampires reflects a conflict that I have discussed throughout this book. Like the ideological and political reactions to vampire integration, the mainstream vampire rights movement itself can be neatly mapped onto the identity-based politics of contemporary LGBT (particularly marriage-equality) activism, and their conflict with the unassimilated vampires is reminiscent of the tension between homonormative gay liberals and those who consider themselves more subversively queer in their resistance to normative cultural values such as property ownership, private intimacy, marriage, and family. The series casts the subversive "queer" vampires as atavistic, antisocial, and complicit in their own oppression, and the liberal, assimilationist vampires are emblematic of desirable social advancement and a reassuring symbol of society's "natural" and inevitable progress toward a predetermined, increasingly liberal end. While this series offers the fantasy of a sexy super-natural world replete with the rippling abs of vampires and the shapely breasts of fairies, the fantasy also lies in its vision of a world readable in its trajectory from chaos to order. Whereas eighteenth-century Gothic novels offered narratives of normalcy disrupted and eventually restored, this series presents a future-oriented timeline—the queer vampires are associated with the chaotic primitivism of the past and the mainstream vampires are associated with an inevitable progressive future. This con-temporary manifestation of gothic queerness is not gothic queer culture but instead mirrors the exploitative conservatism of eighteenth- and nineteenth-century Gothic fiction through a neoliberal lens.

Wendy Brown notes that one hallmark of neoliberalism (in addition to its free-market rationality) is that it "confidently identifies itself with the future, and in producing itself as normal rather than adversarial does not acknowledge any alternative futures."[6] The vampires that appear in the Sookie Stackhouse/*True Blood* series occupy a moment of social upheaval, but the future orientation of the narrative imagines only one future—one of progress toward neoliberal assimilation. The series takes this future for granted as natural and desirable; however, the unques-tioned privileging of progress does not leave room for any kind of future that does not involve assimilation into mainstream capitalist culture. As proper neoliberal subjects, "out" vampires develop an intimate relation to the market—both as consumers and as commodity. Vampire blood circulates on the black market as an illegal drug, yet vampires are only minimally protected by federal law, and police enforcement of those laws is unenthusiastic and underpinned with bias against the vampires they are supposed to protect. Within this atmosphere the vampire rights movement emphasizes the lifestyle choices of mainstreaming vampires, implying that they deserve equal protection under the law *because* they are attempting to be just like humans. This vampire normativity emerges, as does homonormativity, from a "neoliberal 'equality' politics," bypassing any revolutionary approach to politics and anchoring mainstreaming vampires firmly within the realm of "domesticity and consumption."[7] As mainstream vampires gain additional rights and legal protections, they become simply a market demographic and are expected to enter into the economy through their purchasing power, by consuming houses, cars, and clothes rather than humans.

The narrative of progress embedded in this series also depends heavily on race as a backdrop and analogy. As Teresa Goddu notes, the American gothic is "infiltrated" by the "hauntings of history," namely the historical horrors of slavery and racial violence.[8] *True Blood*'s gothicism rests on its historical racial undercurrent.[9] Most strikingly, the series is set in the South during a period of recent integration, and it follows characters as they attempt to navigate this new social reality. The vampires' relationship with the dominant culture reflects the kinds of stereotypes and tensions commonly associated with the uneasy status of blackness in the pre- and newly integrated South of the 1950s and 1960s. The opening credits of the HBO series strongly imply a parallel between vampire integration and the civil rights movement—amid shots of rural culture, sexual exploits, and bloody abstractions, the well-known images of KKK hoods and civil rights marches are interspersed. But the history of racial tensions and hard-won integration are merely part of the backstory in the series, setting the scene but not taking a central role in the narrative.

Society regards vampires as hypersexual creatures—simultaneously lustful, skillful, and dangerous—in a manner that reflects stereotypes of black men historically used to justify lynching. In fact, a lynching-type killing does occur in the first novel of the series when, after several women from the town are murdered, some community members decide that a group of "flamboyant" vampires who recently visited the local bar are to blame. One morning Sookie wakes up to a phone call letting her know that the vampires' "nest" had been burned along with the vampires sleeping inside. She notes that the low quality of police work following the crime was clearly influenced by the officers' own prejudices, since they were not "conducting any serious crime-scene investigation" and cracking jokes about "Southern fried vampires."[10] We eventually learn that the spate of killings was committed not by vampires but by Rene, a local townsperson who originally killed his sister for dating a vampire and then began killing any woman whom he suspected to be in a relationship with a vampire. This reveals that one of the driving forces behind the murders, and by extension the vampire lynching, is a fear of miscegenation, thereby setting up a parallel between the violence against vampires and the racially motivated lynchings that historically plagued the U.S. South. Dale Hudson points to the show's racialized treatment of "debates inflected with fears over 'mixed' blood, illusions about 'pure' bloodlines, and the return of asymmetrical power relations that facilitate exploitation."[11] To underscore the *explicit* parallel between vampire rights and LGBT rights, the narrative circulates almost entirely around this *implicit* racial analogy.

In the adoption of racial stereotypes and civil rights discourse to set the stage for vampire integration, the series effectively sets up the same notion of progress implied by the "like race" arguments used to advance the rights and entitlements of homonormative liberals. In *The Feeling of Kinship* David Eng explains that "queer liberalism's freedom and progress is predicated on the systematic dissociation of race from (homo)sexuality as coeval historical phenomena" since utilizing "like race" arguments forecloses the possibility of reading any legal victory for the LGBT community "as part of a long legal tradition maintaining interlocking, indeed constitutive, systems of white supremacy and heterosexism foundational to liberal modernity's unending march of freedom and progress."[12] The use of analogy, in other words, oversimplifies the complex intersections of identity that work to unevenly distribute rights, power, and wealth in contemporary U.S. society. Instead, the "like race" arguments used to advance liberal LGBT assimilationist causes imply that it is a struggle that follows the successful (and already completed) black civil rights movement. Race in this "color blind" culture is an issue of the past, and the civil rights movement's struggles for freedom and equality simply serve as an analogy on which to model demands for LGBT equality.

Further, homonormative liberalism reframes the discourse of rights to emphasize freedom as dependent on individual choice—both in the context of consumer choice and the choice to buy into normative bourgeois concepts of intimacy, family, and the domestic space. Lisa Duggan notes that homonormative politics adopts and recodes the language of "freedom," "equality," and the "right to privacy," only to create a "corporate culture managed by a minimal state, achieved by the neoliberal privatization of affective as well as economic and public life."[13] This is a neoliberal politics based on personal choice within a market-based society, and all notions of civil rights are recast into these terms. Harris proposes a society in which the struggles of racial integration are firmly located in the past, since the focus has shifted to the vampires' struggle for the right to "choose" assimilation into a heteronormative, neoliberal society. In its racial analogy the Sookie Stackhouse/True Blood series imagines a culture in which all but neoliberal futures are foreclosed because issues around race, class, and sexuality have been entombed as historical relics.

By using a "like race" analogy to examine vampire integration, the tensions involved in the fight for racial integration of the civil rights movement inform the atmosphere of the narrative while remaining distinctly in the past. Season 5 of True Blood features a KKK-like hate group that performs targeted killings of all "supernaturals." Although the group is clearly modeled on the KKK (its leader is the "dragon"), the group's hate is focused only on the nonhuman with no mention of race whatsoever. To emphasize the racial inclusivity of the group, the show features a black man as one of the group members, and instead of white hoods they don Obama masks. There is no element of the plotline that addresses race— this is clearly supposed to be a new, postracial, hate group.[14] Society, it seems, has learned its lesson regarding race but is repeating its mistakes in the context of vampires.

While the series blithely relegates racism and white supremacy to the past, its gothicism also serves as an uncritical reproduction of Islamophobia in the post-9/11 period by imagining a future world in which, as mainstreaming vampires move inevitably toward integration and assimilation, their evolution is predicated on the merging of the subversive queer vampire with the figure of the terrorist.[15] This reflects the logic of what Jasbir Puar calls "homonationalism," or a "brand of homosexuality [that] operates as a regulatory script not only of normative gayness, queerness, or homosexuality, but also of the racial and national norms that reinforce these sexual subjects." Homonationalism produces the "terrorist and citizen bodies" through "sexual exceptionalism, queer as regulatory, and the ascendancy of whiteness." In season 5 of *True Blood*, a group of vampires overthrow the mainstreaming political organization and orchestrate the bombing of all Tru-Blood manufacturing locations, hoping to force assimilationist vampires to revert back to their murderous, hedonistic nature without their supply of synthetic blood. Why would a series so initially invested in the vampire/gay rights analogy create a narrative in which the vampires display their "true" nature as terrorists? Doesn't this undermine the liberal message of integration and progress? In the inevitable march toward progress implied by the "like race" analogy of the series, vampires must shift their queerness onto another figure to move into proper nationalist subjectivity as exceptionalist, capitalist-consumerist, and hetero/homonormative subjects. The queer vampires who refuse to mainstream are cast as terrorists, while the assimilationist vampires move more clearly into the neoliberal cultural mainstream, thereby erasing the presence of subversive queerness. In a world that is supposedly postrace, this is a kind of racialization that Puar describes as the "production of terrorist bodies against properly queer subjects."[16] As mainstreaming vampires become visible as liberal subjects, the ones who refuse to assimilate become "terrorists" cathected to death, while proper subjects (even though they are technically undead) become associated with life and productivity. The fantasy of progress depends on this mechanism to fabricate the erasure of subversive queerness. In tracing the vampires' march from queer to normative, the series moves from a relegation of black racial struggles to a distant past to a relegation of subversive queerness to the past as those queers become terrorists, leaving only properly assimilated liberal subjects. A new fantasy binary emerges—no longer between subversive queer and homonormative assimilationist but between terrorist and liberal individual.

The series deploys the vampire as queer subject located in a moment of historical transition, but, because of its dependence on the race analogy and on the juxtaposition of the proper vampire with the terrorist one, it implies that this is a moment of inevitable progress. What begins as a narrative of choice ends with a predetermined future—that of the non-normative outsider being properly integrated into society when, and only when, they adopt what Puar describes as "ever-narrowing parameters of white racial privilege, consumption capabilities, gender and kinship normativity, and bodily integrity."[17] The future for the vampires in the Sookie Stackhouse/*True Blood* series is one of "freedom" through assimilative liberalism, in which progress is marked by the use of raced bodies as those buried in the historical past and as those currently undeserving of life, against which the inevitable neoliberal subject emerges.

The Sookie Stackhouse/*True Blood* series seems to be a forward-looking, equality-minded treatment of contemporary subjectivity. After all, the series presents a world filled with familiar prejudice, murder, injustice, and violent sexuality while it explores the integration of a previously oppressed group of people. The decade following 9/11 (in which this series achieved widespread popularity) was filled with prejudice and injustice engendered by the nebulous War on Terror and the government's apparent support of practices such as the racial profiling and indefinite detainment of Muslims. This decade also saw intense battles for marriage equality in several states, bringing the oppression of LGBT communities into the forefront of the U.S. popular consciousness.[18] The Sookie Stackhouse/*True Blood* series, however, turns out to be simply another fantasy screen that masks the racism implicit in the post-9/11 decade by imagining a world in which these racial prejudices are solved and located firmly in the past, allowing society to move on to other issues of injustice, such as vampire rights. This narrative of progress seems to adopt a hopeful future orientation, but in proper neoliberal fashion, its future is limited to the analogy of what has come before.[19] The predetermined future is that of nonnormative outsiders being properly integrated into society when, and only when, they adopt normative values and behaviors. The future, then, for the vampires in the Sookie Stackhouse/*True Blood* series is one of "freedom" through liberal assimilation, in which progress is marked by the once primitive and promiscuous vampires slowly assuming the normative notions of the private sphere and "bourgeois respectability." Within a neoliberal rationality this is a fantasy of progress that not only promises a prescribed future in which freedom and liberation are marked by "privacy, intimacy, domesticity, marriage, and the unfettered ability 'to shop until you drop'" but that also masks the unpleasant reality that U.S. culture and institutions are founded on racism and white supremacy that is certainly not past.[20]

Beyond its supernaturalism the fantasy the series peddles is indeed gothic, but it is not gothic queer culture. Instead of emerging as a cultural expression of insidious trauma, the Sookie Stackhouse/*True Blood* series appropriates the rhetoric of gothic queer culture in the service of curtailing queerness. In this context gothicism (and I would argue the same for *Twilight* and most other popular twenty-first-century vampire narratives) works as a *tool* of insidious trauma by erasing and demonizing those who don't assimilate properly and casting all progress in relation to free-market values. Gothic queer culture has not disappeared, but it functions in the shadow of this flashy appropriation that, in many ways, is merely a contemporary return to eighteenth- and nineteenth-century Gothic fiction. This is a gothicism that sneaks past the senses of the liberal-minded in the guise of progress but that ultimately buttresses racist, heteropatriarchal, and neoliberal norms that continue to create intersectional and insidious trauma for queer folks.

There are myriad traumatic experiences that do not conform to the definitions of trauma that would validate them and that cannot be effectively represented by traditional historical or trauma narrative structures.

Maurice Stevens describes history as "haunted by stories that have gone unincluded in the realm of the historiography 'trauma narratives' require. History grows gaunt and distracted in its confrontation with events that test its ability to represent, and in its encounter with affect that won't stay still and is difficult to inscribe with any accuracy."[21] Echoing Sigmund Freud, Cathy Caruth once claimed, "the experience of a trauma repeats itself, exactly and unremittingly, through the unknowing acts of the survivor and against his very will" as "a human voice that cries out from the wound," but what happens when the experience of trauma actually occurs again and again through institutional and social structures that traumatize in ways that reach beyond the confines of the bounded "traumatic experience?"[22] What happens when even those who claim to study and treat trauma refuse to acknowledge insidious traumatic experience *as* trauma, thereby silencing and erasing it? What happens when the survivor has both survived and continues to experience daily insidious traumas, and what if they dive into traumatic "possession" not "against [their] very will" but with agency and intention? I have argued that the insidious manifestation of trauma occurs daily and accumulates, and, like bounded traumatic experience, it too drives narrativization and repeats itself through both unknowing and *knowing* acts. These acts often turn to gothicism as a means of expressing the unspeakable, because gothicism reveals a wound that won't close and that refuses to be healed, indeed cannot be healed, because it is continually ripped open by repeated and incessant traumatic recurrences.

Creative production is an inherent byproduct of trauma, and the productions covered in this project are all examples of the "frayed ends of incomplete narratives, hidden transcripts, dream images, and unruly sensations" emerging from the attempts to account for the open wounds of insidious trauma.[23] Gothic queer culture occupies that wound, its festering a testament to traumatic experiences that otherwise go invalidated and silenced. Gothic queer culture acknowledges the material realities and effects of violent marginalization and insidious trauma while developing a rich cultural aesthetic that challenges structures of oppression and that has the potential to continue the radical queer work of social transformation.

In queer culture's contemporary moment, the gothic emerges once again as a battleground where society can work through its anxieties, where the marginalized can reappropriate dehumanizing narratives used against them, and where the battle between queer resistance and LGBT assimilation rages on through a rhetoric of haunting, live burial, monstrosity, and sadomasochism. This book has focused on the way cultural productions addressing nonnormative genders and sexualities in the context of insidious trauma take shape as gothic queer culture—a mode of exploration that utilizes gothicism to both narrativize trauma and at times piece together the traumatically fragmented social narratives about queerness in new and subversive (though never finite or reparative) ways. This vision of ongoing, accumulated traumatic experience as an opportunity for restructuring a hegemonic society as one more egalitarian and inclusive may be taken up by some, but other cultural productions attempt to appropriate traumatic queer gothicism in ways that reestablish the pretrauma status quo, or they take the opportunity to piece together a new but less egalitarian society in which power is even more highly concentrated among the few. Regardless of the drive, it remains clear that insidious trauma opens up a battleground space, a location in which society struggles over the fantasies of queerness and hetero/homonor-mativity. If we recognize that a traumatically informed gothic aesthetic was and continues to be central to queer cultural production—critical theory, popular culture, literature, art, performance—it becomes clear that resistant and subversive queer culture is gothic at its core.

Preface

1. Jocelyn Vena, "Lady Gaga Meat Dress Designer Tells How to Re-create His VMA Look," MTV News, September 16, 2010, www.mtv.com/news /articles/1647978/lady-gaga-meat-dress-designer-tells-how-re-create-his -vma-look.jhtml.

2. Brett Zongker, "Lady Gaga Meat Dress Joins Museum Exhibit Featuring Rock n' Roll Relics," *Huffington Post*, September 6, 2012, www .huffingtonpost.ca/2012/09/06/lady-gaga-meat-dress-museum_n_1860235 .html. The meat dress became part of the permanent exhibit at the Rock and Roll Hall of Fame in 2015.

3. Anderson Cooper, "Lady Gaga's Meat Dress: Outfit with a Message?" CBS News, February 13, 2011, www.cbsnews.com/8301-18560_162-20031711.html.

4. Denise Winterman and Jon Kelly, "Five Interpretations of Lady Gaga's Meat Dress," BBC *News Magazine*, September 14, 2010, www.bbc.co.uk /news/magazine-11297832. This article, for example, offers several options for interpretation: an antifashion statement, a feminist statement, a commentary on aging and decay, a reflection on our hypocritical attitude to meat, or nothing at all.

5. Ingrid E. Newkirk, "Lady Gaga's Meat Dress," People for the Ethical Treatment of Animals, September 13, 2010, www.peta.org/blog/lady-gagas-meat-dress/.

6. Franc Fernandez, qtd. in Vena, "Meat Dress Designer."

7. Jun Francisco, "Does Lady Gaga's Meat Dress Smell? (And Everything Else You Wanted to Know about the Dress)," interview by Ivan Sheehan, Rock and Roll Hall of Fame, September 11, 2015, http://rockhall.com/blog /post/13456_lady-gagas-meat-dress-at-the-rock-hall/.

8. Ventzislavov, "Time Is Now," 62.

9. Jennex, "Diva Worship, 351.

10. Michael Musto, "The 12 Greatest Female Gay Icons of All Time," *OUT*, August 25, 2014, www.out.com/entertainment/michael-musto/2014/08 /25/12-greatest-female-gay-icons-all-time-also-nathan-matthew.

11. Jennex, "Diva Worship," 349, 350. In *How to Be Gay* Halperin explains that "Born This Way" "was a defiant defense of individual differences, particularly of stigmatized ones which 'left you outcast, bullied or teased,' and an implicit rebuke to biblically based homophobia, especially of the evangelical Christian variety, which holds homosexuality to be a sinful choice rather than a natural, or innate, condition" (115).

12. Weber, "Born This Way," 113.

13. Jennex, "Diva Worship," 352.

14. Edelman, *No Future*, 6–7, 35.

15. This is also the Gaga that Horn reads as adopting camp, a "decidedly queer and countercultural strategy" that uses irony and emotional distance to question the notion of the "natural." Gaga's version of camp parodies the "performativity and product-like status" of contemporary pop stars. Horn claims that Lady Gaga intentionally draws on queer camp tradition to "take advantage of this position as well-known pop icon to relativize dominant discourses" and cites Cho's determination that Lady Gaga makes it her "mission to foreground the artifice of her own performance." Similarly, Macfarlane argues that Gaga's iconic queer monstrosity challenges even the notion of citationality itself, instead creating her persona through a "series of uncannily familiar but citationless references"—a nod to the citationless circulation of texts on the internet (128). Halberstam, too, theorizes on the potential of Lady Gaga's outrageous approach to identity, gender, and sexuality. He proposes a new form of feminism, "Gaga feminism," inspired by Gaga and involving an embrace of "the phony, the unreal, the specula-

tive . . . a celebration of the joining of femininity to artifice" (xii–xiii). Horn, "Camping with the Stars"; Cho, "Lady Gaga, Balls-Out"; Macfarlane, "Monstrous House of Gaga"; Halberstam, *Gaga Feminism*.

16. The Supreme Course decision, of course, followed decades of LBGT activism. Lady Gaga's brief but flashy contribution to the cause should not receive credit for this milestone.

17. Huba's study, *Monster Loyalty*, breaks down Gaga's career moves into a series of business strategies (with worksheets!) for those aspiring to build their own successful commercial brand, including chapters on leading with values, building community, giving your fans a name, embracing shared symbols, making them feel like rock stars, and generating buzz.

18. Halperin, *How to Be Gay*, 112.

Introduction

1. Walpole, *Castle of Otranto*, 106.
2. Haggerty, *Queer Gothic*, 25.
3. For examinations of Horace Walpole's queerness, see Haggerty, "Queering Horace Walpole"; and Mowl, *Horace Walpole*.
4. Kilgour, *Gothic Novel*, 11.
5. Halberstam, *Skin Shows*, 2.
6. Herman, *Trauma and Recovery*, 34–35; Stevens, "Trauma," 27, 29.
7. L. Brown, "Not Outside the Range," 107.
8. In *Literary Women* Moers used the term "Female Gothic" in 1976 to describe Gothic fiction written by women and the influence that their gendered experiences had on the content of the writing.
9. Haggerty, *Queer Gothic*.
10. Kilgour, *Gothic Novel*, 4.
11. Haggerty, *Gothic Fiction/Gothic Form*, 7–8; Sedgwick, *Coherence of Gothic Conventions*, 6.
12. Haggerty, *Gothic Fiction/Gothic Form*, 10.
13. Kilgour, *Gothic Novel*, 6.
14. Botting and Townshend, *Gothic*, 3, 6.
15. Watt, "Time and Family." Kilgour also emphasizes that the Gothic developed as "part of the reaction against the political, social, scientific, indus-

trial, and epistemological revolutions of the seventeenth and eighteenth centuries which enabled the rise of the middle class" (*Gothic Novel*, 10–11).

16. Auerbach, *Our Vampires, Ourselves.*
17. Sedgwick, *Coherence of Gothic Conventions*, ix.
18. Kilgour, *Gothic Novel*, 8.
19. Fincher, *Queering Gothic*, 4.
20. Sedgwick, *Tendencies*, 7.
21. Haggerty, *Queer Gothic*, 2.
22. Palmer's *The Queer Uncanny* rests on the foundational claim that the uncanny is always queer. Haggerty argues that the indeterminacy of meaning in the Gothic results from its "uncanny structure" or the ubiquitous "shadow-presence of the real" and the "distortions of the symbolic" (*Queer Gothic*, 9). In other words, the repeated themes, the multiplicity of interpretations, and often the apparent critical failure of Gothic literature lies in its obsession with, what Žižek terms, the "Real," or the traumatic "kernel" that defies symbolization (*Sublime Object of Ideology*, 6). This leads Gothic writers to perform a compulsive revisiting of cultural "primal scenes" that are invariably queer, creating a genre of literature that offers a compelling discourse on sexuality that both predates Freud and deserves a place in contemporary versions of the history of sexuality (Haggerty, *Queer Gothic*, 9).
23. Lloyd-Smith, *American Gothic Fiction*, 4.
24. Poe, *Selected Writings.*
25. Auerbach and Dyer straddle the gothic–queer theory divide with their work highlighting implied sexual and gender transgression in vampire fiction. Dyer's "It's in His Kiss" offers insights into the reciprocal relationship between gothicism and queerness, and Auerbach's "Grave and Gay" explores the queer uses of vampirism during the AIDS crisis, for example. Sedgwick's *Between Men* serves as a bridge between her early Gothic literary criticism, *The Coherence of Gothic Conventions*, and her later fame as queer theory scholar. In *Between Men* Sedgwick illustrates the concepts of homosocial desire, triangulation, and homosexual panic through readings of English culture, "chiefly as embodied in the mid-eighteenth- to mid-nineteenth-century novel" (1). While not all the literary texts she uses are

strictly Gothic, she devotes two chapters to Gothic literature because "the Gothic was the first novelistic form in England to have close, relatively visible links to male homosexuality" (91). In the introduction to the 1986 reissue of *The Coherence of Gothic Conventions*, Sedgwick inserts a queer reading to the text's predominantly literary focus by drawing a parallel between the themes of British Gothic fiction and media coverage of the AIDS crisis: "The current discourse of AIDS in the United States . . . confronts the reader of the Gothic with an uncircumnavigable familiarity, made only the more paralyzing by the 'bizarreness' of the nightmare-intimate shocks dealt by every morning's newspaper" (xii). This move recursively links Sedgwick's thinking around queerness with her work on the Gothic, illustrating that her later queer theory is inextricable from its Gothic roots. Halberstam, another queer theory scholar, began his career with *Skin Shows*, a text that traces gothicism from nineteenth-century Gothic texts such as *Frankenstein* and *Dracula* through twentieth-century horror films such as *The Texas Chainsaw Massacre* and *Silence of the Lambs*.

26. See, for example, Massé, *Name of Love*; Haggerty, *Queer Gothic*; Fincher, *Queering Gothic*; Hughes and Smith, *Queering the Gothic*; and Marshall, *Romanticism, Gender, and Violence*.

27. As I explore in chapter 1, the gothicism in queer theory is not relegated to the 1990s but continues to thread through queer theory in its contemporary permutations. For example, Lorenz's *Queer Art* turns to the figure of "the freak," those who embodied monstrous difference in historical freak shows and exhibitions, to propose a theory that queers art production and reception. Notably, trauma is central to the gothicism of Lorenz's queer theory in the "violent histories of exclusion, exposure, staring, and differentiating" that bolstered the popularity of freak shows (26).

28. Russo, *Celluloid Closet*.

29. Dyer, *Culture of Queers*, 70. Hughes and Smith reinforce Dyer's observation, noting that in addition to Gothic fiction's attention to "taboo issues—such as sexual deviance, arbitrary power, miscegenation and apostasy," there is a "literal queerness—in the popular, sexual, sense of the term—about many of the authors conventionally regarded as being central to the development of the Gothic" (*Queering the Gothic*, 1, 2).

30. Sue, *Microaggressions in Everyday Life*, xv; Nadal, *That's So Gay*, 7, 27; Lorde, "Age," 116.

31. Root, "Reconstructing the Impact of Trauma"; L. Brown, "Not Outside the Range," 100. According to the American Psychiatric Association's *Diagnostic and Statistical Manual* (3-R, 1987), a traumatic event must be "outside the range of human experience" to potentially cause post-traumatic stress disorder. Brown acknowledges in her epilogue that in the DSM 4 (1994) the APA updated the PTSD definition to focus instead on "the person's subjective perceptions of fear, threat, and risk to well-being" (111). Regardless of this revision, as well as the more recent revisions in the DSM 5 (2013), Brown's argument regarding the marginalizing assumptions of normalcy remains valid.

32. L. Brown, "Not Outside the Range," 101. Though Brown does not cite Lorde, this definition certainly depends on Lorde's theorization of the "mythical norm" (Lorde, "Age," 116).

33. L. Brown, "Not Outside the Range," 106.

34. Caruth, introduction to *American Imago*, 3; Caruth, *Unclaimed Experience*, 4. Though contemporary trauma theorists like Stef Craps, Irene Visser, Roger Luckhurst, and Michael Rothberg highlight the limitations of Caruth's event-based trauma theory and its "Eurocentric bias," the ghostly metaphors describing traumatic experience persist in contemporary trauma theory. Craps, *Postcolonial Witnessing*, 4. See also Visser, "Decolonizing Trauma Theory"; Luckhurst, *Trauma Question*; and Rothberg, "Decolonizing Trauma Studies."

35. Luckhurst, *Trauma Question*, 81, 98.

36. Schwab, *Haunting Legacies*, 1.

37. In their 2016 collection, *Critical Trauma Studies*, Casper and Wertheimer succinctly trace the development of trauma studies as a field of medical, psychological, and cultural inquiry. Beginning with nineteenth-century investigations of the psychiatric and biological impact of traumatic events such as train accidents, war, and natural disaster, trauma studies shifted in the late twentieth century to bring the "study of trauma firmly within the purview of the humanities and social sciences, recognizing and naming 'trauma' not only as a condition of broken bodies and shattered minds,

but also and primarily as a cultural object" (3). Freud's musings (primarily in *Beyond the Pleasure Principle* and *Moses and Monotheism*) on train accidents, war neuroses, and the "repetition compulsion" that follows such traumatic experiences serve as the basis of most early theories on trauma. Critical and postcolonial trauma studies, however, have largely shifted focus away from this psychoanalytic approach.

38. Casper and Wertheimer call for a critical trauma studies invested in an "ethics of intellectual *and* moral engagement" and that interrogates the "political and cultural work that 'trauma' does" (*Critical Trauma Studies*, 5).

39. Stevens, "Trauma," 20.

40. Stevens, "Trauma," 21, 20–21.

41. Perhaps, in this examination, the book itself falls under the first instance Stevens proposes—an attempt to "beat back the loathing" by creating histories that feature those memories ghosted in the popular imagination ("Trauma," 20–21).

42. Caruth, *Trauma*, 7; Luckhurst, *Trauma Question*, 5.

43. Freud first identifies this as a "repetition compulsion," and Felman and Laub develop an extended theory in *Testimony*. As Visser succinctly points out, Caruth's formulation of trauma implies that trauma narratives therefore lead to "increased indeterminacy," whereas Herman's approach casts trauma narratives as therapeutic, "enabling psychic integration and eventual resolution of trauma" (Visser, "Decolonizing Trauma Theory," 256). In *The Unsayable* Rogers, a clinical psychologist, explores this linguistic, communicative disruption resulting from traumatic experience and reiterates the survivor's paradoxical need to testify and failure to satisfyingly do so. She explains her clinical experience with survivors of childhood sexual abuse, the link between the physical and mental wounds they suffered and continue to suffer through treatment, and their inability to put their experience into language: "I saw what is so terrible about trauma is not abuse itself, no matter the brutality of treatment, but the way terror marks the body and then becomes invisible and inarticulate" (44).

44. Visser, "Decolonizing Trauma Theory"; Kaplan, *Trauma Culture*, 19; McCormack, *Queer Postcolonial Narratives*, 3.

45. Halberstam, *Queer Art of Failure*, 2, 15; Berlant and Edelman, *Sex*, vii–viii, xiv.
46. Kilgour, *Gothic Novel*, 31.
47. Luckhurst, *Trauma Question*, 81.
48. Freccero's *Queer/Early/Modern*.
49. Nadel, *Containment Culture*.
50. Forrest, *Lesbian Pulp Fiction*, x.
51. Bannon, *Odd Girl Out*; Bannon, *I Am a Woman*; Bannon, *Women in the Shadows*; Bannon, *Journey to a Woman*; Bannon, *Beebo Brinker*.
52. Shelley, *Frankenstein*, 53.
53. Kilgour, *From Communion to Cannibalism*, 4.

1. Haunted Epistemologies

1. Hall, *Well of Loneliness*, 505–6. This passage appears in Love's *Feeling Backward*, Ahmed's *Promise of Happiness*, and Castle's *Apparitional Lesbian*, to name a few. References to the novel in general appear throughout LGBTQ+ studies. For example, in *Second Skins* Prosser points to *Well of Loneliness* not only as a lesbian novel but as a touchstone in trans* studies.
2. Luckhurst explains that "trauma psychology frequently resorts to the Gothic or supernatural to articulate post-traumatic effects" (*Trauma Question*, 98).
3. L. Brown, "Not Outside the Range," 107.
4. Sedgwick, *Tendencies*, 1.
5. Halberstam, *Skin Shows*, 29.
6. In *Queer Gothic* Haggerty notes, "Freud relied on gothic writing to help him articulate his notions of uncanny and various delusional behaviors" (5). See Freud, "Psychoanalytic Notes."
7. Freud, "Psychoanalytic Notes," 135–36.
8. Freud, "Psychoanalytic Notes," 89, 94–95, 100. The use of the word *intercourse* here explicitly refers not to sexual intercourse but to any means of interaction and communication between God and humans. The choice of a word that also evokes sexuality is not coincidental in a text that theorizes repressed homosexual desires and that also speaks overtly of Schreber's explicit references to sexual intercourse with God.

9. Clery, *Rise of Supernatural Fiction*, 108. This definition comes from "Fatal Revenge," Walter Scott's 1810 critique of Radcliffe and her followers (predominately women), who were known for instances of the explained supernatural in their fiction. Radcliffe is perhaps best known for this device. For example, Emily, from *The Mysteries of Udolpho*, stumbles on a rotting corpse hidden behind a veil only to learn that it was, in fact, a wax effigy, and the mysterious ghostly noises plaguing a chateau turn out to be outlaws trying to scare people away from the dwelling.
10. Freud, "Psychoanalytic Notes," 111n2, 111, 123, 101, 131.
11. Fincher describes this formal characteristic of Gothic fiction as "Chinese-box narrative structures" and "multiple narrators and interrupted stories," explaining that these structures "invite a circuitous reading attitude" (*Queering Gothic*, 4).
12. Freud, "Psychoanalytic Notes," 101.
13. Maturin, *Melmoth the Wanderer*; Lewis, *Monk*; Shelley, *Frankenstein*.
14. J. Gordon, "Narrative Enclosure," 57. Gordon explores at length this correlation between Gothic architectural structures and embedded Gothic narratives in Walpole's *Castle of Otranto*, William Godwin's *Adventures of Caleb Williams*, Stoker's *Dracula*, Maturin's *Melmoth the Wanderer*, Lewis's *Monk*, Radcliffe's *Mysteries of Udolpho*, Jane Austen's *Northanger Abbey*, Hogg's *Justified Sinner*, Anne Brontë's, *Tenant of Wildfell Hall*, and Emily Brontë's *Wuthering Heights*.
15. J. Gordon, "Narrative Enclosure," 59.
16. Sedgwick, *Between Men*, 116. She also returns to the concept of the paranoid Gothic in *Epistemology of the Closet*: using the relationship between Victor Frankenstein and his creature, Sedgwick puts Frankenstein in conversation with Freud's "Psychoanalytic Notes" to show that the "paranoid Gothic powerfully signified, at the very moment of crystallization of the modern, capitalism-marked oedipal family, the homosocial constitution," meaning that Freud's text has "everything to do with the foregrounding, under the specific foundational historic conditions of the early Gothic, of intense male homosocial desire as at once the most compulsory and the most prohibited of social bonds" (187).

17. Freud, "Psychoanalytic Notes," 88.
18. Eng, *Feeling of Kinship*, 56, 55.
19. Freud, "Psychoanalytic Notes," 147.
20. Trauma theorists describe the shattering, or fracturing, that occurs both during a traumatic event and after. Survivors often describe a separation from the body or an ability to see the scene from a third-person perspective during a severe trauma. Post-traumatic reactions are often characterized by a temporal fracturing as well as the inability to reconstruct a unified narrative of the event. See, for example, Herman's *Trauma and Recovery*.
21. Sedgwick, "Paranoid Reading."
22. Sedgwick writes, "As I pointed out in a 1986 essay . . . 'The gorgeous narrative work done by the Foucauldian paranoid, transforming the simultaneous chaoses of institutions into a consecutive, drop-dead-elegant diagram of spiraling escapes and recaptures, is also the paranoid subject's proffer of himself and his cognitive talent, now ready for anything *it* can present in the way of blandishment or violence, to an order-of-things *morcelé* that had until then lacked *only* narratibility, a body, cognition' (*Coherence* xi)" (Sedgwick, "Paranoid Reading," 131–32).
23. Sedgwick, "Paranoid Reading," 126.
24. Sedgwick, "Paranoid Reading," 146–48.
25. The concept of straight temporality versus queer temporalities has been picked up by queer theorists again and again, often utilizing the gothic language of haunting or sadomasochism.
26. Sedgwick, "Paranoid Reading," 149, 151.
27. Shelley, *Frankenstein*, 53.
28. J. Butler, *Precarious Life*.
29. Shelley, *Frankenstein*, 177.
30. Foucault, *Abnormal*, 63, 60, 67, 74–75.
31. Foucault, *Herculine Barbin*, 140. The doctors' goal was to demonstrate that this "monstrous" physicality could be known, named, and contained through developing notions of "true sex" as a medically diagnosable identity determined by a combination of physical characteristics and sexual desires. Foucault explains that society once believed that intersex

individuals simply had two sexes. A paternal figure determined which gender they would function as until they became marriageable, and then they could decide whether to remain their assigned gender or switch, giving them a certain degree of agency. During the nineteenth century the practice changed so that a medical authority conducted an investigation and assigned a gender based on the "true sex" that existed beneath the ambiguous physicality, assuming that it merely had to be discovered and documented.

32. Foucault, *Herculine Barbin*, xii–xiii.

33. Indeed, monstrous terms such as "chimera" creep into Foucault's description of contemporary perceptions of "sexual irregularity" (*Herculine Barbin*, x).

34. Foucault, *Herculine Barbin*, xiii–xiv.

35. Puar and Rai, "Monster, Terrorist, Fag," 117, 119.

36. Puar, *Terrorist Assemblages*, 37.

37. Mbembe, "Necropolitics," 40.

38. Puar, *Terrorist Assemblages*, 35.

39. Haritaworn, Kuntsman, and Posocco argue that "since it helps us make sense of the symbiotic co-presence of life and death, manifested ever more clearly in the cleavages between rich and poor, citizens and non-citizens (and those who can be stripped of citizenship at any moment); the culturally, morally, economically valuable and the pathological; queer subjects invited into life and queerly abjected populations marked for death" (*Queer Necropolitics*, 20). Snorton and Haritaworn extend this frame to focus specifically on transgender people of color in a transnational context (see "Trans Necropolitics").

40. Edelman, *No Future*, 2, 11, 38.

41. Cohen, "Monster Culture," 12.

42. Edelman, *No Future*, 48, 35. Edelman puns mercilessly throughout *No Future*, another gothic element of the text. Jack Halberstam identifies punning as a specifically gothic narrative device "employed repeatedly within both nineteenth-century Gothic novels and twentieth-century Gothic cinema" to provide some "light (very light) relief to the dark dramas of blood and mutilation" (*Skin Shows*, 178) According to Hal-

berstam, punning has an economy of meaning—a single word may have multiple interpretive possibilities—and as a result the punned sentence embodies an excess of meaning and often causes meanings to slip into their opposite, making "mincemeat out of any notion of binaries." He adds that "puns posit a surface relation but absolutely eschew a depth relation" (179, 180). Edelman's punning can be read as a gothic play of surfaces whose function is epistemological disruption. Like the undead and *sinthom*osexual, Edelman's linguistic playfulness challenges meaning by drawing attention to the surface, or the words on the page, and foregrounds the pleasure of his indulgence in the written word. The gothic punning embodies the primacy of pleasure in the present, in the surface, while drawing attention to the fantasy that words can ever avoid slippage. Edelman's words are designed to slip into one another, refusing "the Symbolic logic that determines the exchange of signifiers" and serving as the site where "meaning comes undone"—a perfect description of the sinthome itself but also making the text formally gothic (*No Future*, 35).

43. Edelman, *No Future*, 142.
44. Stryker, "My Words," 243. I use "trans*" with an asterisk to "to open up transgender or trans to a greater range of meanings." Tompkins, "Asterisk," 26.
45. Stryker, "My Words," 238, 40.
46. Koch-Rein, "Monster," 135.
47. Halberstam, *Queer Time and Place*, 97.
48. SymbioticA, qtd. in Halberstam, *Queer Time and Place*, 113.
49. Halberstam, *Queer Time and Place*, 110, 113.
50. Halberstam, *Queer Time and Place*, 114, 116, 115.
51. For example, references to A. Gordon's *Ghostly Matters* and Derrida's hauntology appear in Halberstam's *Queer Art of Failure*; Freeman's *Time Binds*; Freccero's *Queer/Early/Modern*; and Puar's *Terrorist Assemblages*, to name a few.
52. Derrida, *Specters of Marx*, xviii; A. Gordon, *Ghostly Matters*, xvi; Ferreday and Kuntsman, "Haunted Futurities," 2 (emphasis mine).
53. Willey's *Undoing Monogamy* also includes epigraphs from Haraway's "Promises of Monsters" and Puar's *Terrorist Assemblages*.
54. Castle, *Apparitional Lesbian*, 63.

55. Haggerty, *Queer Gothic*, 2.
56. Haggerty, *Queer Gothic*, 22.
57. Bersani, *Freudian Body*, 41.
58. O'Higgins and Foucault, "Sexual Choice, Sexual Act," 20, 21.
59. Foucault, "Sex, Power, and the Politics of Identity," 169.
60. Deleuze's argument—that the torturer in the masochistic situation "cannot be sadistic precisely because she is *in* the masochistic situation, she is an integral part of it, a realization of the masochistic fantasy"—reinforces the unlikely dominance that the masochist holds in the masochistic scene, even when being dominated by another. Deleuze, *Coldness and Cruelty*, 41.
61. Bersani, "Shame on You," 93, 99, 102, 103, 99.
62. Dean, *Unlimited Intimacy*, 10, 57, 51.
63. Dean, *Unlimited Intimacy*, 88, 143.
64. Freeman, *Time Binds*, 98.
65. Freeman, *Time Binds*, 137, 168, 145, 162. She later compares this reanimation to *Frankenstein*, since "the dead come back to life as and through layers of skin; here, leather serves as a doubling of black skin and binds contemporary Afro-British and African American subjects to their enslaved (or even slave-trading) ancestors" (165).
66. Freccero, *Queer/Early/Modern*.
67. Freccero, *Queer/Early/Modern*, 75, 99.
68. Freccero, *Queer/Early/Modern*, 104, qtd. in Freeman, *Time Binds*, 147.
69. Freccero, *Queer/Early/Modern*, 76.
70. Tongson, *Relocations*, 212, 210, 212.
71. Tongson, *Relocations*, 212, 160, 213, 211.
72. Tongson, *Relocations*, 213.
73. Halberstam, *Queer Art of Failure*, 2–3, 15, 2.
74. Utopian queer theorists, though arguably oppositional to both antirelationality and negativity more broadly, are not immune to the infusion of gothicism. In *Cruising Utopia* Muñoz advocates for the disruption of "any ossified understanding of the human" in a turn away from the properly human to the monstrous and the undead (26). In *Disidentifications* he advocates for an adoption of melancholia, since it disrupts temporality with an eye to the "decay of the present." Here Muñoz deploys gothic lan-

guage to recognize death and decay while queering temporality in ways later echoed by Freeman's treatment of sadomasochistic temporality (52).

75. Love, *Feeling Backward*, 1, 21.

76. Freud, *Beyond the Pleasure Principle*.

77. Rigby, "Uncanny Recognition."

2. Live Burial

1. Highsmith, *Price of Salt*. This is the novel on which the 2015 movie *Carol* is based.

2. Haut, *Pulp Culture*, 6.

3. Stryker, *Queer Pulp*, 7–8. Like Stryker, I use *queer* in this chapter to broadly denote those with nonnormative gender or sexuality, not in the sense of later political movements that have adopted *queer* as a political orientation that pushes against assimilative politics.

4. Stryker, *Queer Pulp*, 8.

5. For a curated collection of gay male pulp, see Bronski, *Pulp Friction*.

6. Gunn and Harker, *1960s Gay Pulp Fiction*, 19.

7. Stryker, *Queer Pulp*, 12.

8. L. Brown, "Not Outside the Range," 107. See this book's introduction for a more in-depth exploration of insidious trauma.

9. In Lewis's Gothic novel *The Monk*, Ambrosio and the Prioress famously utilize the crypt as a means of containment and control; when their victims are imprisoned within those subterranean passages, the villains can find them, study them, and act on them as they please. Radcliffe, too, frequently features the convent, an isolated space with its own winding passages and crypts, as a location of imprisonment and surveillance. See, for example, Radcliffe's *Mysteries of Udolpho* and *The Italian*.

10. Nadel, *Containment Culture*, 4.

11. Kennan, "Sources of Soviet Conduct," 575.

12. Nadel, *Containment Culture*, 17, 2–3, 14, 24.

13. Nadel, *Containment Culture*, 117.

14. Lorde, who grew up in the United States during the era of McCarthyism, would later name this privileged identity intersection the "mythic

norm": "white, thin, male, young, heterosexual, christian, and financially secure" ("Age," 116).

15. Forrest, *Lesbian Pulp Fiction*, x.
16. Keller, "Her Brother's Wife," 402.
17. Zimet, *Strange Sisters*, 83.
18. Zimet features these examples and other medicalized cover copy in the chapter "Psycho-Babble," in *Strange Sisters*, 83–89.
19. Haut, *Pulp Culture*, 5.
20. In *Odd Girls* Faderman explains that the words *twilight* and *odd* specifically signal lesbian content by representing the shame and self-hatred that lesbian characters display in pulp novels. "Lesbians," however, "could ignore their homophobic propaganda and moralizations and peruse the pulps for their romance and charged eroticism" (147). In *The Apparitional Lesbian* Castle claims that "a subterranean 'lesbian' meaning may be present in *odd* and its derivatives—I would argue—as early as 1755" (9n).
21. Aldrich, *We Walk Alone*; Dumont, *I Prefer Girls*; Holk, *Strange Friends*.
22. Kilgour, *Gothic Novel*, 8.
23. Taylor, *Stranger on Lesbos*; Lucchesi, *Strange Breed*; Stryker, *Queer Pulp*, 36.
24. Corber, "All about the Subversive Femme." Corber explains that there was a fear of "invisibility" that facilitated infiltration and linked "gays and lesbians to the communists and fellow travelers who were supposedly conspiring to overthrow the nation, a link that encouraged the view that gender and sexual nonconformity were un-American" (37).
25. The notion of the "lesbian sicko" came into public consciousness most strongly during World War II and the years following. See Faderman, *Odd Girls*.
26. Said, *Orientalism*; Kennan, "Sources of Soviet Conduct," 574; Nadel, *Containment Culture*, 32.
27. Stryker, *Queer Pulp*, 64.
28. Belletto and Grausam, *American Literature and Culture*, 167 (emphasis mine).

29. Adlon, *One Between*; Emery, *Queer Affair*; Priest, *Forbidden*.
30. Carr, *Unnatural Wife*.
31. Modleski, *Loving with a Vengeance*, 71.
32. Saglia, "Material-Discursive Orient," 79.
33. Said, *Orientalism*, 4.
34. The concept of a "third sex" has Orientalist implications as well. Lee argues that, beginning in the nineteenth century, the Oriental figure functioned in the United States as a third sex—"ambiguous, inscrutable, hermaphroditic"—representing sexual possibility (*Orientals*, 85). The model-minority myth later developed to cast Asian Americans as an idealized "third" race (not white but also not black), characterized by political silence and cultural assimilation in contrast to the perceived militancy of African American politics. This shift from third sex to third race maintains the Oriental's position in the popular imagination as a potentially threatening, yet controllable, other—a narrative "through which America's anxieties about communism, race mixing, and transgressive sexuality might be contained and eventually tamed" (146). The language of the third sex on pulp covers is yet another Orientalizing gesture that signals transgression but ultimately controls it, while simultaneously distancing itself from the racial tension ramping up around African American civil rights.
35. Westad, *Global Cold War*, 2.
36. Ellis, *Third Street*.
37. Faderman, *Odd Girls*, 161, 158.
38. Stryker, *Queer Pulp*, 61.
39. Packer, *Spring Fire*, vi, vii, ix.
40. Packer, *Spring Fire*, ix.
41. Zimet reviews lesbian pulp covers thematically in *Strange Sisters*, with entire sections devoted to sorority, dormitory, and prison novels.
42. Bannon's official website lists these five novels as the Beebo Brinker Chronicles; however, some scholars note that Bannon published a sixth novel, *The Marriage* (1960), that was originally part of the series. Carter explains that *The Marriage*, the story of a marriage of convenience between a lesbian and a gay man, was dropped from the chronicles when

Cleis Press reprinted them in 1983, stating that it was "not of interest to lesbians" in the context of the lesbian-feminist culture of the 1980s ("Gay Marriage," 585).

43. Though *The Well of Loneliness* was originally published in 1928, it was reprinted as a pulp novel by Perma Books in 1951, 1955, and 1960, once publishers realized the market appeal of novels with lesbian content.

44. Bannon, introduction to Bannon, *Odd Girl Out*, x.

45. In twentieth-century U.S. literature gothicism in tales with queer undercurrents is not uncommon. For example, Hellman's dark play *The Children's Hour*, originally produced in 1934 and revived in 1952, controversially addressed lesbianism in the context of a residential girl's school. Later Jackson published *The Haunting of Hill House* in 1959, a gothic tale of lesbian obsession. *The Talented Mr. Ripley* by Highsmith, published in 1955, is also a gothic vehicle for queer sexuality, although more gay male oriented. With this in mind, it is important to note that gothicism, or what Palmer identifies specifically as "lesbian gothic," already existed as a trope for tales of transgressive sexuality by the time Bannon entered the literary scene; however, one can see that Bannon's particular lesbian gothic is inflected by the containment conversation of its moment. It emerges as a gothicism that specifically redeploys the tropes of paranoid victimization and confined spaces—a lesbian gothic that is, perhaps, so iconic because of its timely participation in containment discourse. See Palmer, *Lesbian Gothic*.

46. Gay and lesbian bars feature prominently in LGBT literary classics such as Hall's *Well of Loneliness*, Baldwin's *Giovanni's Room*, and Feinberg's *Stone Butch Blues*. Because the bar scene was often the only option for lesbian-community formation (with an often distinctly working-class clientele), Daughters of Bilitis was formed as a "private social group to give middle-class lesbians an alternative to the gay bar scene" (Faderman, *Odd Girls*, 149).

47. Faderman, *Odd Girls*, 162, 167, 161.

48. Bannon, *Beebo Brinker*, 39, 41.

49. Kristeva, *Powers of Horror*, 1.

50. Bannon, *Beebo Brinker*, 41, 42.

51. Bannon, *Beebo Brinker*, 63, 64.

52. Carter, "Gay Marriage," 594. Carter sources these figures from Israel, *Bachelor Girl*, 187; and Coontz, *Marriage*, 226.

53. Bannon, *I Am a Woman*, 32, 33.

54. Belletto and Grausam, *American Literature and Culture*, 168.

55. Bannon, *I Am a Woman*, 34.

56. Bannon, *I Am a Woman*, 7, 11.

57. Bannon, *I Am a Woman*, 4.

58. Isabella is initially engaged to be married to young Conrad, but he is killed by the giant helmet. In a semi-incestuous turn, Conrad's father Manfred decides to marry Isabella himself, setting off the erotically charged pursuit that occurs in the dark passages underneath the crumbling estate.

59. Haggerty, *Queer Gothic*, 22.

60. Bannon, *I Am a Woman*, 168.

61. Bannon, *I Am a Woman*, 166, 208.

62. Bannon, *Women in the Shadows*, 105.

63. Carter depends on Muñoz's theory of "disidentification," a form of "critical recycling" of dominant ideologies about identity in which minority subjects neither adopt dominant frameworks nor fully resist them but instead use them to construct new sites of identification. Carter, "Gay Marriage"; Muñoz, *Disidentifications*.

3. Monstrosity

1. Therese Frare, photograph of David Kirby, *Life*, November 1, 1990.

2. Joe Morgan, "Survivors of 1980s AIDS Crisis Reveal What Happened to Them," *Gay Star News*, February 2, 2015, www.gaystarnews.com/article /survivors-1980s-aids-crisis-reveal-what-happened-them020215/.

3. Edmund White, qtd. in Elizabeth Landau, "HIV in the '80s: 'People Didn't Want to Kiss You on the Cheek,'" CNN, May 25, 2011, www.cnn.com/2011 /HEALTH/05/25/edmund.white.hiv.aids/index.html.

4. Evan Thomas, Cathy Booth, and Michael G. Riley, "The New Untouchables: Anxiety over AIDS Is Verging on Hysteria in Some Parts of the Country," *Time*, September 23, 1985, http://content.time.com/time /magazine/article/0,9171,959944,00.html.

5. Shelley, *Frankenstein*, 96.
6. L. Brown, "Not Outside the Range," 107.
7. *Post-AIDS* is a contested term since to many it implies that HIV is no longer a global threat, which is certainly not the case. In *Dry Bones Breathe* Rofes conceptualizes "post-AIDS" as an era in which "AIDS is not seen as the central, overarching trauma visited on gay communities." He goes on to note that the term "claims that the communal experience of AIDS-as-crisis has ended, but does not imply that the epidemic of AIDS is over" (75).
8. Cohen, "Monster Culture," 6; Halberstam, *Skin Shows*, 29.
9. Cohen outlines seven characteristics of the monster as cultural theory: "Thesis I: The Monster's Body Is a Cultural Body"; "Thesis II: The Monster Always Escapes"; "Thesis III: The Monster Is the Harbinger of Category Crisis"; "Thesis IV: The Monster Dwells at the Gates of Difference"; "Thesis V: The Monster Polices the Borders of the Possible"; "Thesis VI: Fear of the Monster Is Really a Kind of Desire"; "Thesis VII: The Monster Stands at the Threshold . . . of Becoming" ("Monster Culture," 3–25). Halberstam's definition of the Gothic monster provides the foundation for Cohen's later classification, explaining that monsters have served as a "screen" on which cultural anxieties are projected, allowing "for a whole range of specific monstrosities to coalesce in the same form" (*Skin Shows*, 29).
10. Shelley, *Frankenstein*, 53.
11. Halberstam, *Skin Shows*, 29.
12. Like Cohen's seven characteristics of the monster, E. Butler lists four defining principles of the vampire: "first, the vampire is neither wholly dead nor entirely alive"; "second, the vampire goes about its work by expropriating and redistributing energy"; "third, when vampires draw life from their victims, they infuse them with death and make the living resemble them"; and "fourth . . . the vampire defies the boundaries of space and time, and it seeks to spread terror actively" (*Metamorphoses of the Vampire*, 11).
13. Kilgour, *From Communion to Cannibalism*, 4, 6.
14. Berglund, *Cannibal Fictions*, 19 (emphasis mine).
15. E. Butler explains that "all vampires share one trait: the power to move between and undo borders otherwise holding identities in place. At this

monster's core lies an affinity for rupture, change, and mutation. Because of its inimical relationship to stability, tradition, and order, the vampire embodies the transformative march of history" (*Metamorphoses of the Vampire*, 1).

16. Kilgour, *From Communion to Cannibalism*, 226.

17. Cohen, "Monster Culture," 6.

18. See Pérez-Torres, *Mestizaje*; Allatson, "My Bones Shine"; Mullins, "Subjects of Rights"; and Minich, "Reading Gil Cuadros."

19. In *How to Be Gay* David M. Halperin attributes "gay culture's apparent decline" directly to the AIDS epidemic as one of the three contributing factors to increasing homonormative assimilation. These three structural causes include "the recapitalization of the inner city and the resulting gentrification of urban neighborhoods; the epidemic of HIV/AIDS; and the invention of the Internet" (433). For neoliberalism's impact on queer communities, see Warner, *Trouble with Normal*; Duggan, *Twilight of Equality*; and Eng, *Feeling of Kinship*.

20. Both Camacho's *Migrant Imaginaries* and Viego's *Dead Subjects* address the relevance of melancholia as a strategy for approaching Latinx history and identity.

21. Halberstam, *Skin Shows*, 2.

22. For an overview of the genre of AIDS literature more generally, see O'Connell, "Big One"; and Pearl, *AIDS Literature*. For early anthologies, see Murphy and Poirer, *Writing AIDS*; Pastore, *Confronting AIDS through Literature*; Osborn, *Way We Live Now*; and Miller, *Fluid Exchanges*. For more recent anthologies, see Ellis and Hunter, *Spaces between Us*; Rasebotsa, Samuelson, and Thomas, *Nobody Ever Said AIDS*; and Horton, Hunter, and Thompson, *Fingernails across the Chalkboard*. A piece by Cuadros appears in Wolverton, *Blood Whispers*.

23. Watney, *Policing Desire*, 23. The idea that homosexuality itself is a kind of contagion or seduction was not invented during the AIDS crisis. In *Three Essays* Freud famously posits that sexual perversion may develop through initiation or contact with others.

24. Helms, qtd. in Crimp, "How to Have Promiscuity in an Epidemic," 261–62.

25. Watney, *Policing Desire*, 10.

26. Crimp, *Melancholia and Moralism*, 47.

27. Navarro, "Eso, me está pasando," 317–19.

28. Guzmán, "Between Action and Abstraction," 308.

29. Friedman et al., "AIDS Epidemic," 458.

30. Cuadros, *City of God*, 61, 66, 62, 67, 65, 66.

31. Dean, *Unlimited Intimacy*.

32. Cuadros, *City of God*, 69.

33. Kristeva, *Powers of Horror*, 1.

34. Cuadros, *City of God*, 3, 7.

35. Cuadros, *City of God*, 7, 13.

36. Cuadros, *City of God*, 13–14.

37. Cuadros, *City of God*, 37–38, 87.

38. Cuadros, *City of God*, 42, 43, 44.

39. Bersani, *Freudian Body*, 41, 38.

40. Bataille, "The Practice of Joy before Death," 236, 237, 239.

41. Freud, "Mourning and Melancholia," 249–50. Later Freud would clarify that "the character of the ego is a precipitate of abandoned object-cathexes and that it contains the history of those [lost] object-choices," a characteristic he views as inherent to all ego formation, not just the melancholic ego (Freud, "Ego and the Id," 638).

42. Cuadros, *City of God*, 54, 55, 58.

43. Cuadros, *City of God*, 133, 111, 118, 54.

44. Cuadros, *City of God*, 56; Cheng, *Melancholy of Race*, 30, 25.

45. Cuadros, *City of God*, 58.

46. Dean, *Unlimited Intimacy*, 88.

47. Muñoz, *Disidentifications*, 51. Muñoz argues that disidentification allows minority subjects to refuse both identification and counteridentification with cultural narratives about their identity. Instead, disidentification "neither opts to assimilate within such a structure nor strictly opposes it; rather, disidentification is a strategy that works on and against dominant ideology" (11). "For the minority subject," he argues, "[disidentification] is a mode of recycling or re-forming an object that has already been invested with powerful energy" and thereby constructing a "new model of identity and a newly available site of identification" (39, 41).

48. Muñoz, *Disidentifications*, 52

49. J. Butler, *Psychic Life of Power*, 169. This observation builds directly on Freud's description of the melancholic ego as a "precipitate" of lost objects ("Ego and the Id").

50. J. Butler, *Psychic Life of Power*, 133.

51. Pérez, "Queering the Borderlands," 123.

52. Cuadros, *City of God*, 137, 138, 149, 146, 149, 150.

53. Muñoz, *Cruising Utopia*, 20; Duggan, *Twilight of Equality*; Eng, *Feeling of Kinship*. Duggan's "homonormativity" is a neoliberal orientation that does not challenge heteronormative ideological structures but that adopts assimilative practices in the name of equality, leading to a depoliticized, market-oriented constituency. Eng's "queer liberalism" is an approach to freedom and equality that conflates political and economic spheres and upholds the interlocking forces of white supremacy and heterosexism to achieve equal rights for gays and lesbians under the law.

54. In 2017 Black Lives Matter chapters temporarily shut down the Seattle and Twin Cities' PRIDE marches, and the Toronto and New York City chapters publicly boycotted the PRIDE events, releasing a statement criticizing the police presence, corporate sponsorship, and widespread erasure of "those most marginalized—queer and transgender Black communities." #BlackLivesMatter NYC, "Not Like This—#NoPrideHere," *Medium*, June 25, 2017, https://medium.com/@blmnyc/not-like-this-notopride-8b3f414a3d5a.

55. In 2015 gay and bisexual men "accounted for 82% (26,375) of HIV diagnoses among males and 67% of all diagnoses." African Americans and Latinxs are disproportionately affected: in 2015 "African Americans represented 12% of the US population, but accounted for 45% (17,670) of HIV diagnoses," and "Hispanics/Latinos represented about 18% of the US population, but accounted for 24% (9,290) of HIV diagnoses." "HIV in the United States: At a Glance," Centers for Disease Control and Prevention, June 2017, www.cdc.gov/hiv/statistics/overview/ataglance.html.

56. "In the United States, 6,721 people died from HIV and AIDS in 2014. HIV remains a significant cause of death for certain populations. In 2014, it was the 8th leading cause of death for those aged 25–34 and 9th for those

aged 35–44." "Basic Statistics," Centers for Disease Control and Prevention, June 6, 2017, www.cdc.gov/hiv/basics/statistics.html.

57. Muñoz, *Cruising Utopia*, 26.
58. Muñoz, *Cruising Utopia*, 28.
59. Johnson, "Perverse Martyrologies," 512.
60. In the context of contemporary horror films, Hurley explains that the "narrative told by body horror again and again is of a human subject dismantled and demolished: a human body whose integrity is violated, a human identity whose boundaries are breached from all sides" (205). This disruption of the human body, rendered even more horrific by the fact that it is *not* produced by special effects, is precisely what moves Athey's body into the realm of the monstrous. Hurley, "Reading Like an Alien."
61. Athey, "Raised in the Lord."
62. Johnson, introduction to Johnson, *Pleading in the Blood*, 20.
63. Athey, "Deliverance," 100. Athey describes the motivation behind each of these pieces. The first, *Martyrs and Saints*, is a "meditation fueled by the rage and grief I felt in the early 1990s, tackling the dark ambiance created by the AIDS catastrophe." The second, *4 Scenes in a Harsh Life*, is "still focused on AIDS," while "looking at working-class sexism, drug addiction, suicide attempts, prophetic dream images, Pentecostal evangelism, leather daddy/boy role-playing, and, for a finale, a non-traditional lesbian three-way white wedding" (102, 106). The third, *Deliverance*, is about the "impulse to experience the miraculous" in the face of the promise of "dying from an ugly, AIDS-related illness" (107, 106).
64. Johnson, "Perverse Martyrologies," 508, 513.
65. In *LA Weekly* Athey describes his Premature Ejaculation persona as "monstrous" and later speaks of his work as a process "of learning to love the monster" (Ron Athey, "Rozz Williams, 1963–1998," *LA Weekly*, April 8, 1998, www.laweekly.com/music/rozz-williams-1963-1998-2129452, cited in Johnson, "Perverse Martyrologies," 508). Critics also describe Athey and his work as "monstrous" (Heathfield, "Illicit Transit," 219) as well as a "truth-telling queer soothsayer from beyond the grave" (Johnson, introduction to Johnson, *Pleading in the Blood*, 33); "demonic" (Johnson,

"Bloody Towel," 82); and a "visage . . . at once a death mask and a living face: still moving" (Heathfield, "Illicit Transit," 211).

66. Athey, "Some Thoughts," n.p. Johnson explains that Athey's "'plague' works elegize the generation of men and women lost to AIDS by figuring the specific horrors of the injured, sick or dying body," whereas his "'post-AIDS' works extend these investments through representations of the wound as a breach in the body, and as a potential rupture in the production of meaning" (introduction to Johnson, *Pleading in the Blood*, 32–33).

67. Heathfield, "Illicit Transit," 221.

68. Johnson, introduction to Johnson, *Pleading in the Blood*, 32–33. This definition of *post-AIDS* aligns with Rofes's description of the term as not implying that the disease has been cured but as an era in which "AIDS is not seen as the central, overarching trauma visited on gay communities" (*Dry Bones Breathe*, 75).

69. Johnson, "Bloody Towel," 67.

70. Mary Abbe, "Bloody Performance Draws Criticism," *Minneapolis Star Tribune*, March 24, 1994, 1A, qtd. in Johnson, "Bloody Towel," 69, 72.

71. 140 Cong. Rec. s98 (July 25, 1994), Government Publishing Office, accessed November 13, 2018, www.gpo.gov/fdsys/pkg/CREC-1994-07-25/html/CREC-1994-07-25-pt1-PgS17.htm.

72. "Senate Session: Consideration of the Fiscal Year 1995 Interior Department Appropriations Bill," C-Span 2, July 25, 1994, www.c-span.org/video/?58938-1/senate-session.

73. Athey received only $150 in travel funds for his participation in the Minneapolis event (Johnson, "Bloody Towel," 72).

74. Warner, *Publics and Counterpublics*, 122.

75. Warner, *Publics and Counterpublics*, 27, 23.

76. Bowers v. Hardwick, 478 U.S. 186 (1986); Lawrence v. Texas, 539 U.S. 558 (2003). Eng points out that this move ushered in "queer liberalism" as an extension of the "right of privacy to gay and lesbian U.S. citizen-subjects willing to comply with its normative dictates of bourgeois intimacy, and able to afford the comforts of bourgeois domesticity," but Eng also notes that race is subsumed in these conversations around sodomy laws and access to private intimacy. He explains that "intimacy might be regarded

as a type of racialized property right that remains unequally and unevenly distributed" (*Feeling of Kinship*, 45).

77. Girard, *Scapegoat*, 21, 22.

78. E. Butler, *Metamorphoses of the Vampire*, 11.

79. E. Butler, *Metamorphoses of the Vampire*, 113.

80. Stoker, *Dracula*, 180, 177.

81. Jones, "How Ron Athey Makes Me Feel," 167.

82. Critic Amelia Jones explains the relationality of Athey's work: "exposing the hole(s) in the body is exposing the hole(s) in the self is pointing to the ultimate source of human aggression on both personal and political (global) levels" ("Holy Body," 168).

83. Jones, "How Ron Athey Makes Me Feel," 153.

84. Athey, qtd. in Johnson, "Perverse Martyrologies," 512.

85. Jones, "How Ron Athey Makes Me Feel," 153.

86. McClintock, *Imperial Leather*, 28.

87. Goldberg points out that in addition to charges of cannibalism, the "accusation of sodomy" was used not only to mark difference and justify genocide but also to "offer an uncanny mirror of Spanish desires, above all the desire to violate"—again, that which is used to establish difference ultimately reveals the lack thereof. Goldberg explains that sodomy "names something otherwise unnameable, something that goes beyond the evidentiary and the logical; it is a category of a violation that violates categories" (*Sodometries*, 196–97).

88. Goldberg, *Sodometries*, 196. Freccero reiterates Goldberg's observation that "what marks the indigenous man as sodomical is also the spectacle of a pierced and porous male body, a male body riddled with holes" (*Queer/Early/Modern*, 97).

89. Though Stoker's Dracula feeds only on women and is therefore less explicitly queer, E. Butler notes that "Dracula's Brides (two of whom share his features) are extensions of him, and the impurity of their embrace stems at least in part from its latent homosexual charge. Harker's entries in his journal provide a breeding ground for undead perversion, a medium in which the vampire can mutate and take on unprecedented forms of terror" (*Metamorphoses of the Vampire*, 111). Other more contemporary

vampires, such as Anne Rice's Louis and Lestat, are perhaps more closely aligned with sodomical sexuality, and Hanson argues that gay men during the AIDS crisis were linked to vampires in the popular imagination in their association with death and disease and the public's "irrational fear of PWAS [people with AIDS] and gay men who 'bite.'" He explains, "I am talking about essentialist representations of gay men as vampiric: as sexually exotic, alien, unnatural, oral, anal, compulsive, violent, protean, polymorphic, polyvocal, polysemous, invisible, soulless, transient, superhumanly mobile, infectious, murderous, suicidal, and a threat to wife, children, home, and phallus" (Hanson, "Undead," 325). Whether predominately hetero- or homosexually oriented, vampires are perverse puncturers and therefore at least metaphorically sodomical (324–40).

90. Freccero touches on cannibalism in her search for a more ethical relationship to history through haunting, or what she calls "queer spectrality," a historiography receptive to the returns of the past (*Queer/Early/Modern*, 70). To illustrate this approach, she looks to Jean de Léry's *History of a Voyage to the Land of Brazil*, a sixteenth-century text in which Léry describes his year living with the indigenous, cannibalistic Tupinamba people. Freccero juxtaposes a spectral approach with a cannibalistic one, noting that "cannibalism is in some sense haunting's double, its evil twin. A literalization of melancholic incorporation through the ingestion of the other, cannibalism is the flip side of the excorporation that a ghost might be said to be" (87). But her description of queer spectrality depends on the cannibalistic spectacle, as she holds up Léry's memories of his time with the Tupinamba as an example of "receptive witnessing." Léry recalls observing a ritual that "at first inspires fear but then produces ravishment" and goes on to haunt him decades later ("Whenever I remember it, my heart trembles, and it seems their voices are still in my ears"). Essential to the queer spectral approach is the notion of "penetrative reciprocity," or a relationship to witnessing in which "witness is both penetrator and penetrated," leading to the kind of masochistic self-shattering I discussed earlier in the context of Cuadros (99).

91. Freccero, *Queer/Early/Modern*, 102.

92. Heathfield, "Illicit Transit," 206–7.

93. See McClintock's description of "America, ca. 1600 engraving by The-odore Galle after a drawing by Jan van der Straet (ca. 1575)" (*Imperial Leather*, 25–27).

94. Heathfield, "Illicit Transit," 221.

95. Johnson, "Perverse Martyrologies," 506–7.

96. Kilgour, *From Communion to Cannibalism*, 16.

97. Halberstam, *Skin Shows*, 21.

4. Sadomasochism

1. In *Queer History* Bronski points to an uptick in mainstream representation of homosexual communities in the 1950s and 1960s by briefly mentioning this article, showing the centrality of s/m to queer history (182).

2. Rubin, "Catacombs," 224–40, 233. A description of the Catacombs also appears several times in Califia's *Public Sex*.

3. Rubin, "Catacombs," 226. Jeffery Weeks adds that the larger national debates around sadomasochism at the end of the twentieth century were "stimulated by the emergence of explicit subcultures and activist groupings of gay and lesbian s/mers in the 1970s" (*Sexuality and Its Discontents*, 236).

4. Rubin, "Catacombs," 226; "Folsom Street Fair," Folsom Street Events, accessed January 15, 2016, www.folsomstreetevents.org/folsomstreetfair/.

5. Kathleen Connell and Paul Gabriel, "The Power of Broken Hearts: The Origin and Evolution of the Folsom Street Fair," Folsom Street Events, accessed January 15, 2016, www.folsomstreetevents.org/heritage.

6. For more on the ethics of consent in the BDSM community, visit the National Coalition for Sexual Freedom (https://ncsfreedom.org/), the National Leather Association–International (www.nla-international.com /home.html), the Eulenspiegel Society (www.tes.org/), and the Society of Janus (http://soj.org/).

7. Rubin, "Catacombs," 239.

8. Weeks, *Sexuality and Its Discontents*, 236–37.

9. Lamar's, Cassils's, and Drucker's restaging of trauma might be charac-terized as a Freudian "repetition compulsion," in which one passively or actively revisits a traumatic experience as a way of "binding" and thereby mastering the stimulus. Freud's theories around traumatic repetition are

foundational to the trauma theory developed in the 1990s by theorists such as Cathy Caruth, Shoshana Felman, Dori Laub, and Judith Herman. But critics such Irene Visser have more recently called this model a problematically "Eurocentric, event-based, individualistic orientation" that doesn't take into account the "prolonged, cumulative hurt of long years of repression that constitutes the trauma of colonialism, with its repeated and cumulative stressor events" ("Decolonizing Trauma Theory," 252). Since I argue that the work of Lamar, Cassils, and Drucker responds to this kind of cumulative, insidious trauma, I attempt to perform a socially and materially based reading of these artists that moves away from Freudian-centered trauma theory, though Freud's concepts necessarily echo throughout any discussion of trauma or sadomasochism; see Freud, *Beyond the Pleasure Principle*.

10. Haggerty, *Queer Gothic*, 2. Massé similarly points to the "masochism at the center of the Gothic," arguing that Gothic romances circulate around the pain of female characters as a kind of repetition compulsion to work through the trauma of feminine socialization (*Name of Love*, 2).

11. Bersani, *Freudian Body*, 64.

12. Psychoanalytic theorists of sadomasochism also recognize sadomasochism's complexity and resistance to simple definitions. In *Three Essays* Freud originally privileges sadism as the primary phenomenon when he claims that "masochism is nothing more than an extension of sadism turned round upon the subject's own self" (24). But he later revises and complicates this assertion by positing a primary "erotogenic" masochism that, when directed to "objects in the external world," becomes "sadism proper" ("Economic Problem of Masochism," 163). Bersani remarks on Freud's paradox that "the pleasurable unpleasurable tension of sexual stimulation seeks not to be released, but to be increased" (*Freudian Body*, 34). This observation, along with Freud's implication that sexual excitement can result from any powerful emotion, even a distressing one, leads Bersani to conclude that all sexuality involves a shattering of the self and "could be thought of as a tautology for masochism" (*Freudian Body*, 39). Deleuze, more so than Freud or Bersani, maintains the separation of

sadism and masochism, and he insists on operating completely outside the assumption that they are anything more than coincidentally related.

13. Freud, *Three Essays*, 23.

14. Silverman, *Male Subjectivity*, 187.

15. In the 1980s antipornography feminists Dworkin (*Intercourse*) and MacKinnon ("Sexuality, Pornography, and Method") used sadomasochism as a metaphor for oppressive patriarchal power relations, claiming that sexuality itself is based on an oppressive and colonizing system of dominance and submission. Rubin ("Catacombs") and Califia (*Public Sex*) counter the MacKinnon-Dworkin position by pointing out the possibilities for queer and feminist agency in BDSM practices and emphasizing the constructive presence of fantasy, performance, and egalitarianism integral to the sadomasochistic relationship.

16. Freeman, *Time Binds*, 189. For race-based critiques of sadomasochism, she refers readers to anthologies such as Reti, *Unleashing Feminism*; and Linden et al., *Against Sadomasochism*. Reid-Pharr writes about the controversy of racialized dominance and submission in Gary Fisher's posthumously published "difficult" work, *Gary in Your Pocket*. He explains that Fisher's formation of a black gay identity through the recreation of the master-slave dynamic and his own sexual degradation incites readers to "righteous indignation" and "maddening inarticulateness" (*Black Gay Man*, 149). Though Reid-Pharr claims he does not defend Fisher, he notes that "Fisher's work leaves one with the distinct understanding that the white master is necessary to the project of black historical recovery precisely because his abuse of flesh . . . is what truly connects the black modern to her enslaved ancestors" (147).

17. Freeman, *Time Binds*, 138, 143.

18. Musser, *Sensational Flesh*, 23.

19. Nicole Disser, "M. Lamar's Black Radical Impulse Brings Together Metal and Devil-Worshipping Blues," *Bedford + Bowery*, September 17, 2015, http://bedfordandbowery.com/2015/09/m-lamars-black-radical-impulse -brings-together-metal-and-devil-worshipping-blues/; Emily Colucci, "The Plantation Is Still Here: Inside M. Lamar's 'Negrogothic, a Mani-

festo,'" *Vice*, October 3, 2014, www.vice.com/read/the-plantation-is-still
-here-inside-m-lamars-negrogothic-a-manifesto-exhibition?utm_source
=vicetwitterus. For more on the relationship between goth, metal, and
punk subcultures, see Goodlad and Bibby's *Goth*.

20. Emily Nathan, "Southern Gothic and Goth-Kid Makeup: M Lamar on
Racialized Art and Black Leather," *Observer*, February 16, 2015, http://
observer.com/2015/02/southern-gothic-and-goth-kid-makeup-m-lamar
-on-racialized-art-and-black-leather/.

21. Jonathan Curiel, "Fully Cocked: Provocateur M. Lamar Reclaims African-
American Male Sexuality in New Show," *SF Weekly*, February 4, 2015,
www.sfweekly.com/sanfrancisco/san-francisco-arts-culture-m-lamar
-negrogothic-badass-nigga-robert-mapplethorpe-san-francisco-art
-institute-walter-mcbean-galleries/Content?oid=3377180; Laverne Cox
and M. Lamar, "Laverne Cox and M. Lamar Discuss Identity, Collective
Trauma, Celebrating the Black Penis and More," *Queer Voices*, February 2, 2016, www.huffingtonpost.com/2012/02/08/laverne-cox-m-lamar
-lgbt-black-communities_n_1262990.html; Paisley Dalton, "Interview:
Laverne Cox's Queer Brother M. Lamar Says, 'I'm Not Gay, But It's OK
If You Are!,'" *World of Wonder (WOW) Report*, March 16, 2016, http://
worldofwonder.net/interview-laverne-coxs-queer-brother-m-lamar-says
-im-not-gay-but-its-ok-if-you-are/.

22. Curiel, "Fully Cocked."

23. Michael Eric Dyson, "What White America Fails to See," *New York Times*,
July 7, 2016, www.nytimes.com/2016/07/10/opinion/sunday/what-white
-america-fails-to-see.html. Interestingly, only four days after the original
publication date, this article was "updated to reflect news developments,"
including a title change to "Death in Black and White" and a complete
removal of the quote cited here. These changes, following the shooting
of five Dallas police officers by Micah Xavier Johnson, downplay Dyson's
original rhetoric criticizing white failure to see the racism structuring
police brutality.

24. Nathan, "Southern Gothic."

25. Nathan, "Southern Gothic."

26. Nadal, *That's So Gay*, 6.
27. Kaplan, *Trauma Culture*, 19.
28. Freud, *Beyond the Pleasure Principle*, 37.
29. Dalton, "Interview."
30. M. Lamar, *Negrogothic, a Manifesto: The Aesthetics of M. Lamar*, multimedia solo show, at Participant Inc., New York, 2014.
31. Nathan, "Southern Gothic."
32. Kilgour, *Gothic Novel*, 3; Goodlad and Bibby, *Goth*, 15.
33. Nathan, "Southern Gothic."
34. Goodlad and Bibby defend the goth emphasis on white skin, claiming that by "employing various techniques to lighten complexions that a mainstream culture already regards as white, white goths seem to reject the transparent status of whiteness—making skin tone a site of theatrics rather than nature. The subculture thus encourages those who might otherwise take their whiteness for granted to experience this key aspect of race as mutable and constructed" (*Goth*, 26–27). Nonetheless, they concede that in many ways goth subculture "is complicit with the normative status of whiteness in mainstream culture" (25).
35. *Negrogothic, a Manifesto: The Aesthetics of M. Lamar*, exhibition press release (New York: Participant Inc., 2014).
36. Colucci, "Plantation Is Still Here."
37. *Negrogothic, a Manifesto*, press release.
38. Mercer, *Welcome to the Jungle*, 173.
39. Notably, Lamar's adoption of the goth aesthetic itself functions as a commentary on gender, as contemporary goth subculture is founded on "resistance toward normative masculinity," according to Goodlad and Bibby (*Goth*, 19). "At its most utopian," they add, "goth subculture helps to cultivate antiheteronormative sexualities, unconventional genders, and nonbinaristic social relations between the sexes" (20). But Ferguson's queer of color critique would add that the concept of "normative masculinity" is always already racialized and embedded in narratives of class and liberal identity. Lamar's gothicism makes these intersections visible (*Aberrations in Black*).

40. Colucci, "Plantation Is Still Here."

41. These novels include Lewis's *The Monk*, Radcliffe's *The Italian*, and Maturin's *Melmoth the Wanderer*, among others.

42. Doyle, *Hold It against Me*, 23, 22.

43. Brandon Peter Masterman, "In the Belly of the Ship: Paraontological Blackness and Sonic Abjection in the Music of M. Lamar," M. Lamar.com, accessed January 22, 2016, www.mlamar.com/critical-theory/. Interestingly, Lamar has chosen to highlight this academic article on his official website by creating a "Critical Theory" tab that displays the full text of the article. Though apparently not published in a monograph or refereed journal, Masterman's observations are resonant enough with Lamar's sense of himself as an artist that he has built the article into his virtual presence, indicating that the notion of dissonance and sonic abjection are, indeed, central to the intended effects of Lamar's work.

44. Lamar, qtd. in Kathleen Massara, "Birds in Flight," *Guernica*, September 15, 2014, www.guernicamag.com/art/birds-in-flight/.

45. Curiel, "Fully Cocked."

46. Disser, "M. Lamar's Black Radical Impulse"; Michelle Carlson, "A Punishing Perspective: M. Lamar's 'Negrogothic,'" KQED, February 12, 2015, http://ww2.kqed.org/arts/2015/02/12/a-punishing-perspective-m-lamars-negrogothic/.

47. Disser, "M. Lamar's Black Radical Impulse."

48. Hartman, *Scenes of Subjection*, 20.

49. Ferguson, *Aberrations in Black*, 17–18.

50. Doyle, *Hold It against Me*, xi.

51. Priscilla Frank, "10 Transgender Artists Who Are Changing the Landscape of Contemporary Art," *Huffington Post*, March 26, 2014, www.huffingtonpost.com/2014/03/26/trans-artists_n_5023294.html.

52. Sue, *Microaggressions in Everyday Life*, xv.

53. Lorde describes this phenomenon: "It is the responsibility of the oppressed to teach the oppressors their mistakes. I am responsible for educating teachers who dismiss my children's culture in school. Black and Third World people are expected to educate white people as to our humanity.

Women are expected to educate men. Lesbians and gay men are expected to educate the heterosexual world" ("Age," 114–15).

54. Williams, "Transgender," 232; Stryker, *Transgender History*, 19. The TSQ: *Transgender Studies Quarterly*'s inaugural issue defines the keywords in the field of transgender studies. They note that, since 2010, the use of an asterisk following "trans" has been used regularly "to open up *transgender* or *trans* to a greater range of meanings" (Tompkins, "Asterisk," 26). They explain, "Although *transgender* has been used since the early 1990s as an umbrella term to cover the widest possible range of gender variation, it is now understood in some circles to represent only binary notions of transness" (Killermann 2012). Proponents of adding the asterisk to trans argue that it signals greater inclusivity of new gender identities and expressions and better represents a broader community of individuals" (Tompkins, "Asterisk," 27). But there is some debate about the use of "trans" versus "trans*." Organizations such as Trans Student Educational Resources note that the asterisk "did well for explicitly noting that being trans is not limited to trans men and trans women (as trans without the asterisk was misinterpreted as meaning) but it subtly began working with this misinterpretation and contributed to the incorrect thought that 'trans' by itself only means binary trans people." My usage of "trans*" will fall in line with the definition in TSQ, arguably the most authoritative source in transgender studies to date, to denote both binary and nonbinary transgender identities. Danie Diamond and Eli Erlick, "Why We Used Trans* and Why We Don't Anymore," Trans Student Educational Resources, accessed July 16, 2016, www.transstudent.org/asterisk.

55. Cox, qtd. in Katy Steinmetz, "The Transgender Tipping Point," *Time*, May 29, 2014.

56. Carter, "Transition," 235.

57. Stryker, *Transgender History*, 6.

58. Janet Mock, "A Note on Visibility in the Wake of 6 Trans Women's Murders in 2015," Janet Mock.com, February 16, 2015, http://janetmock.com /2015/02/16/six-trans-women-killed-this-year/. The Human Rights Campaign reported that there were at least twenty-three trans* murders in 2016 and twenty-eight trans* murders in 2017. GLAAD puts the 2017

number at twenty-six. Both organizations note that many transgender deaths were not reported or were not counted because of misgendering by police, media, and family. "Violence against the Transgender Community in 2017," Human Rights Campaign, accessed January 10, 2018, www.hrc.org/resources/violence-against-the-transgender-community-in-2017; Nick Adams, "Honoring Known Cases of Deadly Anti-trans Violence in 2017," GLAAD, December 14, 2017, www.glaad.org/blog/glaad-calls-increased-and-accurate-media-coverage-transgender-murders.

59. Mock, "Note on Visibility."

60. Spade, *Normal Life*, 32. For example, the "majority of ID-issuing agencies in the United States" require that individuals show proof that they have "undergone gender-confirming health care, especially surgery" to be issued an ID that reflects their lived gender (12). Those who cannot afford treatment or do not wish to have any "gender-confirming" medical interventions may not be able to access services that require identification. The lack of accurate ID frequently outs people as trans* in public circumstances, making them vulnerable to assault and harassment. This type of administrative policy demonstrates hostile indifference to the experience of many whose circumstances bar them from accessing medical transition services or whose gender identity falls outside of or in between the male/female binary.

61. Lorde, "Age," 116.

62. Musser, *Sensational Flesh*, 2.

63. Cassils uses plural gender-neutral pronouns (they/them/their).

64. Cassils, interview by the author, September 20, 2013.

65. Doyle, *Hold It against Me*, 23.

66. Deleuze, *Coldness and Cruelty*, 93.

67. Cassils, interview.

68. In *Queer Art* Lorenz theorizes the turn to the exaggerated body as a means of visualizing power and its hierarchical constructions of norm and other. A freak theory "undermines a logic of norm and deviation in that it produces or confirms the norm by deploying highly unstable narratives about the 'other,' so that a kind of pleasure arises precisely from the instability of the narrative.... The appearances present conspicuous

bodies but as a performance: a visualization of bodies that in a certain way fictionalizes and unsettles these bodies, thus coming into a deviant and ambivalent relationship to norms, destabilizing and contesting those norms, or even abandoning them" (162). Notably, this theory combines the gothicism of the freak, the artistic visualization of traumatic social hierarchies, and the potential for pleasure in destabilizing power relations.

69. Zackary Drucker, *The Inability to Be Looked At and the Horror of Nothing to See*, live performance video, 2008–9, www.zackarydrucker.com/performance/2018/11/27/nz2plik6kwt9aq7ss3bunvqf4hxw0k.

70. Marshall, *Romanticism, Gender, and Violence*, 12–13.

71. Jennifer Doyle, "Plucked: Zackary Drucker's 'The Inability to Be Looked At and the Horror of Nothing to See,'" *I. E. You Belong to Me: Meditations on Two Weeks of Performance Art in the Riv*, March 2, 2009, http://ieyoubelongtome.blogspot.com/2009/03/plucked-zackary-druckers-inability-to.html.

72. George, "Negotiating the Spectacle," 274 (emphasis mine).

73. In "Demarginalizing the Intersection" Crenshaw coins the term "intersectionality" to describe a means of accounting for the complexities of intersecting social forces to avoid the "conceptual limitations of the single-issue analyses" (149).

74. Sue, *Microaggressions in Everyday Life*, xv.

75. López, "Emotional Contraband," 27.

76. Kaplan, *Trauma Culture*, 23, 122.

77. Tal, *Worlds of Hurt*, 122, 115–16, 119, 7.

78. Tal, *Worlds of Hurt*, 122.

79. J. Butler, *Precarious Life*, 48, 49.

80. Lamar, qtd. in Colucci, "Plantation Is Still Here."

81. Lamar, qtd. in Nathan, "Southern Gothic."

82. Cassils, interview.

83. "Cassils: Monumental," Cassils.net, accessed January 11, 2018, http://cassils.net/news-2/.

84. "Zackary Drucker: About," Zackary Drucker.com, accessed August 28, 2015, http://zackarydrucker.com/about/.

85. Kaplan, *Trauma Culture*, 23.

Conclusion

1. L. Brown, "Not Outside the Range," 107.
2. Harris, *Dead until Dark*, 1.
3. Harris, *Living Dead in Dallas*.
4. In her reading of the show, Chaplin argues that the vampires' political self-positioning as oppressed minority demanding equality under the law in fact represents "the subject pushed toward an apocalyptic confrontation with the *failure* of law" ("Contemporary Gothic," 41; emphasis mine).
5. Harris, *Dead until Dark*, 169, 106, 169.
6. W. Brown, "American Nightmare," 699.
7. Duggan, *Twilight of Equality*, 50.
8. Goddu, *Gothic America*, 8.
9. Lloyd reflects Goddu's claim but links the "hauntings of history" specifically to *traumatic* reverberations of southern history. *True Blood* is a vaguely racialized extension of the southern gothic genre, engaging "dark traumas from the region's past" ("Southern Gothic," 81). Marrati reads the bloody abstractions in the opening sequence of the show as a depiction of the "blood that haunts human history as such" ("True Blood," 987).
10. Harris, *Dead until Dark*, 151, 176.
11. Hudson, "Werewolves and Vampires," 664.
12. Eng, *Feeling of Kinship*, 25, 41.
13. Duggan, *Twilight of Equality*, 66.
14. The unacknowledged dependence on blackness as a metaphor of liberal progress reflects what Morrison describes in *Playing in the Dark* as the "construction of a history and a context for whites by positing history-lessness and context-lessness for blacks" (53).
15. For more on the post-9/11 implications of the show, see Blake, "Vampires."
16. Puar, *Terrorist Assemblages*, 2, xiii.
17. Puar, *Terrorist Assemblages*, xii.
18. Eng notes that the intersection of these phenomena is not coincidental—the post-9/11 decade, he argues, is a moment in which "the enfranchisement of the normative gay and lesbian US citizen-subject 'over here' as 'liberated' and 'free' is accompanied by the simultaneous annihilation

of Muslim populations deemed 'unfree' and 'uncivilized' 'over there,'" a similar claim to the one Puar posits in *Terrorist Assemblages*. Historically, the advancement of "liberty" for those LGBT subjects willing to conform to normative mandates functions in direct relation to the alienation and exclusion of raced subjects in this country, and, according to Eng, this line of reasoning applies specifically to the inverse relationship between gay and lesbian rights and the rights of Muslim subjects during the War on Terror (*Feeling of Kinship*, 48).

19. W. Brown, "American Nightmare," 699.
20. Eng, *Feeling of Kinship*, 43, 30.
21. Stevens, "Trauma," 34.
22. Caruth, *Unclaimed Experience*, 2, 3.
23. Stevens, "Trauma," 34.

Adlon, Arthur. *The One Between*. New York: Beacon Signal, 1962.

Ahmed, Sara. *The Promise of Happiness*. Durham: Duke University Press, 2010.

Aldrich, Ann. *We Walk Alone through Lesbos Lonely Groves*. New York: Gold Medal, 1955.

Allatson, Paul. "'My Bones Shine in the Dark': AIDS and the De-scription of Chicano Queer in the Work of Gil Cuadros." *Aztlán: A Journal of Chicano Studies* 32, no. 1 (2007): 23–52.

American Psychiatric Association. *Diagnostic and Statistical Manual of Mental Disorders*. 3rd ed. Washington DC: American Psychiatric Association, 1987.

———. *Diagnostic and Statistical Manual of Mental Disorders*. 4th ed. Washington DC: American Psychiatric Association, 1994.

———. *Diagnostic and Statistical Manual of Mental Disorders*. 5th ed. Washington DC: American Psychiatric Association, 2013.

Athey, Ron. "Deliverance: The 'Torture Trilogy' in Retrospect." In Johnson, *Pleading in the Blood*, 100–109.

———. "Raised in the Lord: Revelations at the Knee of Miss Velma." In Johnson, *Pleading in the Blood*, 180–93.

———. "Some Thoughts on the Politics of the Body and the Problematics of Documentation." In *Exposures*, edited by Lois Keidan and Manuel Vason, n.p. London: Black Dog, 2002.

Auerbach, Nina. "Grave and Gay." In Auerbach, *Our Vampires, Ourselves*, 163–92.

———. *Our Vampires, Ourselves*. Chicago: University of Chicago Press, 1995.

Baldwin, James. *Giovanni's Room*. 1956. Reprint, New York: Random House, 2000.

Bannon, Ann. *Beebo Brinker*. 1962. Reprint, San Francisco: Cleis, 2001.

———. *I Am a Woman*. 1959. Reprint, Tallahassee: Naiad, 1986.

———. *Journey to a Woman*. 1960. Reprint, New York: Arno, 1975.

———. *Odd Girl Out*. 1957. Reprint, New York: Arno, 1975.

———. *Women in the Shadows*. 1959. Reprint, New York: Arno, 1975.

Bataille, Georges. "The Practice of Joy before Death." In *Visions of Excess: Selected Writings, 1927–1939*, edited by Allan Stoekl, 235–39. Minneapolis: University of Minnesota Press, 1994.

Beckford, William. *The History of Caliph Vathek*. 1787. Reprint, Oxford: Oxford University Press, 1998.

Belletto, Steven, and Daniel Grausam, eds. *American Literature and Culture in the Age of Cold War: A Critical Reassessment*. Iowa City: University of Iowa Press, 2012.

Berglund, Jeff. *Cannibal Fictions: American Explorations of Colonialism, Race, Gender, and Sexuality*. Madison: University of Wisconsin Press, 2006.

Berlant, Lauren, and Lee Edelman. *Sex, or the Unbearable*. Durham: Duke University Press, 2013.

Bersani, Leo. *The Freudian Body: Psychoanalysis and Art*. New York: Columbia University Press, 1986.

———. "Shame on You." In *After Sex? On Writing since Queer Theory*, edited by Janet Halley and Andrew Parker, 91–109. Durham: Duke University Press, 2011.

Blake, Linne. "Vampires, Mad Scientists and the Unquiet Dead: Gothic Ubiquity in Post-9/11 US Television." In Edwards and Soltysik Monnet, *Gothic in Contemporary Literature*, 37–56.

Boone, Joseph Allen. *The Homoerotics of Orientalism*. New York: Columbia University Press, 2014.

Botting, Fred, and Dale Townshend, eds. *Gothic: Critical Concepts in Literary and Cultural Studies*. Vol. 1. London: Routledge, 2004.

Bronski, Michael, ed. *Pulp Friction: Uncovering the Golden Age of Gay Male Pulps*. New York: St. Martin's Griffin, 2003.

———. *A Queer History of the United States*. Boston: Beacon, 2011.

Brown, Charles Brockden. *Weiland, or The Transformation, an American Tale*. 1798. Reprint, New York: Dover, 2010.

Brown, Laura. "Not Outside the Range: One Feminist Perspective on Psychic Trauma." In Caruth, *Trauma*, 100–112.

Brown, Wendy. "American Nightmare: Neoliberalism, Neoconservatism, and De-democratization." *Political Theory* 34, no. 6 (2006): 690–714.

Butler, Erik. *Metamorphoses of the Vampire in Literature and Film: Cultural Transformations in Europe, 1732–1933*. Rochester: Camden House, 2010.

Butler, Judith. *Precarious Life: The Powers of Mourning and Violence*. London: Verso, 2004.

———. *The Psychic Life of Power: Theories in Subjection*. Stanford: Stanford University Press, 1997.

Califia, Pat. *Public Sex: The Culture of Radical Sex*. 2nd ed. San Francisco: Cleis, 2000.

Camacho, Alicia Schmidt. *Migrant Imaginaries: Latino Cultural Politics in the U.S.-Mexico Borderlands*. New York: New York University Press, 2008.

Carr, Jay. *Unnatural Wife*. New York: Beacon Signal, 1962.

Carter, Julian. "Gay Marriage and Pulp Fiction Homonormativity, Disidentification, and Affect in Ann Bannon's Lesbian Novels." *GLQ: A Journal of Lesbian and Gay Studies* 15, no. 4 (2009): 583–609.

———. "Transition." *TSQ: Transgender Studies Quarterly* 1, nos. 1–2 (2014): 235–37.

Caruth, Cathy. Introduction to *American Imago* 48, no. 1 (1991): 1–12.

———, ed. *Trauma: Explorations in Memory*. Baltimore: Johns Hopkins University Press, 1995.

———. *Unclaimed Experience: Trauma, Narrative, and History*. Baltimore: Johns Hopkins University Press, 1996.

Casper, Monica J., and Eric Wertheimer, eds. *Critical Trauma Studies: Understanding Violence, Conflict, and Memory in Everyday Life*. New York: New York University Press, 2016.

Castle, Terry. *The Apparitional Lesbian: Female Homosexuality and Modern Culture*. New York: Columbia University Press, 1993.

Chaplin, Susan. "Contemporary Gothic and the Law." In *The Cambridge Companion to the Modern Gothic*, edited by Jerrold E. Hogle, 37–51. Cambridge: Cambridge University Press, 2014.

Chavoya, C. Ondine, and David Evans Frantz, eds. *Axis Mundo: Queer Networks in Chicano L.A.* Los Angeles: USC Libraries, 2017.

Cheng, Anne Anlin. *The Melancholy of Race: Psychoanalysis, Assimilation, and Hidden Grief*. Oxford: Oxford University Press, 2001.

Cho, Alexander. "Lady Gaga, Balls-Out: Recuperating Queer Performativity." *Flow* 10, no. 5 (2009). http://flowtv.org/?p=4169.

Clery, Emma J. *The Rise of Supernatural Fiction, 1762–1800*. Cambridge: Cambridge University Press, 1995.

Cohen, Jeffrey Jerome. "Monster Culture (Seven Theses)." In *Monster Theory: Reading Culture*, edited by Jeffrey Jerome Cohen, 3–25. Minneapolis: University of Minnesota Press, 1996.

Coontz, Stephanie. *Marriage: A History*. New York: Viking, 2005.

Corber, Robert J. "All about the Subversive Femme: Cold War Homophobia in *All about Eve*." In *American Cold War Culture*, edited by Douglas Field, 34–49. Edinburgh: Edinburgh University Press, 2005.

Craps, Stef. *Postcolonial Witnessing: Trauma Out of Bounds*. New York: Palgrave Macmillan, 2013.

Crenshaw, Kimberlé. "Demarginalizing the Intersection of Race and Sex: A Black Feminist Critique of Antidiscrimination Doctrine, Feminist Theory and Antiracist Politics." *University of Chicago Legal Forum*, no. 1 (1989): 139–67.

Crimp, Douglas. "How to Have Promiscuity in an Epidemic." In *AIDS: Cultural Analysis/Cultural Activism*, edited by Douglas Crimp, 237–71. Cambridge: MIT Press, 1988.

———. *Melancholia and Moralism: Essays on AIDS and Queer Politics*. Cambridge: MIT Press, 2002.

Cuadros, Gil. *City of God*. San Francisco: City Lights Books, 1994.

Dacre, Charlotte. *Zofloya, or The Moor*. 1806. Reprint, Oxford: Oxford University Press, 2008.

Dean, Tim. *Unlimited Intimacy: Reflections on the Subculture of Barebacking.* Chicago: University of Chicago Press, 2009.

Deleuze, Gilles. *Coldness and Cruelty.* In Deleuze and Sacher-Masoch, *Masochism*, 15–138.

Deleuze, Gilles, and Leopold von Sacher-Masoch. *Masochism: "Coldness and Cruelty" and "Venus in Furs."* New York: Zone Books, 1991.

Derrida, Jacques. *Specters of Marx: The State of the Debt, the Work of Mourning and the New International.* Translated by Peggy Kamuf. New York: Routledge, 1994.

Doyle, Jennifer. *Hold It against Me: Difficulty and Emotion in Contemporary Art.* Durham: Duke University Press, 2013.

Duggan, Lisa. *The Twilight of Equality? Neoliberalism, Cultural Politics, and the Attack on Democracy.* Boston: Beacon, 2003.

Dumont, Jessie. *I Prefer Girls.* Derby: Monarch, 1963.

Dworkin, Andrea. *Intercourse.* 1987. Reprint, New York: Basic Books, 2007.

Dyer, Richard. *The Culture of Queers.* London: Routledge, 2002.

———. "It's in His Kiss: Vampirism as Homosexuality, Homosexuality as Vampirism." In Dyer, *Culture of Queers*, 70–89.

Edelman, Lee. *No Future: Queer Theory and the Death Drive.* Durham: Duke University Press, 2004.

Edwards, Justin, and Agnieszka Soltysik Monnet. *The Gothic in Contemporary Literature and Popular Culture.* New York: Routledge, 2012.

Ellis, Joan. *The Third Street.* New York: Tower, 1964.

Ellis, Kelley Norman, and M. L. Hunter, eds. *Spaces between Us: Poetry, Prose and Art on HIV/AIDS.* Chicago: Third World, 2010.

Emery, Carol. *Queer Affair.* New York: Beacon, 1957.

Eng, David L. *The Feeling of Kinship: Queer Liberalism and the Racialization of Intimacy.* Durham: Duke University Press, 2010.

Faderman, Lillian. *Odd Girls and Twilight Lovers: A History of Lesbian Life in Twentieth-Century America.* New York: Columbia University Press, 1991.

Feinberg, Leslie. *Stone Butch Blues.* Ithaca: Firebrand Books, 1993.

Felman, Shoshana, and Dori Laub. *Testimony: Crises of Witnessing in Literature, Psychoanalysis and History.* New York: Routledge, 1991.

Ferguson, Roderick. *Aberrations in Black: Toward a Queer of Color Critique.* Minneapolis: University of Minnesota Press, 2004.

Ferreday, Debra, and Adi Kuntsman. "Haunted Futurities." *Borderlands* 10, no. 2 (2011): 1–14.

Fincher, Max. *Queering Gothic in the Romantic Age: The Penetrating Eye.* New York: Palgrave Macmillan, 2007.

Forrest, Katherine V., ed. *Lesbian Pulp Fiction: The Sexually Intrepid World of Lesbian Paperback Novels, 1950–1965.* San Francisco: Cleis, 2005.

Foucault, Michel. *Abnormal: Lectures at the Collège de France: 1974–1975.* Edited by Valerio Marchetti and Antonella Salomoni. Translated by Graham Burchell. London: Verso, 2003.

———. *Herculine Barbin: Being the Recently Discovered Memoirs of a Nineteenth-Century French Hermaphrodite.* New York: Pantheon Books, 1980.

———. "Sex, Power, and the Politics of Identity." In *Ethics: Subjectivity and Truth*, edited by Paul Rabinow, 163–73. Vol. 1 of *Essential Works of Foucault, 1954–1984*. New York: New Press, 1997.

Freccero, Carla. *Queer/Early/Modern.* Durham: Duke University Press, 2006.

Freeman, Elizabeth. *Time Binds: Queer Temporalities, Queer Histories.* Durham: Duke University Press, 2010.

Freud, Sigmund. *Beyond the Pleasure Principle.* Edited and translated by James Strachey. 1920. Reprint, New York: Norton, 1961.

———. "The Economic Problem of Masochism." In *The "Ego and the Id" and Other Works*, 155–70. Vol. 19 of Freud, *Standard Edition*.

———. "The Ego and the Id." 1923. In *The Freud Reader*, edited by Peter Gay, 628–58. London: Norton, 1989.

———. *Moses and Monotheism.* Translated by Katherine Jones. New York: Vintage Books, 1939.

———. "Mourning and Melancholia." In *On the History of the Psycho-Analytic Movement, Papers on Metapsychology and Other Works*, 239–58. Vol. 14 of Freud, *Standard Edition*.

———. "Psychoanalytic Notes upon an Autobiographical Account of a Case of Paranoia (Dementia Paranoides)." In *Three Case Histories*, edited by Philip Riefe, 83–160. New York: Simon and Schuster, 1993.

———. *The Standard Edition of the Complete Psychological Works of Sigmund Freud*. 24 vols. Edited and translated by James Strachey. London: Hogarth, 1953–74.

———. *Three Essays on the Theory of Sexuality*. Edited and translated by James Strachey. New York: Basic Books, 2000.

Friedman, Samuel R., Jo L. Sotheran, Abu Abdul-Quader, Beny J. Primm, Don C. Des Jarlais, Paula Kleinman, Conrad Maugé, Douglas S. Goldsmith, Wafaa El-Sadr, and Robert Maslansky. "The AIDS Epidemic among Blacks and Hispanics." Supplement 2, *Milbank Quarterly* 65, pt. 2 (1987): 455–99.

George, Doran. "Negotiating the Spectacle in Transgender Performances of Alexis Arquette, Zackary Drucker, DavEnd, Niv Acosta, and Tobaron Waxman." *TSQ: Transgender Studies Quarterly* 1, nos. 1–2 (2014): 273–79.

Gilman, Charlotte Perkins. *"The Yellow Wallpaper" and Other Stories*. New York: Dover, 1997.

Girard, René. *The Scapegoat*. Translated by Yvonne Freccero. Baltimore: Johns Hopkins University Press, 1986.

Goddu, Teresa A. *Gothic America: Narrative, History, and Nation*. New York: Columbia University Press, 1997.

Goldberg, Jonathan. *Sodometries: Renaissance Texts, Modern Sexualities*. New York: Fordham University Press, 2010.

Goodlad, Lauren M. E., and Michael Bibby. *Goth: Undead Subculture*. Durham: Duke University Press, 2007.

Gordon, Avery F. *Ghostly Matters: Haunting and the Sociological Imagination*. Minneapolis: University of Minnesota Press, 1997.

Gordon, Jan B. "Narrative Enclosure as Textual Ruin: An Archeology of Gothic Consciousness." In Botting and Townshend, *Gothic*, 55–82.

Gunn, Drewey Wayne, and Jaime Harker. *1960s Gay Pulp Fiction*. Amherst: University of Massachusetts Press, 2013.

Guzmán, Joshua Javier. "Between Action and Abstraction." In Chavoya and Frantz, *Axis Mundo*, 303–15.

Haggerty, George E. *Gothic Fiction/Gothic Form*. University Park: Pennsylvania State University Press, 1989.

———. *Queer Gothic*. Urbana: University of Illinois Press, 2006.

———. "Queering Horace Walpole." *SEL: Studies in English Literature, 1500–1900* 46, no. 3 (2006): 543–61.

Halberstam, Jack. *Gaga Feminism: Sex, Gender, and the End of Normal.* Boston: Beacon, 2012.

———. *In a Queer Time and Place: Transgender Bodies, Subcultural Lives.* New York: New York University Press, 2005.

———. *The Queer Art of Failure.* Durham: Duke University Press, 2011.

———. *Skin Shows: Gothic Horror and the Technology of Monsters.* Durham: Duke University Press, 1995.

Hall, Radclyffe. *The Well of Loneliness.* Garden City: Blue Ribbon Books, 1928.

Halperin, David M. *How to Be Gay.* Cambridge: Belknap, 2012.

Hanson, Ellis. "Undead." In *Inside/Out: Lesbian Theories, Gay Theories*, edited by Diana Fuss, 324–40. New York: Routledge, 1991.

Haraway, Donna J. "The Promises of Monsters: A Regenerative Politics for Inappropriate/d Others." In *Cultural Studies*, edited by Lawrence Grossberg, Cary Nelson, and Paula Treichler, 295–337. New York: Routledge, 1992.

Haritaworn, Jin, Adi Kuntsman, and Silvia Posocco, eds. *Queer Necropolitics.* New York: Routledge, 2014.

Harris, Charlaine. *Dead until Dark.* New York: Ace Books, 2001.

———. *Living Dead in Dallas.* New York: Ace Books, 2002.

Hartman, Saidiya V. *Scenes of Subjection: Terror, Slavery, and Self-Making in Nineteenth-Century America.* New York: Oxford University Press, 1997.

Hastings, March. *The 3rd Theme.* Chicago: Newsstand Library Books, 1961.

Haut, Woody. *Pulp Culture: Hardboiled Fiction and the Cold War.* London: Serpent's Tail, 1995.

Hawthorne, Nathaniel. *"Young Goodman Brown" and Other Tales.* Oxford: Oxford University Press, 2009.

Heathfield, Adrian. "Illicit Transit." In Johnson, *Pleading in the Blood*, 206–22.

Hellman, Lillian. *The Children's Hour.* 1934. Reprint, New York: Dramatists Play Service, 1953.

Herman, Judith. *Trauma and Recovery: The Aftermath of Violence; From Domestic Abuse to Political Terror.* New York: Basic Books, 1992.

Highsmith, Patricia. *The Price of Salt.* New York: Bantam, 1953.

———. *The Talented Mr. Ripley.* 1955. Reprint, New York: Norton, 2008.

Hogg, James. *The Private Memoirs and Confessions of a Justified Sinner*. 1824. Reprint, New York: New York Review Books, 2002.

Holk, Agnete. *Strange Friends*. 1955. Reprint, New York: Pyramid, 1963.

Horn, Katrin. "Camping with the Stars: Queer Performativity, Pop Intertextuality, and Camp in the Pop Art of Lady Gaga." COPAS: *Current Objectives of Postgraduate American Studies* 11 (2010). https://copas.uni-regensburg.de/article/view/131/155.

Horton, Randall, M. L. Hunter, and Becky Thompson, eds. *Fingernails across the Chalkboard: Poetry and Prose on HIV/AIDS from the Black Diaspora*. Chicago: Third World, 2007.

Huba, Jackie. *Monster Loyalty: How Lady Gaga Turns Followers into Fanatics*. New York: Penguin, 2013.

Hudson, Dale. "'Of Course There Are Werewolves and Vampires': *True Blood* and the Right to Rights for Other Species." *American Quarterly* 65, no. 3 (2013): 661–87.

Hughes, William, and Andrew Smith, eds. *Queering the Gothic*. Manchester: Manchester University Press, 2009.

Hurley, Kelly. "Reading Like an Alien: Posthuman Identity in Ridley Scott's *Alien* and David Cronenberg's *Rabid*." In *Posthuman Bodies*, edited by Jack Halberstam and Ira Livingston, 203–24. Bloomington: Indiana University Press, 1995.

Israel, Betsy. *Bachelor Girl: The Secret History of Single Women in the Twentieth Century*. New York: Morrow, 2002.

Jackson, Shirley. *The Haunting of Hill House*. 1959. Reprint, New York: Penguin, 2013.

Jennex, Craig. "Diva Worship and the Sonic Search for Queer Utopia." *Popular Music and Society* 36, no. 3 (2013): 343–59.

Johnson, Dominic. "'Does a Bloody Towel Represent the Ideals of the American People?': Ron Athey and the Culture Wars." In Johnson, *Pleading in the Blood*, 64–93.

——— . Introduction to Johnson, *Pleading in the Blood*, 10–40.

——— . "Perverse Martyrologies: An Interview with Ron Athey." *Contemporary Theatre Review* 18, no 4 (2008): 503–13.

————, ed. *Pleading in the Blood: The Art and Performances of Ron Athey*. Chicago: Intellect/University of Chicago Press, 2013.

Jones, Amelia. "Holy Body: Erotic Ethics in Ron Athey and Juliana Snapper's *Judas Cradle*." TDR: *The Drama Review* 50, no. 1 (2006): 159–69.

————. "How Ron Athey Makes Me Feel: The Political Potential of Upsetting Art." In Johnson, *Pleading in the Blood*, 152–78.

Kaplan, E. Ann. *Trauma Culture: The Politics of Terror and Loss in Media and Literature*. New Brunswick: Rutgers University Press, 2005.

Keller, Yvonne. "'Was It Right to Love Her Brother's Wife So Passionately?': Lesbian Pulp Novels and U.S. Lesbian Identity, 1950–1965." *American Quarterly* 57, no. 2 (2005): 385–410.

Kennan, George. "The Sources of Soviet Conduct." *Foreign Affairs* 25, no. 4 (1947): 566–82.

Kilgour, Maggie. *From Communion to Cannibalism: An Anatomy of Metaphors of Incorporation*. Princeton: Princeton University Press, 1990.

————. *The Rise of the Gothic Novel*. London: Routledge, 1995.

Kinsey, Alfred C., Wardell B. Pomeroy, and Clyde E. Martin. *Sexual Behavior in the Human Male*. Philadelphia: Saunders, 1948.

Koch-Rein, Anson. "Monster." TSQ: *Transgender Studies Quarterly* 1, nos. 1–2 (2014): 134–35.

Krafft-Ebing, Richard von. *Psychopathia Sexualis: A Medico-Forensic Study*. Translated by Harry E. Wedeck. New York: Putnam's Sons, 1965.

Kristeva, Julia. *Powers of Horror: An Essay on Abjection*. Translated by Leon S. Roudiez. New York: Columbia University Press, 1982.

Lee, Robert G. *Orientals: Asian Americans in Popular Culture*. Philadelphia: Temple University Press, 1999.

Lewis, Matthew. *The Monk: A Romance*. 1796. Reprint, London: Penguin Books, 1998.

Linden, Robin Ruth, Darlene R. Pagano, Diana E. H. Russell, and Susan Leigh Star, eds. *Against Sadomasochism: A Radical Feminist Analysis*. San Francisco: Frog in the Well, 1982.

Lloyd, Christopher. "Southern Gothic." In *American Gothic Culture: An Edinburgh Companion*, edited by Joel Faflak and Jason Haslam, 79–91. Edinburgh: Edinburgh University Press, 2016.

Lloyd-Smith, Allan. *American Gothic Fiction: An Introduction*. New York: Continuum, 2004.

López, Tiffany Ana. "Emotional Contraband: Prison as Metaphor and Meaning in U.S. Latina Drama." In *Captive Audience: Prison and Captivity in Contemporary Theater*, edited by Thomas Fahy and Kimball King, 25–40. New York: Routledge, 2003.

Lord, Sheldon. *The Third Way*. New York: Beacon, 1962.

Lorde, Audre. "Age, Race, Class, and Sex: Women Redefining Difference." In *Sister Outsider: Essays and Speeches by Audre Lorde*, 114–23. 1984. Reprint, Berkeley: Crossing, 2007.

Lorenz, Renate. *Queer Art: A Freak Theory*. New Brunswick: Transaction, 2012.

Love, Heather. *Feeling Backward: Loss and the Politics of Queer History*. Cambridge: Harvard University Press, 2007.

Lucchesi, Aldo. *Strange Breed*. New York: Tower, 1960.

Luckhurst, Roger. *The Trauma Question*. London: Routledge, 2008.

Macfarlane, Karen E. "The Monstrous House of Gaga." In Edwards and Soltysik Monnet, *Gothic in Contemporary Literature*, 114–34.

MacKinnon, Catherine A. "Sexuality, Pornography, and Method: 'Pleasure under Patriarchy.'" *Ethics* 99, no. 2 (1989): 314–46.

Marrati, Paola. "True Blood, Bon Temps Louisiana, 2008–2012." *MLN* 127, no. 5 (2012): 981–96.

Marshall, Nowell. *Romanticism, Gender, and Violence: Blake to George Sodini*. Plymouth: Bucknell University Press, 2013.

Massé, Michelle A. *In the Name of Love: Women, Masochism, and the Gothic*. Ithaca: Cornell University Press, 1992.

Maturin, Charles. *Melmoth the Wanderer*. 1820. Reprint, Oxford: Oxford World Classics, 2008.

Mbembe, Achille. "Necropolitics." *Public Culture* 15, no. 1 (2003): 11–40.

McClintock, Anne. *Imperial Leather: Race, Gender and Sexuality in the Colonial Contest*. New York: Routledge, 1995.

McCormack, Donna. *Queer Postcolonial Narratives and the Ethics of Witnessing*. New York: Bloomsbury Academic, 2014.

Mercer, Kobena. *Welcome to the Jungle: New Positions in Black Cultural Studies*. New York: Routledge, 1994.

Miller, James L., ed. *Fluid Exchanges: Artists and Critics in the AIDS Crisis*. Toronto: University of Toronto Press, 1992.

Minich, Julie Avril. "Reading Gil Cuadros in the Aftermath of HIV/AIDS." *GL/Q* 23, no. 2 (2017): 167–93.

Modleski, Tania. *Loving with a Vengeance: Mass-Produced Fantasies for Women*. 2nd ed. New York: Routledge, 2008.

Moers, Ellen. *Literary Women*. Garden City: Doubleday, 1976.

Morrison, Toni. *Playing in the Dark: Whiteness and the Literary Imagination*. New York: Vintage Books, 1993.

Mowl, Timothy. *Horace Walpole, the Great Outsider*. London: Murray, 1996.

Mullins, Greg A. "Subjects of Rights in Another City of God: Violence, Sexuality, and the Norms of Human Rights." *Ilha do Desterro: A Journal of English Language, Literatures in English and Cultural Studies* 54 (2008): 107–21.

Muñoz, José Esteban. *Cruising Utopia: The Then and There of Queer Futurity*. New York: New York University Press, 2009.

——. *Disidentifications: Queers of Color and the Performance of Politics*. Minneapolis: University of Minnesota Press, 1999.

Murphy, Timothy F., and Suzanne Poirer, eds. *Writing AIDS: Gay Literature, Language, and Analysis*. New York: Columbia University Press, 1993.

Musser, Amber Jamilla. *Sensational Flesh: Race, Power, and Masochism*. New York: New York University Press, 2014.

Nadal, Kevin L. *That's So Gay! Microaggressions and the Lesbian, Gay, Bisexual, and Transgender Community*. Washington DC: American Psychological Association, 2013.

Nadel, Alan. *Containment Culture: American Narratives, Postmodernism, and the Atomic Age*. Durham: Duke University Press, 1995.

Navarro, Ray. "'Eso, me está pasando,' 1990." In Chavoya and Frantz, *Axis Mundo*, 316–19.

O'Connell, Shaun. "The Big One: Literature Discovers AIDS." *New England Journal of Public Policy* 4, no. 1 (1988): 485–506.

O'Higgins, James, and Michel Foucault. "Sexual Choice, Sexual Act: An Interview with Michel Foucault." *Salmagundi* 58–59 (1982–83): 10–24.

Osborn, M. Elizabeth, ed. *The Way We Live Now: American Plays and the AIDS Crisis*. New York: Theatre Communications Group, 1990.

Packer, Vin. *Spring Fire*. 1952. Reprint, San Francisco: Cleis, 2004.

Palmer, Paulina. *Lesbian Gothic: Transgressive Fictions*. London: Cassell, 1999.

———. *The Queer Uncanny: New Perspectives on the Gothic*. Cardiff: University of Wales Press, 2012.

Pastore, Judith Laurence, ed. *Confronting AIDS through Literature*. Champaign: University of Illinois Press, 1993.

Pearl, Monica B. *AIDS Literature and Gay Identity: The Literature of Loss*. New York: Routledge, 2013.

Pérez, Emma. "Queering the Borderlands: The Challenges of Excavating the Invisible and Unheard." *Frontiers: A Journal of Women Studies* 24, nos. 2–3 (2003): 122–31.

Pérez-Torres, Rafael. *Mestizaje: Critical Uses of Race in Chicano Culture*. Minneapolis: University of Minnesota Press, 2006.

Poe, Edgar Allan. *The Selected Writings of Edgar Allan Poe*. Edited by Gary Richard Thompson. New York: Norton, 2004.

Priest, J. C. *Forbidden*. New York: Beacon, 1952.

Prosser, Jay. *Second Skins: The Body Narratives of Transsexuality*. New York: Columbia University Press, 1998.

Puar, Jasbir K. *Terrorist Assemblages: Homonationalism in Queer Times*. Durham: Duke University Press, 2007.

Puar, Jasbir K., and Amit Rai. "Monster, Terrorist, Fag: The War on Terrorism and the Production of Docile Patriots." *Social Text 72* 20, no. 3 (2002): 117–48.

Radcliffe, Ann. *The Italian*. 1797. Reprint, Oxford: Oxford University Press, 2008.

———. *The Mysteries of Udolpho, a Romance Interspersed with Some Pieces of Poetry*. 1794. Reprint, London: Penguin Books, 2001.

Rasebotsa, Nobantu, Meg Samuelson, and Kylie Thomas, eds. *Nobody Ever Said AIDS: Poems and Stories from Southern Africa*. Cape Town: Kwela NB, 2004.

Reid-Pharr, Robert. *Black Gay Man*. New York: New York University Press, 2001.

Reti, Irene, ed. *Unleashing Feminism: Critiquing Lesbian Sadomasochism in the Gay Nineties*. Santa Cruz: Herbooks, 1993.

Rigby, Mair. "Uncanny Recognition: Queer Theory's Debt to the Gothic." *Gothic Studies* 11, no. 1 (2009): 46–57.

Rofes, Eric. *Dry Bones Breathe: Gay Men Creating Post-AIDS Identities and Cultures*. New York: Routledge, 1998.

Rogers, Annie. *The Unsayable: The Hidden Language of Trauma*. New York: Random House, 2006.

Root, Maria P. P. "Reconstructing the Impact of Trauma on Personality." In *Personality and Psychopathology: Feminist Reappraisals*, edited by Laura S. Brown and Mary Ballou, 229–65. New York: Guilford, 1992.

Rothberg, Michael. "Decolonizing Trauma Studies: A Response." *Studies in the Novel* 40, no. 1 (2008): 224–34.

Rubin, Gayle. "The Catacombs: A Temple of the Butthole." In *Deviations: A Gayle Rubin Reader*, 224–40. Durham: Duke University Press, 2011.

Russo, Vito. *The Celluloid Closet: Homosexuality in the Movies*. New York: Harper and Row, 1981.

Sacher-Masoch, Leopold von. *Venus in Furs*. In Deleuze and Sacher-Masoch, *Masochism*, 143–271.

Sade, Marquis de. *120 Days of Sodom*. 1785. Reprint, Radford: Wilder, 2008.

———. *Justine, or The Misfortunes of Virtue*. 1791. Reprint, Oxford: Oxford University Press, 2012.

Saglia, Diego. "William Beckford's 'Sparks of Orientalism' and the Material-Discursive Orient of British Romanticism." *Textual Practice* 16, no. 1 (2002): 75–92.

Said, Edward. *Orientalism*. 1978. Reprint, London: Penguin Books, 2003.

Schwab, Gabriele. *Haunting Legacies: Violent Histories and Transgenerational Trauma*. New York: Columbia University Press, 2010.

Scott, Walter. "Fatal Revenge, or The Family of Montorio: A Romance." *Quarterly Review* 3, no. 6 (1810): 339–47.

Sedgwick, Eve Kosofsky. *Between Men: English Literature and Male Homosocial Desire*. New York: Columbia University Press, 1985.

———. *The Coherence of Gothic Conventions*. 1980. Reprint, New York: Methuen, 1986.

———. *Epistemology of the Closet*. Berkeley: University of California Press, 1990.

———. "Paranoid Reading and Reparative Reading, or You're So Paranoid, You Probably Think This Essay Is about You." In *Touching Feeling: Affect, Pedagogy, Performativity*, 123–51. Durham: Duke University Press, 2003.

———. *Tendencies*. London: Routledge, 1994.

Shelley, Mary. *Frankenstein, or The Modern Prometheus*. 1818. Reprint, London: Penguin Group, 1992.

Silverman, Kaja. *Male Subjectivity at the Margins*. New York: Routledge, 1992.

Smith, Artemis. *The Third Sex*. New York: Beacon, 1959.

Snorton, C. Riley, and Jin Haritaworn. "Trans Necropolitics: A Transnational Reflection on Violence, Death, and the Trans of Color Afterlife." In *The Transgender Studies Reader 2*, edited by Susan Stryker and Aren Z. Aizura, 66–76. New York: Routledge, 2013.

Spade, Dean. *Normal Life: Administrative Violence, Critical Trans Politics, and the Limits of Law*. Brooklyn: South End, 2011.

Stevens, Maurice E. "Trauma Is as Trauma Does: The Politics of Affect in Catastrophic Times." In Casper and Wertheimer, *Critical Trauma Studies*, 19–36.

Stevenson, Robert Louis. *The Strange Case of Dr. Jekyll and Mr. Hyde*. 1886. Reprint, New York: Dover, 1991.

Stoker, Bram. *Dracula*. 1897. Reprint, Garden City: Black and White Classics, 2014.

Stryker, Susan. "My Words to Victor Frankenstein above the Village of Chamounix: Performing Transgender Rage." gl/q: *A Journal of Lesbian and Gay Studies* 1 (1994): 237–54.

———. *Queer Pulp: Perverted Passions from the Golden Age of the Paperback*. San Francisco: Chronicle Books, 2001.

———. *Transgender History*. Berkeley: Seal, 2008.

Sue, Derald Wing. *Microaggressions in Everyday Life: Race, Gender, and Sexual Orientation*. Hoboken: Wiley and Sons, 2010.

Tal, Kalí. *Worlds of Hurt: Reading the Literatures of Trauma*. Cambridge: Cambridge University Press, 1996.

Taylor, Valerie. *Stranger on Lesbos*. Greenwich: Fawcett Crest, 1960.

Tompkins, Avery. "Asterisk." *TSQ: Transgender Studies Quarterly* 1, nos. 1–2 (2014): 26–27.

Tongson, Karen. *Relocations: Queer Suburban Imaginaries*. New York: New York University Press, 2011.

Torres, Tereska. *Women's Barracks*. New York: Gold Medal, 1950.

Ventzislavov, Rossen. "The Time Is Now: Acceptance and Conquest in Pop Music." *Journal of Popular Music Studies* 24, no. 1 (2012): 57–70.

Viego, Antonio. *Dead Subjects: Toward a Politics of Loss in Latino Studies*. Durham: Duke University Press, 2007.

Visser, Irene. "Decolonizing Trauma Theory: Retrospect and Prospects." *Humanities* 4 (2015): 250–65.

Walpole, Horace. *The Castle of Otranto*. Edited by Wilmarth Sheldon Lewis. 1764. Reprint, Oxford: Oxford University Press, 1998.

Warner, Michael. *Publics and Counterpublics*. New York: Zone Books, 2005.

———. *The Trouble with Normal: Sex, Politics, and the Ethics of Queer Life*. Cambridge: Harvard University Press, 1999.

Watney, Simon. *Policing Desire: Pornography AIDS and the Media*. 2nd ed. Minneapolis: University of Minnesota Press, 1989.

Watt, Ian. "Time and Family in the Gothic Novel: *The Castle of Otranto*." *Eighteenth Century Life* 10, no. 3 (1986): 159–71.

Weber, Shannon. "Born This Way: Biology and Sexuality in Lady Gaga's Pro-LGBT Media." In *Queer Media Images: LGBT Perspectives*, edited by Jane Campbell and Theresa Carilli, 111–21. Blue Ridge Summit PA: Lexington Books, 2013.

Weeks, Jeffrey. *Sexuality and Its Discontents: Meanings, Myths, and Modern Sexualities*. London: Routledge, 1985.

Weirauch, Anna Elisabet. *The Scorpion*. Translated by Whittaker Chambers. 1932. Reprint, New York: Avon, 1948.

Westad, Odd Arne. *The Global Cold War*. Cambridge: Cambridge University Press, 2005.

Willey, Angela. *Undoing Monogamy: The Politics of Science and the Possibilities of Biology*. Durham: Duke University Press, 2016.

Williams, Cristan. "Transgender." *TSQ: Transgender Studies Quarterly* 1, nos. 1–2 (2014): 232–34.

Wolverton, Terry, ed. *Blood Whispers: L.A. Writers on AIDS*. Vol. 2. Los Angeles: Silverton Books/Los Angeles Gay and Lesbian Community Services Center, 1994.

Zimet, Jaye. "Psycho-Babble." In Zimet, *Strange Sisters*, 83–89.

———. *Strange Sisters: The Art of Lesbian Pulp Fiction, 1949–1969*. New York: Penguin Putnam, 1999.

Žižek, Slavoj. *The Sublime Object of Ideology*. London: Verso, 1989.

Page numbers in italics indicate illustrations.

Fernandez, Franc, xiii
Ferreday, Debra, 51–52
fetishized decay, 33
Fincher, Max, 10, 201n11
Fisher, Gary, 221n16
fisting, 141
Folsom Street Fair, 142
Forbidden (Priest), 77–78, *78*
Forrest, Katherine V., 71
Foucault, Michel, 19, 42–47, 49, 53–
    54, 202n31, 203n33
4 Scenes in a Harsh Life (Athey), 125–
    26, 128–30, 215n63
Francis, Willie, 153
Frankenstein (Shelley), 8–9, 36, 42,
    49, 56, 100, 116, 197n25, 201n16,
    205n65
Frankenstein's creature, xiii–xiv, 24,
    50, 100, 103–5, 122, 201n16
Freccero, Carla, 21, 56–57, 135, 217n88,
    218n90
Freeman, Elizabeth, 22, 55–58, 146–
    47, 153, 205n65, 206n74, 221n16
Freud, Sigmund: and gothicism,
    32–40, 48, 200n6, 201n16; and
    homosexuality, 33–34, 37–39, 71–72,
    200n8, 212n23; and melancholia,
    117, 213n41, 214n49; "Mourning and
    Melancholia," 116–17; and paranoia,
    32–33; "Psychoanalytic Notes upon
    an Autobiographical Account of
    a Case of Paranoia," 32–35, 38–39,
    43, 188–91, 200n6, 200n8, 201n16;
    and repetition compulsion, 62, 151,
    199n37, 199n43, 219n9; and sado-
    masochism, 145–46, 220n12; *Three*

Essays, 145, 220n12; and trauma,
    62–63, 151, 190, 199n37, 199n43,
    219n9
Fudge, Divinity, 128

Gaga feminism, 194n15
gay marriage, xvi, 31, 96, 195n16
Gay Men's Health Crisis, 100
Gay Shame conference (2003), 54
gender failure, 171
George, Doran, 172
Ghostly Matters (Gordon), 51–52, 61
Gilman, Charlotte Perkins, 11–12
Giovanni's Room (Baldwin), 209n46
Girard, René, 48, 129
Give Me Myself (Sherman), 87
Goddu, Teresa, 184, 228n9
Goldberg, Jonathan, 135, 217nn87–88
Goodlad, Lauren, 152, 223n34, 223n39
Gordon, Avery, 51–52, 61
Gordon, J., 201n14
goth aesthetic, 153, 223n34, 223n39
Gothic fiction: British, 6–12; can-
    nibalism in, 3, 7, 24; Chinese-box
    narrative structures of, 10, 201n11;
    containment in, 206n9; definition
    of, 6; doubling in, 7–9; feminization
    of, 6, 195n8; gay men's appropri-
    ation of, xviii; haunting in, 8, 16,
    21–22, 26; homosexuality in, 39–40,
    197n25; homosexual writers of, 13–
    14; monstrosity in, 3, 7–9, 21, 23–24,
    26, 103–5; origins of, 6–12, 195n15,
    196n22, 196n25; overview of, 179–91;
    paranoia in, 8–9, 32–42; and queer
    cultures, 1–27; sadomasochism

in, 142, 171–72, 220n10; "Shadow-Male" of, 78; "Super-Male" of, 78; taboo issues in, 13, 197n29; transgressive sexuality in, 10, 12–13, 21, 30, 208n34, 209n45; trauma in, 2–3, 5, 15–27, 180, 189–91; uncanny structure of, 8–10, 16, 32, 196n22; unspeakability of, 7; U.S., 11–12

gothicism: definition of, 3; and HIV/AIDS, 102; and Lady Gaga, xi–xviii, 194n15, 195nn16–17; in lesbian pulp fiction, 22–23, 65–98; and monstrosity, 23–26, 99–139; and neoliberalism, 179–91; overview of, 3–4, 6–22, 26–27; as response to exclusion and violence, 3–4; and sadomasochism, 25–26, 141–78; and Sigmund Freud, 32–40, 48, 200n6, 201n16; and trauma, 16; in twentieth-century U.S. cinema, 13–14

gothic negativity, 61–62

gothic queer culture: and AIDS literature, 3, 24–25, 107–16; author's definition of, 3; containment crypts as, 85–97; in fiction, 1–27; and lesbian pulp fiction, 68–69, 85–97; and neoliberalism, 20, 26–27, 106, 122–23, 138–39, 180–81, 183; and sadomasochism, 177. See also gothic queer theory; performance art, queer

gothic queer monstrosity, 122–30

gothic queer theory, 29–63; accretion in, 31–32, 41; and cannibalism, 47; and haunting, 21–22, 29–63, 184, 191; and HIV/AIDS, 31; and living dead, 46; and monstrosity, 31–32,

42–51, 56, 122–30; negativity in, 61–62; overview of, 29–32, 197n27; and paranoia, 32–42, 51, 202n22; and sadomasochism, 31–32, 51–58, 202n25; and violence, 38–39, 51–52, 59, 61, 202n22

gothic trauma, 14–21

Haggerty, George, 2, 7, 95, 145–46, 196n22, 200n6

Halberstam, Jack, 4, 12, 19, 49–50, 61, 194n15, 197n25, 203n42, 211n9

Hall, Radclyffe, 29–30, 88, 200n1, 209n46

Halperin, David M., xvii, 194n11, 212n19

Haritaworn, Jin, 203n39

Harris, Charlaine, 26, 180–89

Harris, Sara, 87

Hartman, Saidiya V., 158, 167

Hastings, March, 82, 85

haunting: and cannibalism, 218n90; in Gothic fiction, 8, 16, 21–22, 26; and gothic queer theory, 21–22, 29–63, 184, 191; and historical trauma, 202n25, 228n9; and monstrosity, 136; and sadomasochism, 31–32, 51–58, 202n25

The Haunting of Hill House (Jackson), 209n45

hauntology, 51

Hawthorne, Nathaniel, 12

Heathfield, Adrian, 136–37, 215n65

Hegel, G. W. F., 152

Hellman, Lillian, 209n45

Helms, Jesse, 108, 126–30

insidious trauma: definition of, 15; in Gothic fiction, 2–3, 5, 15–27, 180, 189–91; and HIV/AIDS, 102–3, 123, 137–38, 151; and queer cultures, 2–3, 5, 15–27; and queer performance art, 160, 167, 173–75; and sadomasochism, 143, 147–48, 160, 167, 173–75; and trans* community, 47
intercourse, 34, 200n8
intersectionality, 227n73
intersex, 45, 202n31
I Prefer Girls (Dumont), 73
The Italian (Radcliffe), 66, 206n9, 224n41

Jackson, Shirley, 209n45
Jenner, Caitlyn, 164–65
Jennex, Craig, xiv–xv
Jim Crow, 149, 154–55
Johnson, Kay, 87
Jones, Amelia, 131–32, 134, 217n82
Journey to a Woman (Bannon), 87
Julien, Isaac, 56

Kaplan, Ann, 19, 151, 173–74
Kennan, George, 69–70
Kilgour, Maggie, 7, 20, 104, 137, 152, 195n15
Kinsey, Alfred, 71–72
Kirby, David, 99
Krafft-Ebing, Richard von, 145
Kuntsman, Adi, 51–52, 203n39

Lady Gaga, xi–xviii; business strategies of, xvii, 195n17; as gay icon, xv; gay male following of, xiv; and gay marriage, xvi, 195n16; meat dress of, xii–xviii, 193n2, 193n4; as Mother Monster, xi, xiv, xvii–xviii; and queer camp, 194n15; and queer monstrosity, xvii, 194n15; and sexual assault, xviii; sexuality of, xiv
Lamar, M., 25, 144, 148–60, *155*, 167, 174–78, 219n9, 223n39, 224n43
Latinx communities, 108, 212n20, 214n55
Laub, Dori, 199n43, 220n9
Lawrence v. Texas (2003), 128, 216n76
leather bars, 141, 145
Leave It to Beaver (TV series), 71
Léry, Jean de, 218n90
Lesbian Gothic (Palmer), 209n45
lesbian pulp fiction: censorship of, 67–69, 71–72, 86–87; characters of color in, 75–76; and communism, 22, 70, 80–81, 90, 208n34; containment in text of, 68–69, 85–97; containment on covers of, 73–84, 97–98; cover art, 23, 66–69, 73–85, *76*, *78*, *81*, *82*, *84*, 90, 92, 97; darkness in, 74–75; gothicism in, 22–23, 65–98; and gothic queer culture, 66–69, 85–97; interracial couples in, 75–76; and "lesbian sickos," 75, 207n25; for male voyeuristic pleasure, 79; microaggression in, 84; monstrosity in, 74; moralizing in, 79; Orientalism in, 75–79, 92, 208n34; overview of, 65–73; paranoia in, 23, 66, 71; sadomasochism in, 66, 74; "Shadow-Males" and "Super-Males" of, 78; third sex in, 72, 80, 81–83, 208n34; twilight in,

56, 122–30; and haunting, 136; and HIV/AIDS, 23–24, 99–105, 116–19, 122–27, 129–30; Jeffrey Jerome Cohen's seven characteristics of, 211n9; and Lady Gaga, xvii, 194n15; in lesbian pulp fiction, 74; patchwork, 116–22; in performance art, 122–30; and sadomasochism, 123; and transgender, 49, 165; vampiric, 102; and violence, 113, 116

monstrous sexualities, 46, 74

Monument Push (Cassils), 176

Morrison, Toni, 61, 152, 228n14

Muñoz, José Esteban, 120, 122–23, 205n74, 210n63, 213n47

Musser, Amber, 147, 167

"My Aztlan" (Cuadros), 117–20

My Name Is Rusty (Johnson), 87

The Mysteries of Udolpho (Radcliffe), 8, 201n9, 201n14, 206n9

mythic norm, 15, 206n14

Nadal, Kevin, 14, 70

Nadel, Alan, 69–70

Nathan, Emily, 149–50

National Endowment for the Arts (NEA), 216–17

Navarro, Ray, 108

necrophilia, 33–34

necropolitics, 46–47

necropower, 46

Negrogoth, 148, 150, 175

Negrogothic, a Manifesto, the Aesthetics of M. Lamar (exhibit), 25, 152

neoliberalism, 20, 26–27, 106, 122–23, 138–39, 179–91

No Future (Edelman), xvi, 22, 47, 203n42

nonnormative genders or sexualities, xiv, xviii, 3, 10–14, 26, 32, 39, 79, 97, 100, 112, 159, 180–81, 188–91, 206n3

Normal Life (Spade), 166, 226n60

nuclear gaze, 70

Odd Girl Out (Bannon), 73, 87

Odd Girls (Faderman), 207n20, 209n46

The One Between (Adlon), 77–78, *78*

Orange Is the New Black (TV series), 148

Orientalism, 75–79, 92, 208n34

Packer, Vin, 85–88

Palmer, Paulina, 209n45

paperbacks. *See* lesbian pulp fiction

paranoia: and accretion, 32–42; in Gothic fiction, 8–9, 32–42; and gothic queer theory, 32–42, 51, 202n22; and homosexuality, 33; in lesbian pulp fiction, 23, 66, 71; and Sigmund Freud, 32–33

paranoid Gothic, 37–38, 42, 201n16

"Paranoid Reading and Reparative Reading" (Sedgwick), 39–42, 46–47, 202n22

patchwork monstrosity, 116–22

People for the Ethical Treatment of Animals, xiii

Pérez, Emma, 120–21

performance art, queer, 3, 25–26, 141–78; by Cassils, 25, 144, 160–63, *163*, 167–70, 174, 176–78, 219n9, 226n63; of color, 141–78; dissonance and

Rock and Roll Hall of Fame, xii–xiii, 193n2

Rofes, Eric, 211n7, 216n68

Rogers, Annie, 199n43

Rothberg, Michael, 198n34, 202n20

Rubin, Gayle, 141–43, 221n15

Russo, Vito, 13

Rutledge-Borger, Meredith, xii

Sacher-Masoch, Leopold von, 145

Sade, Marquis de, 145

sadomasochism: in Gothic fiction, 142, 171–72; and gothicism, 25–26, 141–78; and gothic queer culture, 177; and gothic queer theory, 31–32, 51–58, 202n25; and haunting, 31–32, 51–58, 202n25; and HIV/AIDS, 54–56; and homosexuality, 141–42, 154; and insidious trauma, 143, 147–48, 160, 167, 173–75; in lesbian pulp fiction, 66, 74; as metaphor, 221n15; and monstrosity, 123; overview of, 24–25, 141–44; in queer performance art, 3, 25–26, 141–78, 219n3, 220n12, 221n15; resistance to definition of, 144–48, 220n12; and Sigmund Freud, 145–46, 220n12; and transgender, 172, 176; and violence, 144, 147, 149, 153, 156, 160, 165–72, 176–77

Salem, Randy, 85

scapegoats, 23–24, 113, 125–26, 129–30

Schreber, Daniel Paul, 33–39, 220n8

The Scorpion (Weirauch), 77

Sedgwick, Eve Kosofsky, 7, 10, 12, 30, 37, 39–42, 46–47, 196n25, 201n16, 202n22

sedimentation, 120

Self-Obliteration #1, Ecstatic (Athey), 131–34, *134*

"Self-Portrait with a Whip" (Map-plethorpe), 154

seroconversion, 55, 120

serodiscordance, 110

Serrano, Andres, 126

Sexual Behavior in the Human Male (Kinsey et al.), 71–72

sexual identification, 43, 119–20, 210n63, 213n47, 226n60

sexualized power, 1, 6, 8, 52–53, 145, 153, 157

"Shadow-Males," 78

"Shame on You" (Bersani), 54

Shelley, Mary, 8, 49, 100–101

Sherman, Susan, 87

*sinthom*osexuals, 47–48, 204n42

slavery, 11, 51, 143, 147–49, 154–55, 158, 184, 221n16

Smith, Andrew, 197n29

Smith, Artemis, 80–81, 85

Snorton, C. Riley, 203n39

sodomy, 2, 87, 128–29, 135, 216n76, 217nn87–88

Sookie Stackhouse series (Harris), 26, 180–89

"The Sources of Soviet Conduct" (Kennan), 69–70

Spade, Dean, 166, 226n60

Specters of Marx (Derrida), 51

spectrality, 16, 21, 57, 61, 135, 218n90

Spring Fire (Packer), 86–88

Stevens, Maurice E., 5, 17–18, 190, 199n41

tional, 16; vicarious, 14–15. *See also* insidious trauma

"trauma Gothic," 16

trauma theory, 4–6, 16, 18, 30, 198n34, 202n20, 219n9

traumatic communication, 19, 62

traumatic fragmentation, 5, 39, 41, 121, 159

traumatic intrusion, 32

traumatic nostalgia, 5

traumatic remembering, 19–20

traumatic repetition, 219n9

True Blood (TV series), 26, 180–89, 228n9

"true sex," 43, 202n31

TSQ: Transgender Studies Quarterly, 49, 225n54

twilight love, 73–74, 77–80, 90, 94, 207n20. *See also* lesbian pulp fiction

Undoing Monogamy (Willey), 52

Unlimited Intimacy (Dean), 54

Unnatural Wife (Carr), 78, *78*

"Unprotected" (Cuadros), 109–11, 117

The Unsayable (Rogers), 199n43

utopian queerness, 44–45, 61, 123, 205n74, 223n39

vampires, 8, 10, 24, 104–5, 130–39, 180–89, 196n25, 211n12, 211n15, 217n89

Ventzislavov, Rossen, xiii–xiv

vicarious trauma, 14–15

violence: of the frontier, 11; in Gothic fiction, 2; and gothic queer theory, 38–39, 51–52, 59, 61, 202n22; and HIV/AIDS, 101; institutional, 16, 166; and lesbian pulp fiction, 66, 69, 94; and monstrosity, 113, 116; of oppression, 30; against queer people, 3, 6; and sadomasochism, 144, 147, 149, 153, 156, 160, 165–72, 176–77; against trans* community, 25, 165–66, 225n58; against vampires, 185

Visser, Irene, 18, 198n34, 199n43, 220n9

Volcano, Del LaGrace, 50

Walpole, Horace, 1–3, 8, 53, 55, 90, 95, 177, 201n14

Warner, Michael, 128

Watney, Simon, 107

The Wayward Ones (Harris), 87

Weeks, Jeffrey, 143, 219n3

Weiland (Brown), 12

Weirauch, Anna Elisabet, 77

Welch, Paul, 141

The Well of Loneliness (Hall), 29–30, 62, 88, 200n1, 209n43, 209n46

Wertheimer, Eric, 198n37, 199n38

We Walk Alone through Lesbos Lonely Groves (Aldrich), 73

White, Edmund, 100

white supremacy, 149, 152–53, 156–59, 174, 185–86, 189, 214n53

Why We Fight (exhibit), 101

Willey, Angela, 52

Williams, Rozz, 124

Witkin, Joel-Peter, 126

Women in the Shadows (Bannon), 73, 87, 96–97

Women's Barracks (Torres), 86–87

Women Who Rock: Vision, Passion, Power (exhibit), xii

Women without Men (Reed), 87

Worlds of Hurt (Tal), 174–75

"The Yellow Wallpaper" (Gilman), 12

"Young Goodman Brown" (Hawthorne), 12

Zimet, Jaye, 72, 208n41

Žižek, Slavoj, 48, 196n22

Zofloya, or The Moor (Dacre), 33, 79, 145

Zongker, Brett, xii

To order or obtain more information on these or other University of Nebraska Press titles, visit nebraskapress.unl.edu.

www.ingramcontent.com/pod-product-compliance
Lightning Source LLC
Chambersburg PA
CBHW020340270326
41926CB00007B/254